IT Project Portfolio Management

For a complete listing of the *Artech House Effective Project Management Series,* turn to the back of this book.

IT Project Portfolio Management

Stephen S. Bonham

ARTECH
HOUSE

BOSTON | LONDON
artechhouse.com

Library of Congress Cataloging-in-Publication Data
Bonham, Stephen S.
    IT project portfolio management / Stephen S. Bonham.
        p.   cm.—(Artech House effective project management series)
    Includes bibliographical references and index.
    ISBN 1-58053-781-2 (alk. paper)
        1. Information technology—Management.   2. Project management.
    I. Title.   II. Series.
    T58.64.B65 2004
    004'.068'4—dc22

British Library Cataloguing in Publication Data
Bonham, Stephen S.
    IT project portfolio management.—(Effective project management series)
    1. Information technology—Management   2. Project management—data processing
    3. Strategic planning
    I. Title
    658.4'04
    ISBN 1-58053-781-2

Cover design byYekaterina Ratner

International Standard Book Number: 1-58053-781-2
Library of Congress Catalog Card Number: 2004046248

10 9 8 7 6 5 4 3 2

To my Dad, Charlie, and to my dear wife, Olivia

Contents

Preface

While consulting for a large company's information technology (IT) department, I was asked to help find a way to better manage the various IT projects that were spread among all of its business units. The executives wanted me to research tools that would help them prioritize the projects so they would know which ones were healthy contributors to the corporate strategy and which ones could be axed. The market in which they were selling their products was slowing down, and they wanted to centralize corporate governance and trim unnecessary IT projects. Because they also knew that some IT projects were critical to the growth and ongoing operations of the company, they couldn't simply eliminate a random sampling. Though we had experiences in IT program management and executive information systems (EISs), we had little experience in project portfolio management (PPM). After some research, we realized that implementing a project prioritization tool would be just the tip of the iceberg in providing a successful and lasting solution to their problem.

This was a very project-centric company with over 250 ongoing IT projects running at one time. The market was constantly forcing the product line to change. Such pressures to decrease the life cycle and increase the quality of their products directly affected how the executives wanted IT to improve the efficiencies of their units. This ultimately made the company a prime candidate to adopt IT project-centric management techniques. Combining such a need with the realization that the company had dispersed IT governance across all of the business units highlighted the notion that this initiative would be an organizational change exercise similar in scale to an enterprise resource planning (ERP) or customer resources management (CRM) implementation. As it turns out, the long-term solution to centralizing IT project control was too much of a bite for them to take at once—organizational change needed to come piecemeal if it was going to succeed.

After being burned by past IT initiatives, business units felt comfortable in their decisions to resist new large-scale IT-sponsored changes. To combat this complacency, IT professionals have learned to present solutions that provide early wins to maintain support for the long-term goals. Unfortunately, these early wins can come in the form of "dog-and-pony shows" of "vaporware" just to maintain financing. Therefore, how can an organization implement a solid long-term solution to managing their projects while providing short-term, concrete wins for the executive sponsor and the business units?

IT PPM Versus PPM

PPM is a subject that has been around since the 1970s, when manufacturing companies saw how Dr. Harry Markowitz's theories on financial PPM could be applied to projects. However, when we started to research PPM's application to IT, we found that IT projects and programs sufficiently differentiate themselves from non-IT projects to warrant IT-specific PPM processes. Drug companies create a portfolio of drug development projects to attack known diseases; construction companies have a portfolio of contracts to build from a set of blueprints; and accounting firms have a portfolio of companies to audit every year. These examples of project portfolios tend to be filled with projects that best mitigate risk and increase return. If the business climate changes, they tend to cancel projects rather than drastically modify them. Where the projects in the portfolios of drug, construction, and accounting companies have fairly clear objectives, the projects in an IT portfolio rest on shifting objectives. IT projects are designed to satisfy business unit needs, which, in turn, are at the mercy of shifting corporate strategies. These strategies used to be dependable keels on which companies could cruise for many years. But as global markets explode with the increasing speed of information transfer, corporate strategies have become much more flexible.

Flexible Methodologies

In the early days of IT, projects would follow the *waterfall* methodology of requirements-design-implement-QA-rollout. If the business model changed during the project, not much could be done. Nowadays, projects are split into several releases. IT project managers (PMs) know that if a deliverable isn't made within six months, the likelihood of success drops dramatically. They have become very aware that business rules change so quickly that a designed product can easily become misaligned with the needs of the project sponsor. To combat this, iterative methodologies that allow for more frequent deliveries of subsets of the desired functionality have become the norm. These flexible approaches, along with improved scope management techniques, in turn have allowed projects to permit more midstream scope changes required by the market and controlled by the PM.

Since the 1960s, software PMs have come to realize that the success rates of their projects aren't very good. Various methods have been developed to improve the odds of success against the risks of project failure due to poor staff engineers, poor project management, poor organizational support, or poor ideas. With so many ambitious department heads and so many different kinds of projects in large companies, executive staffs continue to be faced with tornadoes of uncontrolled, high-risk projects. Once a process is in place to improve the odds of project successes, how can executives get a better aggregate view of what is going on in their IT project portfolio? How can IT project teams get word of the various methods for success? How can IT departments obtain control of ambitious department heads starting technically redundant projects? Many IT departments have recently adopted techniques that defense and the National Aeronautics and Space Administration (NASA) contractors have used for decades; techniques that are implemented by a project portfolio management office (PMO).

IT PMO

An established IT PMO that is actively supported at the executive level can help solve problems with project auditing and initiative approval. For example, how can project audits be fair between projects if no common initiative or project methodology is followed by every business unit and PM? How can the business units efficiently communicate ideas to upper management if no business case template has been developed? By creating structure for projects and initiatives through business case templates and software development methodologies, projects can be tracked consistently. The PMO can provide an auditing function that can prove health, risk, and valuation of all projects. The PMO can also provide training curricula to evolve and thus help retain the IT staff. By having a clear window view into all corporate projects, the PMO can allow IT to better manage human resources and assets across projects. How can an IT architecture group dictate new technical direction for the company if it doesn't even know what systems are in place? By establishing an architecture branch, the PMO can ensure that new projects leverage existing assets and avoid duplicate, siloed implementations. Finally, by being aware of any interproject dependencies, the PMO can have seemingly uncoupled projects react appropriately to shifts in corporate strategies. The ultimate gain would be for executive management to be able to read and manage their project portfolio as they do their financial portfolio. And because, according to the Gartner Group, technical initiative funding follows the cycles of the economy, such awareness of the project portfolio is critical for fast economic reactions.

Humans, like the marketplace, change the way they do things constantly and unpredictably. IT-related projects, built on a foundation of software, rely on the high risk associated with such shifting human goals and activities. Many of my hardware friends would argue that IT is based on a foundation of reliable chips—it's the shaky gelatin layer of software that is slapped on top of this chip foundation that makes IT projects unpredictable. Most writings on IT PPM focus on establishing a baseline of methods that the suite of projects should follow. What I have found in the field, in fact, counters this premise. PMs, constrained by extremely tight timeframes and budgets, choose the methods they know from experience will guarantee success. PMs are further constrained by the number of resources and assets available to them as well as the corporate IT architecture to which they must adhere. If central offices dictate some new constraining project management methods, then something will burst. More than likely, it will be the success of the project. This book takes an approach that follows the natural fluidity of humans, markets, and software projects: the IT PMO should be the one that flexes to, and yet firmly supports the needs of, its project portfolio and its executive committee.

This book begins with a chapter that defines IT PPM by first drawing links to modern financial portfolio theory and then expanding into IT project and program management approaches. Chapter 2 then introduces the main reason for the existence of IT PPM—corporate-level strategic alignment of the IT portfolio. This requirement first needs to be understood and then applied by an organization that is trying to gain control of its project portfolio. Chapter 3 then overlays strategic approaches that shift with the ever-changing marketplace with flexible project and program management methodologies. How IT PPM supports a project portfolio that is flexible to changes in the marketplace is one of the central themes of the book. Then, before going into the specific tasks and deliverables, the IT PMO is introduced in Chapter 4. At this point, most literature on generic PPM would dive right into project prioritization approaches. However, that subject is saved until Chapter 9 so that we can highlight the differences in IT PPM via Chapters 5 through 8. These chapters introduce asset, architecture, resource, and knowledge (AARK) management as core processes to allow the IT PMO to support and thus improve the health of the portfolio. This unique opportunity in the world of PPM—to go beyond initiative selection and monitoring by using an extended virtual PMO—is the second central theme of the book. After detailing some prioritization techniques in Chapter 9, the book wraps up with a concluding chapter on the final core theme: organizational support. While several chapters will touch on this subject as it applies to specific IT PMO tasks, Chapter 10 will introduce a marketing technique, supporting software tools, and a proposed rollout method that will help ensure continued organizational support.

Acknowledgments

Thanks to Ben Shaull, Bill Sebastian, and Nate Whaley for their early ideas on IT PPM. I'd like to also thank everyone who helped fine tune this book. Reed McConnell provided his experiences in project management, Professor John Bazley ironed out much of the financial sections, Steve Norgaard offered his executive perspectives, and Pamela Bonham dotted the i's and crossed the t's. The hard work and contributions of each of them expanded the book, as well as my understanding of the ever-growing field of IT PPM.

1

Introduction to IT PPM

When a business wants to get control of its IT projects, two paradigms collide: the world of financial portfolio management and the world of IT project management. When implementing IT PPM, companies will either lean more towards the former by supporting executive decisions or they will lean more towards the latter by supporting PMs. The opportunity that IT PPM presents is how to combine the benefits of both approaches to best support an IT project-centric organization. This chapter will begin by looking at the origins of PPM by reviewing modern portfolio theory (MPT). Then a basic review of IT project management will be presented. Once this foundation has been established, we will start to see how the two overlap. Maximizing return, alignment with strategy, balance between investments, and properly leveraging resources are just some of the commonalities. Finally, a common theme of this book will be introduced at the end: IT PPM rollout. As will be seen, implementing IT PPM can be as big a shift in an organization as business process reengineering (BPR) and ERP implementations have been. References to organizational change strategies for rolling out the

IT PPM solution presented in the book will appear in most chapters, culminating in a complete explanation in the final chapter.

1.1 MPT

1.1.1 Financial Investments

When an individual or a company buys a stock or bond, it does so with the hope that the investment will increase in value. These investors are also more comfortable when their level of confidence in the investment's return is based more on certainty than on hope. In other words, those who invest want to place their bets on sure winners. This gives us two basic principles that guide most financial decisions: maximize return for a given risk or minimize risk for a given return. Any financial investment involves some level of risk; even U.S. Treasury bills have inflation risk. An investor will look at a particular investment instrument, establish a level of risk, and then set a level of return they would expect if they decided to go with it. Figure 1.1 shows conceptual risk-return relationships between a set of such investments. If investors decide to purchase a high-quality common stock, they would expect a higher return than if they purchased a high-quality corporate bond because of the relative risk levels. This figure also shows that the lowest level of expected return is based on the return one would receive from a "zero-risk" investment (e.g., U.S. Treasury bills).

However, because most investors understand how unreliable an economy or a business can be, they mitigate their risks (or reduce their uncertainties) further by making several other investments. This set of purchases can be referred to as a financial portfolio.

And how an investor should best manage that portfolio was the subject of the 1952 *Journal of Finance* paper, "Portfolio Selection" by Nobel Laureate Dr. Harry Markowitz. As a result of this paper, Dr. Markowitz went on to become known as the father of MPT. Dr. Markowitz proved that in order to better ensure the two main goals of any portfolio (high and dependable returns), the portfolio manager must not only diversify investments across risk levels but should also tailor the investments to the particular strategy of the investor [1].

Portfolio managers must build investment portfolios that:

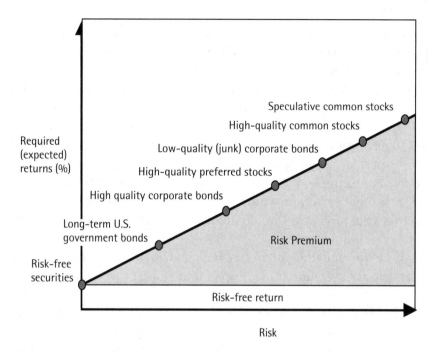

Figure 1.1 Conceptual risk/return tradeoff. (*After:* [2].)

1. Maximize return for a given risk.

2. Minimize risk for a given return.

3. Avoid high correlation.

4. Are tailored to the individual company.

Cash assets kept by companies are usually invested in a financial portfolio and managed by some organization that reports to the chief financial officer. Many times referred to as the treasury department, this organization does its best to fit its portfolio into the four criteria outlined earlier. These criteria are used to prioritize individual investments so the treasurer will quickly know which ones to sell and which ones to keep. The information that the treasurer, or one of the portfolio managers, is able to provide also allows for a structured way to react to immediate strategic shifts. For example, with a prioritized list of investments, executives can quickly sell the lower priority investments when needed.

Risk and rate of return are the most common metrics used in prioritizing a financial portfolio. For each investment approach, investors will first look at what they can earn if they placed their money in a zero-risk investment, such as a U.S. Treasury bond. Though such a bond includes the risk associated with unpredictable inflation rates, it is considered *risk free* because it won't default. Then, after understanding the level of risk other approaches provide, they establish an expected rate of return. This expected rate of return is the zero-free rate plus some risk premium. For example, if someone asked me to cross a country road, I might ask that person for a buck for my time. But if someone asked me to cross a busy freeway, I would up the ante to $100. The risk premium in this case would be $99.

With the inflation premium included in the risk-free rate, the extended risk premium is made up of four risks:

1. *Maturity risk.* The longer an investor keeps their money in a security, the more likely that security will change in an unwanted direction. Therefore, investors will get a higher risk premium for keeping their money in a bond with a longer maturity duration.

2. *Default risk.* Bond rating agencies rate how likely a bond will default, or stop paying what was promised. If the company is rated lower, an investor is taking added risk with that bond.

3. *Seniority risk.* Securities have different rights to the cash flows generated by a company. For example, an investor who has invested in a company's first mortgage bonds has a higher seniority to a return than an investor in a company's common stock.

4. *Marketability risk.* If the security can't be sold very quickly, then the investor will get a higher risk premium. That is, either the cost of the security will be lower or the interest/dividend return will be greater than similar securities that can sell quicker [2].

A portfolio manager needs to apply these (and possibly other) risks to each investment in order to satisfy the first two metrics of portfolio prioritization. But, what can be seen clearly here is the level of subjectivity involved in determining the return on an investment. While much research is spent on determining these risks, the *money out* is heavily based on speculation by rating agencies, the investor, and the market (see Figure 1.2).

In determining how correlated a set of stocks are, a little more research is usually needed. For example, the portfolio manager may need to look at the spread of industries, risk levels, and investment vehicles of the portfolio and then adjust the priority value of each accordingly. Also, portfolio managers would have to be in tune with how their company is shifting their strategy to know whether an investment fits with the goals of the company. "A good portfolio is more than a long list of good stocks and bonds. It is a balanced whole, providing the investor with protections and opportunities with respect to a wide range of contingencies" [1].

Today, modern technology allows such portfolios to be constantly checked in real time. One of the tricks to maintaining a successful portfolio is to make these changes as quickly as the modern markets demand. Each day a strategic shift or some news about the market can change the last three metrics and thus reorder the priority of each investment in the portfolio. For example, if a company suddenly realizes a planned acquisition will require a lot of capital, it may decide to protect its current cash levels by opting for less risky investments with possibly lower returns. Also, if a country is adversely affected by political conflict, a portfolio heavily invested in natural resources from that country may try to reinvest in less correlated risks. Finally, to tailor

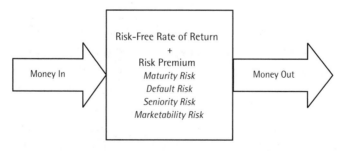

Figure 1.2 Risks associated with financial investments.

investments to the company, PepsiCo may feel that it would be inappropriate to invest in Coca-Cola or Dr Pepper/Seven Up, Inc. The important point here is that a financial portfolio manager doesn't just look at investment return when reprioritizing the portfolio.

1.1.2 Project Investments

As Dr. Markowitz's theories became accepted through the 1950s and into the 1960s, manufacturers saw an analogy to financial portfolios [3]. But when asked if MPT could be applied not just to financial investments, but also to projects, he had some questions. His main concerns focused on the introduction of new uncertainties that aren't found in financial portfolio analysis. "There are different constraints regarding projects, like management expertise, human skill sets, physical production capabilities and other factors that come into play" [4]. To understand what these constraints may be, let's first understand what types of risks projects may encounter. We can start by categorizing the many types of project risks into four buckets:

1. *Market (or commercial) risks.* These risks refer to when unforeseen changes in market demands cause executives to change the strategy, and thus the scope, of an ongoing project. If a company shifts its strategy in the middle of a project, the deliverables can be rejected. Also, if the results of a project are to interface with the external market (e.g., Web portals), they need to be flexible to unforeseen market changes. To maintain a healthy suite of such projects, the IT portfolio will need to be reprioritized quickly to meet such fluid demands.

2. *Organizational risks.* This refers to how well the stakeholders embrace some new IT solution to a business problem. The down side of this risk is the chance that the target organization rejects the IT-based solution (a cause for project failure). If project sponsors aren't satisfied with the end results, they won't dictate its usage among the organization—another cause for project failure. This same risk category, as we will see throughout this book, is central to the success of rolling out an IT PPM initiative.

3. *Technical risks.* This category focuses more on meeting a prede-termined set of functionality. Designs, implementations, interfaces, verification and Q/A, maintenance, specification ambiguity, technical uncertainty, technical obsolescence, and *bleeding-edge* technology are all examples of technical risks. While most of these risks are dictated by the project archi-tect, many of them can be mitigated through the aid of central IT architecture and IT asset management offices (Chapters 6 and 7).

4. *Project (or process) risks.* Meeting a predetermined budget and schedule are the central risks associated with this category. Other risks that fit in this category include gathering the correct requirements from project stakeholders and managing human resources efficiently. A central IT resource management office would be ideal in making sure projects leverage underutilized IT resources in the company (Chapter 8) [5].

Figure 1.3 shows that the core goal of any project is for project investors (or sponsors) to realize the expectations they *ultimately* had

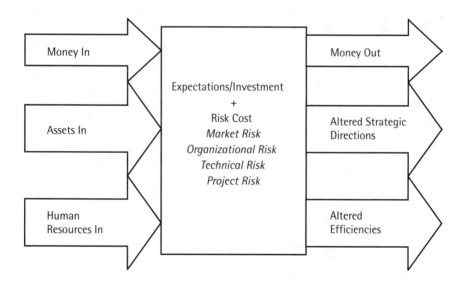

Figure 1.3 Risks associated with project investments.

for the money, assets, and human resources they invested in the project. However, IT projects have a set of risks that can expand or diminish what the sponsor envisioned. The result can be a combination of changes in cash flow, strategic directions, and business efficiencies.

The example of crossing the road was used to explain the additional return one would expect from a riskier crossing—called the *risk premium*. If I decided to build a product that would get me across the road safely (e.g., a tank), I would have to start a project to build it. With a fixed budget and a fixed timeframe, I would want to make sure that there weren't any surprises that would increase the costs or delay getting the tank built and tested. If I don't plan, design, and understand the requirements of the product, the opportunity (and, thus, the cost) of surprises can go up—called the *risk cost*. While financial managers rely on risk management techniques such as trend analysis to calculate the risk premiums, PMs implement risk management techniques such as time buffers, decision-tree analysis, and Monte Carlo analysis to calculate risk costs.

Markowitz proved through quadratic programming that a portfolio of riskier investments had a higher return potential. But "unlike financial investments, higher project risk is not necessarily correlated with higher potential project return. Measuring project risk and return is much more complex" [6]. While financial investors try to increase return (or their risk premium), project investors try to decrease surprises (or their risk expense) by ensuring the desired functionality arrives on time and on budget. When combined into an IT project portfolio, these risk expenses can be mitigated even more efficiently through a central IT portfolio management office. By maintaining awareness of the health and needs of all projects, such a central organization can extend the vision of each project to leverage previously unseen resources.

The IT PPM in Action section at the end of the chapter illustrates the importance that recent government regulations are putting on operational risks, of which project risks are a part. European and U.S. governments are responding to shareholder's, taxpayer's, and insurer's complaints of chaotic (and, in many cases, criminal) organizations. With the Sarbanes-Oxeley, Clinger-Cohen, and Basil II acts, regulators hope to squeeze organizations into adopting better operational control frameworks, such as PPM.

1.2 IT Project Management

The Project Management Body of Knowledge (PMBOK), 2000 release, defines a project as "a temporary endeavor undertaken to create a unique product or service." Projects, as opposed to ongoing corporate operations, are temporary because they have a beginning and an end. In addition, the product or service of the project is unique because it is "different in some distinguishing way." This, and the notion that projects are more strategically focused, is what distinguishes projects from ongoing corporate operations. Still, temporary projects and ongoing operations do have some common traits: they both require resources as input, they both produce an output, and they both can show up as expense in the income statement. "In general, IT can be classified as either systems that address day-to-day operations or project-specific initiatives" [7]. IT-based projects specifically involve the implementation or modification of a business unit's access to information using some technical medium, such as computers, cables, or phone switches. As with other types of projects, the methods used to manage IT projects can vary between countries, companies, and specialty groups. This book will not try to tackle the hundreds of methodologies used in IT project management. Rather, we will start by looking at some basic elements of an IT project. Then, after incorporating some of the concepts found in MPT, we will develop a definition for an IT PMO.

PMs live by an elastic triad of functionality versus schedule versus cost (see Figure 1.4). For example, if cost goes up, schedule may increase and functionality may decrease. As one of these points change, the other two are affected. Since the 1970s, as lessons have been learned from various projects, different views of this triad have evolved. As an example, the Project Management Institute's (PMI) PMBOK adds risk and splits functionality into scope and quality. This modification of the original triad shows the importance PMs also put on mitigating risk and ensuring the quality of the ultimate functionality. A further refinement of the triad would be to prioritize the points by putting weights on

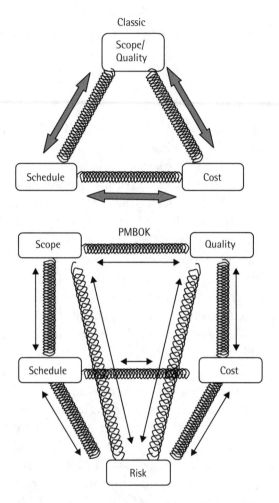

Figure 1.4 Comparison of forces that drive project success.

them. For example, some feel that PMs should stress "quality, schedule, and budget in that order" [8]. However the triad may be modified for each project, it still serves as a good springboard for reviewing project management concepts.

1.2.1 Variable Schedule

The timing of a project deliverable can be critical to how the return on investment (ROI) was calculated. As an example, let's look at a customer relationship management (CRM) system that needs to be modified to handle a larger amount of customer feedback for a marketing campaign. If the CRM system isn't delivered by certain date, then the marketing department could incur added expenses from postponed contracts with advertisers and print shops. So, how can the PM develop a timeline that is reliable enough to reduce these kinds of risks? A time-tested approach would be to use timelines from past projects as a guide and then build in buffers to account for unexpected events.

As long as no unexpected events cause the deadline to change, this approach will do a good job of comforting the investor. One example of an unplanned change that could cause a delay would be if the project sponsor decided to change the final functionality (a tug on the functionality point of the triad) to accommodate some new market requirement. Though the sponsor may feel that the final product may better accommodate the needs of the market, they may not understand the penalties associated with a delayed project [9]. Such penalties can come in the form of additional labor, facility, and licensing costs. That is, a tug on the time point of the triad can cause the cost point of the triad to move as well.

No matter what the changes to functionality are, the PM will try to get the project back on schedule using methods from previously successful projects. But, what if the past project guides are flawed? What if a PM has chosen a corrective timeline from the IT knowledge base that actually was associated with a failed project? The PM needs to feel comfortable that the tools they are using come from a suite of past projects that have succeeded. No company wants to repeat past failures while the competition moves nimbly forward with the market. To combat this, many IT departments will have a staff member maintain a knowledge base of successful project collateral that can be accessed by future PMs. Chapter 8 will show how an IT PMO may be better equipped to manage such a database. Specifically, IT PMOs can ensure that project guidelines associated with successful, rather than flawed, projects are saved when building a central knowledge base.

1.2.2 Variable Cost/Budget

As a PM is working hard to keep a project on schedule, unanticipated costs can appear. And just as time buffers are included in a project's original schedule, so are cost buffers included in the project's original budget. These buffers help keep the final cost, and thus the ROI, of the deliverable within the bounds of the original investment. In some cases, as a project extends beyond the planned timeline, PMs may find comfort in the fact that they are still within their planned budget. However, PMs may be deceiving themselves if they think that though a schedule is not being met, they are still maintaining costs. The example in the previous section explained how a delay in the marketing system's rollout could lead to additional labor, facility, and licensing costs. Other hidden or unforeseen costs that could result from delays include strategic misalignment, resource reallocation delays, salvage costs (if the project is ultimately scrapped), ruined business relationships, and lawsuits. But if a project plan includes well-designed time and cost buffers, it should be able to adjust to many of the blind sides inherent in IT-based projects.

1.2.3 Variable Functionality/Scope/Quality

As mentioned earlier, while a project progresses along the cost/timeline tightrope, project investors may want to change the final functionality to accommodate a market shift or to increase the calculated ROI. As has been explained, such midstream shifts in scope can result in timeline and cost changes. On the other side of the coin, if the project sponsor sees an increase to potential project ROI by rolling it out earlier than planned, then the functionality or quality of the project may decrease. Either way, if a project does not meet the ultimate expectations of the project sponsor, then the final ROI can vary dramatically. Unfortunately, such releases that fail to deliver the expected product are fairly common with IT projects. For example, "surveys indicate that 20%–33% of [completed] projects fail to deliver on sponsor/stakeholder expectations" [10]. If we include projects that fail to stay within budget or fail to deliver on time, this statistic will show an even greater percentage of projects that do not succeed.

Project mismanagement can be another huge factor in causing the final functionality to diverge. A company cannot depend on the quality of project management to be constant. "It changes with the projects and the people. It may be good one year, bad the next" [11]. With such variability comes an increased risk of a sponsor getting a PM that mismanages the project. And a project sponsor surely knows that "a mismanaged implementation can result in a loss equal to ten times the implementation cost" [12]. IT PMOs will look at more than just ensuring quality across the project landscape; they will also look at the quality of the project management staff. Through training classes, knowledge management, and efficient resource management, an IT PMO can help build and maintain the high-quality PMs required for a healthy portfolio.

1.2.4 Risk

The PMI felt that risk is sufficiently central to project management to be given its own balancing point in the classic triad. Others take the approach that risk holds its own separate dimension that is present in all three points of the classical triad. That is, risk exists in the variances of cost, functionality, and schedule. If any of these three points runs into trouble, then other points of the triad can be affected through "side effects of the project and its unforeseen consequences" [13]. Whichever view you take, risk management is a critical piece to any IT project's success.

How can a PM monitor risk levels on their project? Can they categorize and measure increases and decreases in risk levels as a project progresses? While we introduced four types of project risks earlier, we can generalize them from a different angle into two types: technical risk, which is the probability that a project will not complete successfully, and commercial risk, which is the probability that the project's end product or service will not be successful in the marketplace [14]. Two additional risks that we can add to this are the risks associated with budget, cost, and methodology (project/process risk), and the risk associated with the customer not getting involved with the development process (organizational risk). Figure 1.5 shows how by layering these risks, a PM will be able to see how some risks decrease through the life of

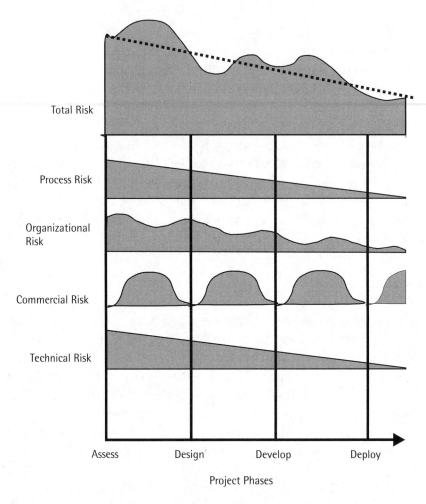

Figure 1.5 Additive nature of risks during a project's lifetime.

the project while others vary. The total risk at any phase in the project is a summation of the various types of risks.

Constructive Cost Model (COCOMO), Monte Carlo, and Real Options analyses are just a few tools a PM can use to gauge the risk his project is in. An IT PMO, on the other hand, is interested in normalizing the risk levels across all projects. It would be impractical for the PMO to rely on the subjective risk levels determined by the different

PMs. Rather, the PMO needs to establish an auditing team that can review a random sampling of projects to ensure they are calculating their risk levels the same as other projects. This is where the IT PMO establishes a common set of metrics to be used by each project to measure risk and to use in the prioritization process.

But IT project portfolio risk doesn't reside solely in the status of ongoing projects. Portfolio risk also must be gauged in the portfolio selection process. "There is more uncertainty about projects which are proposed but not yet underway, as compared to projects which are already underway and for which there is more data available" [14]. If the IT PMO isn't actively managing the IT business initiatives that act as the input stream to the project portfolio, then the opportunity for increased risks can balloon. An IT PMO initiative review committee can establish certain auditable hurdle points for each project before they start. "Any hurdle rate that does not fully account for risk puts the investor in the dangerous position of accepting too much risk in the firm's IT portfolio. And unless companies start managing risk better, they will be forced to require astronomical hurdle rates or get far too little return on their IT investments" [15]. In short, the IT PMO will need to:

1. Provide risk management support to individual projects.

2. Mitigate risk of the portfolio by reviewing the initiative pipeline.

3. Normalize risk assessments through a project audit team.

4. Use risk levels as a metric in prioritizing projects.

Such enterprisewide management of IT project risks has taken on new urgency as governments are passing regulations that require, or strongly recommend, formalized risk management processes (see Appendix 1A).

Project risk management is a well-documented subject that this book will not try to tackle. However, items 2, 3, and 4 are important elements of a successful IT PMO. Chapters 9 and 10 will go into more details on how an IT PMO should address portfolio risk management.

1.3 Portfolio Selection

While MPT shows how to manage the risk of a financial portfolio by selecting the proper range of investments, managing the risk for project portfolios can be more complex. Dr. Markowitz feels that quadratic programming alone can't resolve the additional complexities project management brings to MPT. Though PPM can be more complex than MPT, we can still leverage some of the basics, such as how the portfolio is selected. Three criteria can be used to select and prioritize projects that can be easily mapped to MPT: maximization, balance, and strategic alignment (see Figure 1.6) [16]. While these criteria should be used in selecting projects for the portfolio, resource balancing is the constraining criterion that limits the size of the portfolio. We can thus define project portfolio selection as follows [17]:

> Project portfolio selection is the periodic activity involved in selecting a portfolio, from available project proposals and projects currently underway, that meets the organization's stated objectives in a desirable manner without exceeding available resources or violating other constraints.

1.3.1 Maximization

A project begins by being designed around a set of initial stakeholder expectations. As the project progresses, the expectations of the project stakeholders tend to change. Managing these changing expectations

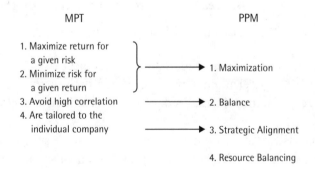

Figure 1.6 Selection and prioritization (S&P) criteria for financial and project portfolios.

falls under the category of project scope management and project rollout marketing. The PM needs to make sure that:

1. The acceptance of scope changes does not adversely affect the success of the project (scope management).

2. The rejection of scope changes does not adversely affect the enthusiasm of the stakeholders (rollout marketing).

The combination of these two make up what we can refer to as expectations management. Being strict with scope management can lead to diminished enthusiasm by the stakeholders and thus ultimate rejection of the solution. Being too loose with scope management can cause the project to increase cost and bypass deadlines (increased risk expenses). Through constant negotiation, the PM must work toward an end result that fits both the managed expectations and the managed enthusiasms of the stakeholder. In other words, a project maximizes its value when the ultimate (or final) expectations of the stakeholder are met or exceeded.

When selecting IT-based business initiatives, a project portfolio team should consider the likelihood that the individual project's end results will satisfy the ultimate expectations of the stakeholders. Then, by attaching auditable metrics to the business case, the project portfolio team will ensure that future auditing teams will be able to gauge whether stakeholders will embrace the end result. For example, a business case could state that an IT implementation will reduce the costs of tracking inventories of *certain* items. After confirming that this is what the end users truly need, the project portfolio team may approve the initiative. Then, during a mid-project audit, if the portfolio team discovers that the end users have changed their needs (e.g., they now want to reduce the costs of tracking the inventories of *different* items), then the project could be rated as unhealthy. This shows how a project portfolio team can contribute to each project's expectation management process.

1.3.2 Strategic Alignment

PPM needs to ensure that the suite of projects furthers the goals of the corporate strategy. If a group of related projects (a program) is focused on building better swimming pools while the executive staff wants to focus on building railroad tracks, then this group of projects would be considered to be out of alignment with the corporate strategy. Figure 1.7 shows how the IT portfolio should first be built and then maintained to ensure strategic alignment.

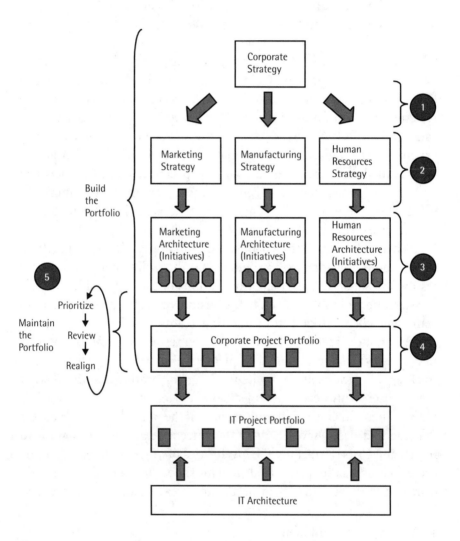

Figure 1.7 Building and maintaining the project portfolio for strategic alignment.

1. A company's resources can be allocated among business units through centralized corporate planning.

2. The corporate strategy can evolve by developing business unit level strategies—similar to the Balanced Scorecard approach.

3. A business unit can implement its strategies for growth or productivity gains by developing detailed plans. This could be in the form of a portfolio of initiatives (or business cases) for projects.

4. A periodic review process for all initiatives that get funded as projects can be established [18].

5. Then, once the portfolio is determined, it can then be maintained through "decision-making, prioritization, review, realignment, and reprioritization" [6].

1.3.3 Balance

Another major goal of portfolio selection is to create and manage a balanced portfolio. The portfolio should first be balanced between what the company needs and what the company is capable of achieving. "Balancing capability and need generally results in defining the best that can be achieved with the limited resources available, rather than attempting to find the perfect solution (which in a perfect world would include infinite resources)" [19]. After determining what the company is capable of successfully implementing, it can then approve those projects that fit its strategic and tactical objectives.

Corporate PPM focuses on balancing the project portfolio among all projects that are critical to furthering the corporate strategy. For a construction company, these projects could include building bridges; for a toy company—new dolls; and for a bank—new financial services. But within each of these companies, projects, products, and services tend to be balanced among a set of risk levels that can provide various levels of return. Similar to how a financial portfolio is balanced among high-risk/high-return stocks and low-risk/low-return bonds, project-oriented companies can also hedge their risks. The construction company could build low-risk foot bridges while also building high-risk interstate suspension bridges. The toy company can produce low-risk dolls for carefree toddlers and high-risk dolls for picky preteens. This same concept applies to how a company balances its portfolio of IT projects across its enterprise. Chapter 9 will show how more elaborate balancing techniques can be used to better tailor the PPM to the company.

1.3.4 Resource Allocation

Most IT projects have a threshold of resources they need in order to satisfy their cost/time/functionality requirements. When developing the business plan for the project, known at this stage as an IT-based business initiative, minimum requirements should be set for hardware, software licenses, human resources, and facilities. While the sponsoring business unit will be best suited to satisfy many of the project expenses, the IT PMO will be best positioned to know what resources are available from within the current portfolio of projects. If these resources are spread too "finely," then each individual project may go below its minimum threshold of resources for success. This, in turn, will lead to an overall failure of the portfolio. Financial portfolio managers, on the other hand, have more control on how finely their resources can be distributed among investment instruments. One major difference between MPT and project portfolio management is in how finely risk is distributed [4]. Dr. Markowitz explains that "in the typical investment situation one can finely subdivide one's funds among many fairly liquid assets. The same cannot be said of portfolios of projects... If a company manager subdivides his resources too finely among many projects in order to diversify, he may give each project too little to succeed" [4].

With PPM, we ask "what mix of potential projects will provide the best utilization of human and cash resources to maximize long-range growth and ROI for the firm?" [20]. We also want to ask, how can the mix of projects best leverage underutilized IT assets to maximize project value? Figure 1.8 shows how IT resources are divided. IT assets on the right are split up into hardware, software, facilities, and contracts/licenses. IT-focused human resources on the left and middle are split into outsourced IT and internal IT technicians. Focusing on the human resources, we see that many large companies allow strategic business units (SBUs) (e.g., marketing, manufacturing, and finance) to have their own quick-response team of technicians. The central IT department will have a more expansive set of IT resources specializing in help desk, database design, systems integration, and IT project management, just to name a few specialties. In short, for a PMO to better leverage IT resources among the various projects, it may be better to categorize those resources into manageable subsets, as shown in Figure 1.8.

1.4 The IT PMO

In order to achieve and maintain a portfolio of projects that meet the selection and prioritization goals outlined in Figure 1.6, certain tasks should be completed. Again, we can look to MPT and map tasks needed to manage financial portfolios to those needed to manage project portfolios. To ensure that the four goals of MPT are satisfied for a financial portfolio, the portfolio manager needs to review investment proposals, monitor the investments as they mature, and constantly valuate and

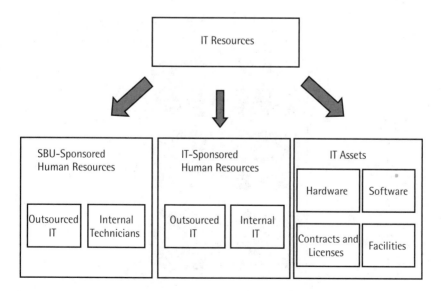

Figure 1.8 Categorizing resources for IT-based projects.

prioritize the portfolio as a whole. As shown in Figure 1.9, these core financial portfolio management tasks can be mapped to the basic processes of project portfolio management: initiative reviews, project audits, and ongoing portfolio valuation.

IT PPM is in the unique position of being able to support the projects in their portfolio and report on them to the executive committee. This support helps reduce the risk expenses by leveraging AARK from other projects. While classic PPM uses resource-balancing techniques to support the PPM S&P process, IT PPM uses an expanded version of resource balancing called AARK management. AARK management splits the classic definition of resources into four subcategories of resources that are each valuable to the success of any IT project. For the rest of this book, when a reference is made to resources, we mean human resources. This is a fairly standard practice in IT, where nonhuman resources can be referred to as assets, architectures, or knowledge. Figure 1.10 shows how the previous figure changes to show the tasks and the goals associated with IT PPM.

With tasks and goals starting to form for IT PPM, we can now introduce the concept of an actual organization charted with the

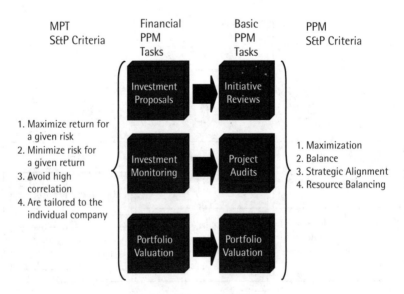

Figure 1.9 Mapping S&P criteria from MPT to PPM via tasks.

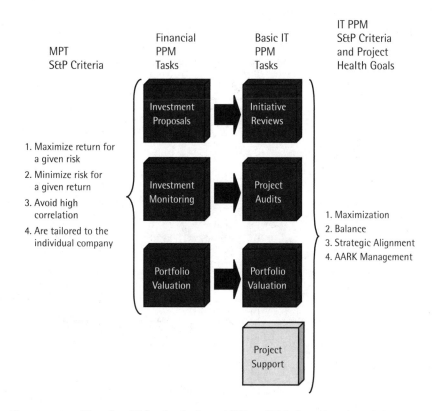

MPT
S&P Criteria

Financial
PPM
Tasks

Basic IT
PPM
Tasks

IT PPM
S&P Criteria
and Project
Health Goals

1. Maximize return for
   a given risk
2. Minimize risk for
   a given return
3. Avoid high
   correlation
4. Are tailored to the
   individual company

Investment
Proposals

Initiative
Reviews

Investment
Monitoring

Project
Audits

Portfolio
Valuation

Portfolio
Valuation

Project
Support

1. Maximization
2. Balance
3. Strategic Alignment
4. AARK Management

Figure 1.10 Mapping S&P criteria from MPT to PPM via tasks with project support.

responsibilities of running IT PPM. While the IT PMO will be covered in much more detail in Chapter 4, we can show how it relates to a corporate PMO. Corporate PMOs need to manage all of the projects in the company, whether they are IT related or not. With such different goals, there are different ways of aligning project with the corporate strategy. Figure 1.11 shows that while the corporate PMO may balance its PPM strategy evenly between growth-oriented projects and productivity-oriented projects, the IT PMO tends to have its strategy lean more towards productivity-oriented projects. Because a company's income relies more on its products or services, IT is used more to improve the efficiency of producing those products or services. Sometimes IT can contribute directly to growth if it develops its own product or service.

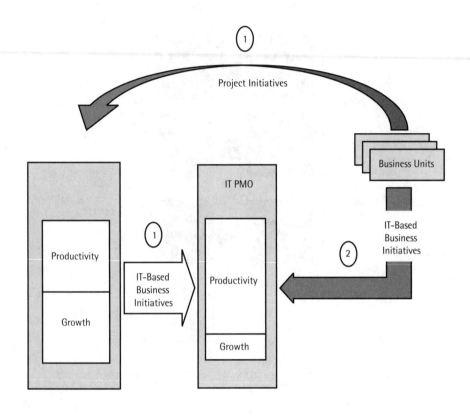

Figure 1.11 Corporate versus IT PMO handling of business initiatives.

However, this is so rare that we can go so far as to claim that "we don't have IT initiatives anymore; we only have business initiatives, and IT supports them" [21].

Figure 1.11 also shows how a corporate PMO receives IT- and non-IT-based project initiatives from business units (path #1). After projects are properly prioritized and then funded, many of them will be passed to an IT PMO—to go through another IT project-specific prioritization. These initiatives tend to fall into one of three required project types [13]:

1. *The sacred cow.* The project is "sacred" in the sense that it will be maintained until successfully concluded or until the boss, personally, recognizes the idea as a failure and terminates it. Sony refers to these types of projects as "skunk works" projects that circumvent the formal project approval process [22].

2. *The operating necessity.* It is needed to keep the business running.

3. *The competitive necessity.* It is needed to keep the business growing.

In some cases, companies can establish their own balance between corporate project control with a central PMO and business unit project control with disparate business unit PMOs. A groundbreaking survey of over 250 companies showed that "a significant number of businesses do both; that is, they operate portfolio management within the business unit, and they also have a centralized or corporate portfolio management method (44.7 percent of respondents)" [19]. This leads to project initiatives coming into an IT PMO from two directions (see Figure 1.11, paths 1 and 2).

As mentioned earlier, an IT prioritization process is much more specific than a general corporate PPM process. Chapter 9 will go into some of the details of how to best prioritize IT projects. But before we can know how to prioritize projects, Chapters 5 through 8 will help us understand the building blocks of an IT PMO. These building blocks will better define how a portfolio should be selected and managed. Figure 1.12 shows how from the goals of an IT PMO we can derive these building blocks. The goals of an IT PMO are to:

1. *Support executives.* Executives need to know the real-time health of their project portfolios so that accurate prioritizations can be made. The PMO can provide this information through project and initiative collaboration tools. Such decision support systems should not only allow decision makers to make adjustments to the portfolio, but these systems should also provide "feedback on the resulting consequences, in terms of

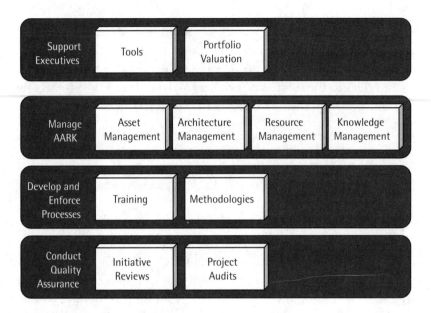

Figure 1.12   IT PMO building blocks.

optimality changes and effects on resources" [17] (see Chapter 9).

2. *Manage AARK.* Redundant and underutilized assets, overlapping architectures, misused resources, and lost experiences are common problems in a large, project-centric organization. These problems are especially acute in organizations that have dispersed power and strategic responsibility among many business units. By getting control of all four of these loose cannons, the PMO can provide a foundation for robust interinitiative and interproject communication (see Chapters 5 through 8).

3. *Develop and enforce processes.* To ensure consistent tracking and evaluation of different initiatives and projects, standard, company-specific touch points need to be added to industry-standard methodologies. Not only should a central body such as the PMO make these modifications, it should develop a training curriculum for the methods. This group would market and train the company on not only these methodology touch points but also on general PMO processes, such as AARK

management, executive support, and project and initiative portfolio quality assurance (QA) (see Chapter 3).

4. *Conduct initiative and project audits (QA).* Because some creative freedom is needed in writing business cases and because project health ratings vary between PMs, a third-party auditing process needs to be supported by a central PMO. This will ensure that a consistent set of metrics will be defined in all business cases that can be monitored throughout the history of its resulting project without impeding the overall format of the business case. Furthermore, some auditing schedule should be made to ensure all projects are rated on the same scale to reduce subjectivity (see Chapters 9).

1.4.1 PMO Rollout

Rolling out an IT PMO draws on the same expectation management techniques used when rolling out an IT program or project. To maximize the value of the IT PMO in the eyes of those who will benefit most from it, the rollout needs to be segmented. That is, a different marketing and functionality release plan needs to be developed to get maximum acceptance and support. This will, in turn, allow the PMO to continue to gather momentum until it is a necessary part of the corporate strategy. The PMO needs to be sold to the different levels of vertical management as well as to the different horizontal groups that will be needed to provide organizational support. (The acompanying CD-ROM provides several examples of presentations that can be used as templates for such IT PMO marketing activities.)

When segmenting the sales and rollout pitch vertically, we need to understand who to market to more vigorously. Some levels of management may be more receptive to such a concept than others. For example, a survey of 205 responding businesses felt that "senior management in technology (CTOs, VPs of R&D, and so forth) attach the most importance to portfolio management; they are followed by senior management overall and then by corporate executives" [23]. This would lead one to develop presentations, updates on progress, and early-win results for the executive committee more frequently than to the other two levels of management.

Because access to executive ears can be limited, the next layer of management will more than likely be where the main battleground will be. Middle to senior management is known for its turf battles. Constant tug of wars over budgets, resources, and executive alliances make any greenhorn organization ripe for pillage. So, let's first learn from those who have taken on the challenge of introducing an IT PMO to a company. Thirty-five leading firms in various industries were interviewed to determine the biggest problems the companies faced in project selection and portfolio management. The keys to failure focused on four areas [16]:

1. Strategic alignment;
2. Resource leveraging;
3. Prioritization;
4. Quality control.

The respondents felt that their PMO initiatives hadn't created and maintained a portfolio of projects that accurately reflected the goals of the corporate strategy or that efficiently leveraged existing resources. They went on to say that their project and initiative prioritization process was inadequate. This was referred to as prioritization "tunnels, not funnels" [16]. One business unit lead exclaimed that, "ten projects enter the process, ten go into development, ten go to launch, and one succeeds!" [16]. But, one of the biggest complaints was that there was a perception of poor-quality portfolios. While selecting and prioritizing portfolios is a major part of an IT PMO, it also needs to focus as much energy on reducing the costs associated with the out-of-control risks inherent in many IT projects. In other words, by helping improve the quality of each project and program, the IT PMO is, in effect, improving the quality of the portfolio as a whole.

Any IT PMO rollout needs to attack each of these four problem areas aggressively in the early stages. The final chapter of this book will show an approach that can be used to roll out the IT building blocks. This approach is designed to gain early and then constant wins throughout the lifetime of the IT PMO and, if successful, the remaining lifetime of the company it serves. Figure 1.13 shows the building blocks that rest

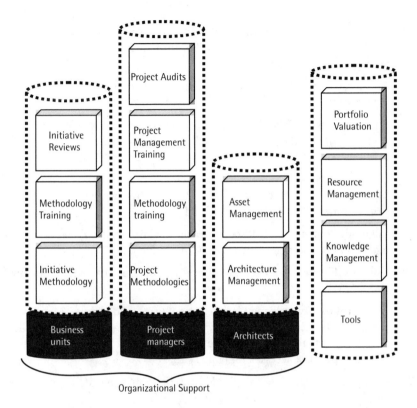

Figure 1.13 Acquiring organizational support for the IT PMO building blocks.

on a foundation of organizational support. Without such a foundation, the PMO spires will topple. Chapter 4 will show how to define a virtual PMO organization that will help start a successful rollout.

References

[1]   Markowitz, Harry M., *Portfolio Selection*, London, England: Basil Blackwell, 1991.

[2]   Moyer, R. Charles, James R. McGuigan, and William J. Kretlow, *Contemporary Financial Management*, 9th ed., Cincinnati, OH: Thomson South-Western, 2003.

[3]   Berinato, Scott, "Do the Math," *CIO Magazine*, October 1, 2001, http://comment.cio.com/comments/6183.html (last accessed on January 15, 2004).

[4]   Harder, Paul, "A Conversation with Dr. Harry Markowitz," *Gantthead.com*, 2002,   http://www.eitforum.com/ForumItem.asp?itemID=1157   (last accessed on January 15, 2004).

[5]   Pressman, Robert S., *Software Engineering: A Practitioner's Approach*, 3rd ed., New York: McGraw-Hill, 1992.

[6]   Sommer, Renee, "Portfolio Management for Projects: A New Paradigm," in *Project Portfolio Management*, Lowell D. Dye and James S. Pennypacker, (eds.), West Chester, PA: Center for Business Practices, 1999, pp. 55–60.

[7]   Chandler, Tamra, "Strategic Analysis Helps Identify IT Issues," *Puget Sound Business Journal*, February 15, 2002, http://www.bizjournals.com/ seattle/stories/2002/02/18/focus11.html.

[8]   Englund, Randall, and Robert Graham, *Creating an Environment for Successful Projects*, San Francisco, CA: Jossey-Bass, 1997.

[9]   Goldratt, Eliyahu, *Critical Chain*, Great Barrington, MA: The North River Press, 1997.

[10] Meta Group, "Centralizing Management of Project Portfolios," *Meta Group*, January 29, 2002, http://www.umt.com/site/Documents/IT_World_- _Leading_Organisation_Centralize_Management_of_Project_Portfolios_- _29Jan02.pdf (last accessed on January 15, 2004).

[11] O'Connell, Fergus, *Successful High-Tech Project-Based Organizations*, Norwood, MA: Artech House Publishers, 1999.

[12] Kaplan, Jeffrey D., "White Paper: Strategically Managing Your IT Portfolio," *PRTM's Insight*, April 1, 2001, http://www.prtm.com (last accessed on January 15, 2004).

[13] Mantel, Samual, and Jack Meredith, "Project Selection," in *Project Portfolio Management*, Lowell D. Dye and James S. Pennypacker, (eds.), West Chester, PA: Center for Business Practices, 1999, pp. 135–168.

[14] Ghasemzadeh, Fereidoun, and Norman Archer, "Project Portfolio Selection Techniques: A Review and a Suggested Integrated Approach," in *Project Portfolio Management*, Lowell D. Dye and James S. Pennypacker, (eds.), West Chester, PA: Center for Business Practices, 1999, pp. 207–238.

[15] Hubbard, Douglas, "Hurdling Risk," *CIO Magazine*, June 15, 1998, http://www.cio.com/archive/enterprise/061598_checks.html (last accessed on January 15, 2004).

[16] Kleinschmidt, Elko, Scott Edgett, and Robert Cooper, "Portfolio Management in New Product Development: Lessons from the Leaders, Phase I," in *Project Portfolio Management*, Lowell D. Dye and James S.

Pennypacker, (eds.), West Chester, PA: Center for Business Practices, 1999, pp. 97–116.

[17] Ghasemzadeh, Fereidoun, and Norman Archer, "An Integrated Framework for Project Portfolio Selection," in *Project Portfolio Management*, Lowell D. Dye and James S. Pennypacker, (eds.), West Chester, PA: Center for Business Practices, 1999, pp. 117–134.

[18] Edgett, Scott, Elko Kleinschmidt, and Robert Cooper, "Portfolio Management in New Product Development: Lessons from the Leaders, Phase II," in *Project Portfolio Management*, Lowell D. Dye and James S. Pennypacker, (eds.), West Chester, PA: Center for Business Practices, 1999, pp. 97–116.

[19] Dye, Lowell, and James Pennypacker, "An Introduction to Project Portfolio Management," in *Project Portfolio Management*, Lowell D. Dye and James S. Pennypacker, (eds.), West Chester, PA: Center for Business Practices, 1999, pp. xi–xvi.

[20] Levine, Harvey, "Project Portfolio Management: A Song Without Words," in *Project Portfolio Management*, Lowell D. Dye and James S. Pennypacker, (eds.), West Chester, PA: Center for Business Practices, 1999, pp. 39–44.

[21] Low, Lafe, and Sarah D. Scalet, "Come Together," *CIO Magazine*, December 15, 2000, http://www.cio.com/archive/010101/together.html (last accessed on January 15, 2004).

[22] Cleland, David, "The Strategic Context of Projects," in *Project Portfolio Management*, Lowell D. Dye and James S. Pennypacker, (eds.), West Chester, PA: Center for Business Practices, 1999, pp. 3–22.

[23] Edgett, Scott, Elko Kleinschmidt, and Robert Cooper, "Best Practices for Managing R&D Portfolios," in *Project Portfolio Management*, Lowell D. Dye and James S. Pennypacker, (eds.), West Chester, PA: Center for Business Practices, 1999, pp. 309–328.

[24] Locher, Christian, Jens I. Mehlau, and Oliver Wild, "Towards Risk Adjusted Controlling of Strategic IS Projects in Banks in the Light of Basel II," *Proceedings of the 37th Hawaii International Conference on System Sciences 2004*, January 2004.

[25] Kersten, Bert and Chris Verhoef, "IT Portfolio Management: A Banker's Perspective on IT," *Cutter IT Journal*, April 2003, http://www.math.vu.nl/~hkersten/pdf/citj0403BK.pdf (last accessed on January 15, 2004).

[26] Crosett, Lex, "Beyond Sarbanes-Oxley Compliance: Improving Operations and Mitigating Risk Through Active Risk Management Practices," *DM Review*, February 6, 2004, http://www.dmreview.com/editorial/newsletter_

article.cfm?nl=dmdirect&articleId=8090 (last accessed on January 15, 2004).

[27] U.S. Congress, "The Sarbanes-Oxley Act of 2002," *107th Congress, 2nd Session,* H.R. 3763, 2002.

[28] Callaghan, Dennis, "Sarbanes-Oxley: Road to Compliance," *eWeek,* February 16, 2004, http://www.eweek.com/article2/0,1759,1527933,00.asp (last accessed on January 15, 2004).

Appendix 1A: IT PPM in Action—Government Regulations

Due to a series of corporate scandals in the late 1990s and early 2000s, new regulations started sprouting up to force corporations (the Sarbanes-Oxley Act), government agencies (the Clinger-Cohen Act), and banks (the Basel II Accord) to be held accountable for lack of risk control. While the Clinger-Cohen Act specifically recommends the usage of IT PPM techniques, Basel II and the Sarbanes-Oxley Act create urgency for IT PPM because of their references to operational risk management. Operational risks have traditionally been managed internally but are now seen as critical sources of information for external entities such as investors, insurers, and governments. Until now, these entities could only rely on the information provided by financial statements and credit ratings agencies to make decisions related to the organization.

To support the requirements of these new regulations, organizations are building IT systems that allow management to have increased visibility into their operational processes. An IT PMO would help ensure that new IT-based business initiatives take new government regulations into account when developing their business cases. Also, IT PPM tools reduce operational risk by providing continuous and clear views of the project portfolio to senior management. Let's now look at the details of these three regulations.

1A.1 Basel II

In 1974, the Basel Committee on Banking Supervision was founded by the G-10 states. In the late 1990s, the Basel II accord was proposed to help central banks better grade the financial strengths of commercial banks. Until Basel II, governmental central banks relied solely on the credit rating (credit risks) and the health of the banking market (market risks) to judge how risky it was to insure or to lend money to particular banks. Basel II provided guidelines for banks to also provide their operational risk levels when determining their minimum equity requirements (e.g., the ratio of cash held to loans outstanding). "The more advanced the risk management system a bank adopts, the lower the cost of capital and the equity requirements central banks will impose" [24]. Such risk management will need to account for potential losses due to IT systems, staff processes, and external events.

> CD-ROM: Two documents are included that provide more detail on this accord, as well as the proposed timeline for introduction by the European Union. The Basel Review—Melbourne article in the CD-ROM reviews the Basel II accord from a fairly academic perspective. The Basel Roadmap shows the timeline that is being followed for the implementation of Basel II.

1A.2 Clinger-Cohen Act

In 1996, the U.S. Congress passed the Clinger-Cohen Act, which compels government agencies to implement IT PPM policies. Such IT PPM standards would be used as a basis to scrutinize proposed initiatives and audit IT-based projects. Historically, after the government imposes new control processes, it tends to require the same processes of its civilian contractors [e.g., ISO 9000, total quality management (TQM)] [25]. Therefore, companies that rely on government contracts are taking a close look at developing IT PPM techniques to maintain an advantage during contract biddings.

> CD-ROM: A grouping of U.S. Department of Defense documents that address approaches to managing IT-based projects is included. The Clinger-Cohen Act is included in this group.

1A.3 Sarbanes-Oxley Act

While the Sarbanes-Oxley Act of 2002 introduced new financial accountability requirements for U.S. corporations, other countries (e.g., Canada) are looking into similar legislation [26]. Section 404 of the Sarbanes-Oxley Act is gaining much attention because it goes beyond just establishing review committees and limiting outside auditors. This section requires companies to expand their financial statements to include a report that "establishes, maintains and assesses the effectiveness of an internal control structure and a set of procedures for financial reporting" [27]. This requirement is similar to the operational risk mitigation controls found in the Basel II Accord. While the Basel II

Accord can impose higher equity requirements for failure to comply, the Sarbanes-Oxley Act can impose criminal penalties. Companies are already incurring costs to comply with this new government regulation. The Hackett Group of Atlanta predicts costs of annual compliance at most companies will be in the range of $5 million to $7 million [28]. IT solutions that automate the new need for process awareness can reduce such costs. However, if enterprise integration isn't considered (e.g., through enterprise IT and business architecture review committees) when introducing such solutions, a company can be taking two steps back for every one step forward. The accompanying CD-ROM includes the complete Sarbanes-Oxley Act.

2

Strategic Alignment

2.1 Corporate Strategy

Strategic planning has been pondered since before Sun Tzu wrote about it over 2,000 years ago in *The Art of War.* He wrote about how an army general in ancient China should best plan to achieve an objective. In some cases, the objective may be conquering an enemy, and in other cases it could be an efficient retreat. The combination of all of these objectives (or microstrategies) may comprise the overriding strategy of a campaign. Different situations require different tactics, but these tactics all need to be connected to one overriding strategy. He explained that strategy is not a competitive game with a goal of "doing more, better, faster." "It does not seek confrontations; instead, it seeks to achieve the objectives with minimum combat" [1]. In recent times, we can see how corporations have adopted or ignored some of these oldest of approaches in developing strategies.

One glaring digression from adopting well-rounded strategies has been the push for quality since the early 1980s. The corporate world began focusing more on improving business and customer-facing quality better and faster than the competitor. Corporate cultures were drastically changed to ensure the smooth rollout and implementation of TQM and Six Sigma programs. Where TQM focuses on improvements in "individual operations with unrelated processes," Six Sigma focuses "on making improvements in all operations within a process" [2]. It was easy to adopt these companywide changes as the overriding strategy of the organization. However, "quality programs help organizations do things right, strategy is about doing the right things" [3].

The strategy is the grand purpose of the organization. Executives first understand the markets they want to attack, then they list out the parts of a strategy that will allow their company to succeed financially. They can follow high-level business paradigms such as just-in-time inventory control, supply-chain management processes, and segmented marketing approaches. Or they can implement classic financial microstrategies through product pricing variations, salary level changes, and capital structure approaches. But the overriding strategy usually follows a combination of two directions: growth and survival [4]. Alternatively, companies have "two basic strategies for driving their financial performance: growth and productivity" [3]. For example, while some focus more on growth by increasing revenue and attacking new markets, others focus more on improving productivity by lowering cost and increasing output. All microstrategies, business objectives, and tactics derive from some combination of these two grand purposes.

No matter what strategy a company chooses, today's volatile high-tech business world can make the strategy obsolete fairly quickly. As the speed of information becomes faster, so does the speed of change in the various marketplaces. To avoid instability, companies must quickly adjust their strategies to accommodate these rapid fluctuations; they need to "be nimble and quick to market" [5]. Moreover, to help reduce complacency during the good times, executives should regularly review the links that bind their corporate strategy with the market. That is, when not moving constantly to stay on top of market shifts, executives must stay vigilant to potential changes. In short, "they must be able to react quickly, innovate ceaselessly, pursue alliances, and handle change continually" [5].

Because advances in economic theory and information technology haven't prevented marketplace upheavals from blindsiding businesses, strategic flexibility continues to be a necessity. However, a company's strategy can only change frequently if the company's culture is flexible enough to support such constant redirection. To both support a flexing market and to create a flexible culture, the leading competitors in the world are moving toward creating "a strategy of flexibility" [6]. The high-level strategy needs to be able to *bend* to marketplace pressures, and the supporting microstrategies need to *negotiate* with less flexible IT projects nearing completion. And, to link these two, the microstrategies need to be written such that they can *accommodate shifts* in the high-level strategy (see Figure 2.1). Keep these plans simple and clear,

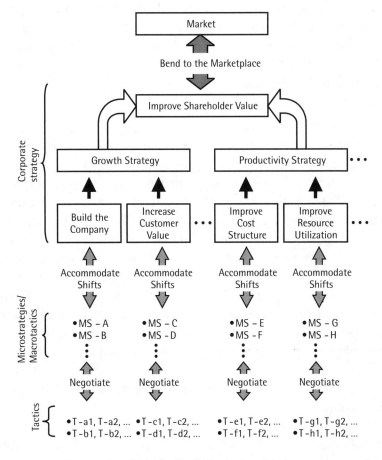

Figure 2.1 Linking market shifts to flexibility in low-level corporate tactics.

however, because "the more sophisticated the planning process becomes, the harder it is to introduce flexibility" [2]. Without such flexibility planned into the various levels of a strategy, the market blind-sides will feel more like a baseball bats to the forehead rather than encouraging nudges.

To balance this concept of flexibility, certain aspects of the strategy need to be kept fairly constant. While parts of the strategy can change to accommodate unforeseen events (e.g., war, new government regulations, and natural disasters), others should stay stable to maintain identity with the customer (e.g., company name, core product suite, and quality of salesmanship). Changes in the latter can cause complete redesign of all microstrategies and cancellation of any supporting projects. In summary "the art of leadership is to delicately balance the tension between stability and change" [3]. By developing a corporate strategy that supports both of these, the executive team is on its way to guiding a company to success.

2.1.1 Problems

When a particular industry experiences rapid growth, companies see the productivity (growth per hours worked) of their competitors increase faster than usual. To ensure they maintain their market share, companies tend to invest this increased revenue stream in productivity-enhancing technology initiatives. Business units in a company scramble to get their technical initiatives funded so they won't be left in their competitor's dust. For example, human resources departments may scream for online recruiting sites and payroll systems tied to changing local laws; marketing departments may insist on GPS information system (GIS)–based demographics and campaigns linked to call center graphical user interfaces (GUIs); and manufacturing departments may beg for business to business (B2B) design extranets and robotic inventory control systems. In short, a whirlwind of IT-based project chaos can whip through companies mesmerized by sudden growth numbers.

There can be some bad side effects, however, from such a rapid spread of IT-based business initiatives in a company. As Scott McLagan, a partner at Intergistic Solutions Consulting, put it, such "growth can wallpaper over efficiency." For example, inefficiency during rapid growth can be seen in the positive business cycle of the late 1990s. The IT project chaos during this growth period had executives gunning to get to the Web yesterday. Executive teams were even "leaving CIO's and the IS department out of the loop altogether" [5] and were instead relying more on IT outsourcers. By leaving out internal technicians who knew the strategy best, IT initiatives became generalized across industries. As a result, commercial off-the-shelf (COTS) packages pushed companies towards generic business models. Services companies pushed industry-standard business processes to allow for quicker implementations. And complex, custom software implementations had countless ways to diverge from a stakeholder's vision. These programs and projects that everyone thought were perfectly consistent with strategic, tactical, and operational business objectives were, in fact, the tail that was wagging the corporate dog.

As a business cycle starts downhill, executives start feeling that their return on IT investment isn't up to snuff. New market demands require that they start slashing outlays for expensive technical initiatives. However, in order to do so without damaging the forward growth of the company, they need an ability to prioritize all of the proposed and ongoing initiatives. This proves difficult because what they find out is that business units have been implementing technical initiatives independently and without IT governance or support. Ultimately, because different business units are approving and running initiatives differently, there are no consistent ways to measure initiative health between business units. So, without a consistent way to compare initiatives, management is forced to clean up the project chaos created by the IT spending explosion of the business cycle upslope.

2.1.2 Solutions

This feeling of lost control can come about if there aren't any links in place to ensure continual alignment between the executives' strategy and the IT project implementations. Some have established these links (and a new corporate culture) by implementing a Balanced Scorecard [3]. Others have just cleaned house and started over. As an analogy, imagine how many households choose to put off deciding whether to keep a piece of junk or throw it out. It isn't until they move to another location that they have to address the "pile of junk in the garage." This is similar to the popular BPR business fad of the 1990s. By not ensuring continued alignment of their IT initiatives, executives feel forced to implement sweeping garage cleanings or BPR initiatives. BPR efforts are referred to as corporatewide innovations that cause radical changes in the business processes. The problem with BPRs, is that "many BPR projects have failed because those involved in the business or the environment objected to the radical changes" [7]. Such organizational resistance coupled with poorly designed business processes ensured many BPR failures.

While many continue to engage in BPR initiatives, others have chosen to take less risky, iterative approaches. One example, known as the business process improvement (BPI) approach, introduces business process changes in increments. For example, if an ERP system such as SAP or Oracle Financials were introduced to end users in pieces, it would be following a BPI approach. If, on the other hand, all departments switch over to such a system at the same time, the organizational backlash typical of BPR initiatives could result. The benefit of BPI is that by establishing a culture receptive to continuous change, it can be easier to get the organizational support for change that is critical to success. BPI allows for constant communication and *buy in* to set expectations before each business process change. "When an opportunity for improvement is identified, a new business model is produced to demonstrate how the business should look after those changes are implemented" [7]. A BPI process supported by a complete IT PMO can ensure that the portfolio of business initiatives follow the lead of the corporate strategy and not the other way around.

2.2 IT Projects

2.2.1 Changing Directions

While business units strive to make organizational strategy a reality by implementing business initiatives, they may, in fact, be leading the company astray. These initiatives, such as increasing a sales force, building a bridge, or distributing disaster relief, have concrete deliverables.

Management can see, in real time, how things are going and whether the intermediate project results are in line with the goals of the company. However, projects that require IT implementations are more difficult to track; their intermediate deliverables can be much less concrete. By forcing projects to have intermediate deliverables that map to auditable project methodologies, a central auditing group can prove real progress. Without such rigor, misaligned IT projects can continue to fly below the radar. This, in turn, will force the sponsoring business unit's microstrategies to accommodate the IT projects rather than the other way around.

2.2.2 Vector Analysis

Figure 2.2 illustrates that while uncertainties in the market can mold the high-level strategy of a company, uncertainties in IT-based projects can affect the low-level microstrategies. That is, because so many factors can

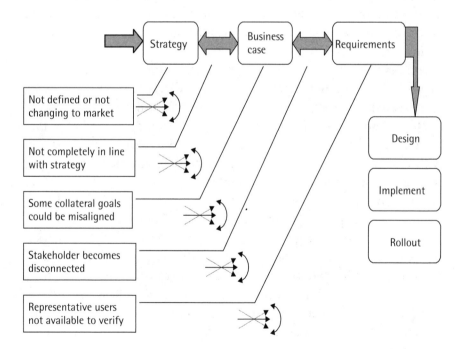

Figure 2.2 Various problems that can misdirect a project from its original strategy.

affect the outcome of an IT-based project, the final deliverable may have changed from what the stakeholder originally and ultimately envisioned. Figure 2.2 shows some of the events that can alter the original goals of a technical business initiative. The central of the three arrows for each event represents the path to take to product delivery as envisioned by the stakeholder. The two other dotted lines for each event represent digressions that could put the project off course. In this example, we see that a strategy that is not well defined or that hasn't kept pace with the market can be a reason that any project goes off course. "It is a business fundamental that the strategy must be correct for the tactics to succeed" [2]. Then, if the business case for an initiative isn't properly aligned with a well-maintained strategy, the final project deliverable may not be what the company needs. And many times, project sponsors will put some unaligned functionality into their project that doesn't align with the strategy. From kickoff to rollout, there are even more issues that can cause an IT-based project to become misaligned with what a company actually needs. The auditing tasks of an IT PMO can ensure continued alignment of the IT portfolio and help projects avoid taking these wrong turns.

In describing how projects progress, the vectors (time and scope) in Figure 2.3 represent the general goals (or directions) of a corporate strategy and those of an IT-based project. We can see that when the strategy changes direction during a project, it can require a little more effort to realign the project vector. Figure 2.3(a) shows how a project with one iteration (requirements gathering, design, implementation, testing, rollout) and a constant strategy can stray off course. Figure 2.3(b) shows a project with multiple iterations (or functional releases: F1, F2, ...) doing the same thing. And finally, Figure 2.3(c) shows this with a corporate strategy that is flexing appropriately to the market place. This latter example can cause the most problems for a portfolio of projects that all started with the goal of supporting the original strategy. Not only does the PM and project sponsor need to keep the project from straying, they need to be able to realign projects to new corporate directions. "The most dangerous time for an organization is when the old strategies are discarded and new ones are developed to respond to competitive opportunities" [6].

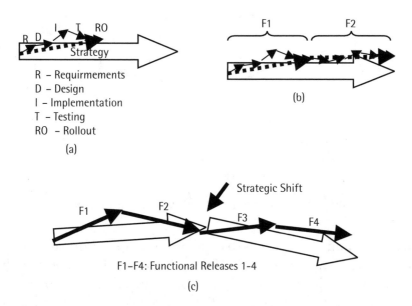

R – Requirements
D – Design
I – Implementation
T – Testing
RO – Rollout

(a)

(b)

F1–F4: Functional Releases 1-4

(c)

Figure 2.3 Project directions versus corporate strategic directions: (a) project with one release (five phases); (b) project with a second release to realign the corporate strategy; and (c) project with multiple releases and shifting corporate strategies.

Because this vector analysis approach can only explain things so far, let's look at some real-world examples. The following two examples of projects undertaken at Joe's Telecommunications will show two different ways a company can react to imperfect project deliverables and shifting corporate strategies. The figures from these next few sections can be further reviewed from a different perspective in the strategic alignment PowerPoint presentation in the accompanying CD-ROM.

2.2.3 Project A—Growth

Joe's Telecommunications is a provider of long-distance phone service. Because gaining and keeping customers is cutthroat in this business, the executive staff decides to develop a strategic goal of having the marketing department react quickly to customer losses (see S1 in Figure 2.4). To help with this, they commission an IT project to track customer loss rates by geography. After the new PM gets approval for his design, the project is released two months later (F1). Unfortunately, the reports can

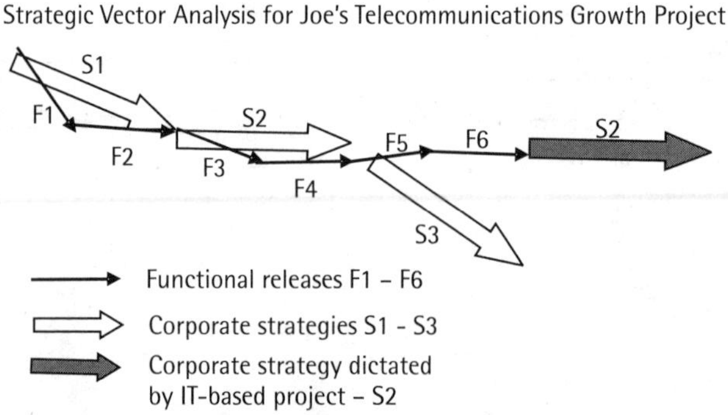

Strategic Vector Analysis for Joe's Telecommunications Growth Project

Functional releases F1 – F6
Corporate strategies S1 - S3
Corporate strategy dictated
by IT-based project – S2

Figure 2.4 Corporate strategy being guided by misaligned projects.

only be run on the weekends so as not to affect the performance of the database. So a second iteration of the project completes three months later. This iteration includes a GUI that accesses real-time customer loss data off of a replicated database (F2). The problem with this release is that the marketing department has old PCs that can't support the new GUI. Only the vice president of marketing has a new computer. Even though the staff can only get its data when this computer is free, the project's functionality is becoming more in line with the executive's original strategy.

As the third iteration (F3) begins, the executive staff announces an updated strategy that they have been considering for a while: regain lost customers more actively (S2). The PM decides to finish F3 before designing new functionality to support the new strategy. While F3 finally gets the project in line with the original strategy by rolling out new computers to the necessary marketing personnel, the deliverables are now out of alignment with the updated strategy. With additional funding, the PM designs, implements, and rolls out new functionality (F4) that passes lost customer data to the call center. The PM has also lobbied for and received approval for call center agents and supervisors to receive commissions when they successfully win back lost customers. Unfortunately, the PM didn't realize the need for the call centers to hire and train new outbound calling agents.

As the PM is working with the call center managers to complete this last phase of the project (F5), the executive staff decides to partner with smaller competitors to create long-distance boutiques in shopping malls to better compete against the nationwide long-distance firms (S3). Unknown to the PM, this strategic shift will put the output of the project at great odds with the goals of upper management. As the agents get online, they quickly learn to work with their supervisors to increase the commissions by engaging in slamming, or winning back a customer against their will. The fact that the new partners are losing their customers to Joe's in such a way causes the partnership to enter rough water. The PM tries to resolve this problem by setting up regular feeds from the partners that reconcile Joe's lost customers with the partners' customers. This multicompany integration effort winds up taking so long that the executives decide that S2 is more important than S3 and dissolve the partnership.

2.2.4 Project B—Productivity

Joe's Telecommunications also has a local digital subscriber line (DSL) service in three metropolitan areas. As this service has been expanding, Joe's has had to hire more field service representatives. A new strategy to improve productivity has been announced (see Figure 2.5) that requires field reps to increase the number of appointments from three to four per day (S1). The director of field operations responds to this by requesting and then getting funding for a new IT project. The PM decides to roll the project out in two iterations. Iteration one (F1) would allow field reps to keep their trucks at home and be assigned appointments daily over the phone. Truck restocking would occur after

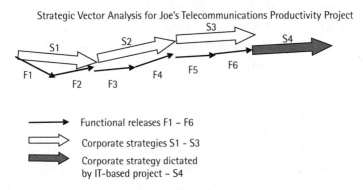

Figure 2.5 Small corporate strategy accommodation to misaligned project.

the biweekly staff meetings. Iteration 2 (F2) would decrease call center agent responsibilities by rolling out mobile devices to the reps. This requires a GUI development effort for the devices and a long-term, discounted contract with the wireless signal providers (carriers).

As F2 is being developed, Joe's wins bids on a couple of mom-and-pop cable companies in the metropolitan areas in which Joe's offers DSL. As a result, this growth strategy forces executives to modify one of their productivity strategies by requiring field reps to service not just more appointments per day, but also more types of appointments per day (S2). With more funding, the PM designs, implements, and rolls out an updated GUI for the mobile devices that includes repair and installation manuals for the cable modems as well as the DSL modems (F3). Unfortunately, with field reps still learning the new system, scrolling through the manuals while on site slows their productivity, and appointments per day fall to an average of 3.25. This forces the PM to successfully lobby for more funding for the call centers to hire and train agents to be on call for technical assistance for the field reps (F4).

As the appointment rate starts climbing back up to four per day, Joe's expands DSL service to two more metropolitan areas (S3). Unfortunately, these cities are areas in which the mobile carrier is piloting a new communications protocol. And the mobile device company won't support this new protocol for another year. To make matters worse, the long-term contract requires continued hardware purchases or the 50% discount will be voided and Joe's will owe on past discounts. The alternative is for the field reps in these new areas to upload from the network intranet daily (F5). But due to security issues and the mobile device's lack of phone modems, the field reps are forced to drive in for data uplinks. This causes a small shift in strategy for the next year. Basically allowing three appointments per day for two areas while still requiring four per day in Joe's original areas (S4).

2.2.5 Lessons

Strategies, like project plans, are road maps to successfully deliver on goals. But when obstacles are met, both need to be agile enough to change course in midstream [5]. How quickly the course changes occur is another matter. For example, a PM knows well the need to manage scope creep. Because there is so much ramp-up work to get a project moving in a certain direction, midcourse changes can be difficult. To combat this, Joe's Telecommunications uses iterative development methodologies that allow for direction (scope) changes during the lifetime of the project. "[Y]ou must mount a sort of ongoing rescue of your project to return it to the place you believe it should be heading" [8]. However, if the end point doesn't match with new strategies, the final project deliverable can still adversely affect the corporate goals. If only the PM was kept more aware of pending strategy shifts, he may have been able to adjust his next iteration's deliverables more efficiently. This would have allowed the strategic direction of Joe's Telecommunications to not be dictated by some IT project that couldn't keep up with the new desires of the executive staff. An IT PMO would have bridged the gap between the project and strategy road maps to ensure aligned deliverables.

The Royal Caribbean case study at the end of this chapter shows how project priorities can change on a dime when the corporate strategy changes. In this case, the new strategy focused not on growth or productivity increases, but rather on the survivability of the organization. Rather than writing off canceled projects, microstrategies were developed to rephase in projects that were tabled due to the new strategy.

2.3 Strategic Frameworks

2.3.1 Alignment

David P. Norton, coauthor of *The Strategy-Focused Organization,* [3], introduced the balanced scorecard as a way to efficiently propagate a corporate strategy throughout an organization. By starting with a vision and then recursively developing microstrategies and macrotactics (or, as D. W. McDavid, author of "A Standard for Business Architecture Description," calls them, business functions [9]), a company can establish links all the way down to the business activities. Figure 1.7 showed that the corporate strategy is made up of a list of high-level strategic goals. Then microstrategies or macrotactics are derived to support these goals. "Strategies at any level are the tactics of the next lower level in the chain of command" [2]. Figure 2.6 shows that if one strategic element is to increase customer value, then a microstrategy would be to react quickly to customer needs. Because the goals of such activities can be based on subjective views of the corporate strategy, it is important to be as explicit as possible when partitioning the strategy into subelements [9]. A strategic map, clearly traced to tactics at the business unit level, can help these units present well-aligned initiatives for review by the IT PMO.

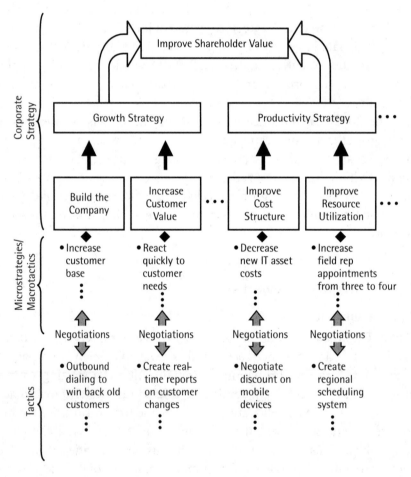

Figure 2.6 Financial perspective of Balanced Scorecard for Joe's Telecommunications.

These initiatives that make up the IT project portfolio also define the lower part of a Balanced Scorecard called the tactical implementation. "The tactical implementation plan is as important as the strategic plan because it takes the vision and strategy to the point of contact" [2]. If this lower level has been kept aligned and flexible, problems can be kept from percolating up and disrupting the higher-level goals of the executives. Figure 2.6 shows the financial perspective of a Balanced Scorecard that Joe's Telecommunications could have developed. The tactical implementation plan is at the bottom, and the high-level strategy is at the top. At Joe's, we saw how the project deliverables changed between iterations to accommodate changing microstrategies. And we saw how some microstrategies needed to accommodate inflexible technical barriers. If a good strategy map is developed, negotiations between ongoing projects and strategy can be kept at the microstrategy level.

"Ongoing software projects usually have little standalone value unless they are linked by a suite of micro-strategies" [3]. These strategies, in turn, need to be a part of one large strategic architecture that can flex rapidly to changing market conditions. When initiatives are first introduced for review by an IT PMO, they are scrutinized for their alignment with the corporate strategy. If a good strategy map has been developed and maintained, such initiatives can align with microstrategies, as shown in Figure 2.6. This is an example of how to make the upper levels of the corporate strategy align with the underlying IT tactics (or projects). As initiatives turn into projects, either the projects can stray off course or the microstrategies can shift. Either way, compromises at this level can be made to be transparent to the executives and to the general, desired course of the company.

2.3.2 Portfolio Selection and Tracking

After initiatives are checked for alignment and then approved, they need to be tracked by the PMO for continued alignment through the lifetime of the project. Too often, IT projects are graded only on a standard set of metrics tied to the project triad shown in Chapter 1: Is the project on time, on budget, and meeting the goals of the stakeholder? If these key performance indicators (KPIs) are not linked to a central strategy in the business case, then project health can be a "dangerous illusion...Both KPI and stakeholder scorecards omit the linkages for driving breakthroughs higher up in the strategy map" [3] (i.e., for customers and internal stakeholders). The project may look like a real winner to the business unit when it delivers, but if the greater company doesn't need it after all, it can be a loser. A PMO that continually prioritizes the IT initiative pipeline and IT project portfolio can help alleviate this.

Mapped microstrategies can also act as a guideline for business units when designing their initiatives. To help business units know where the corporate priorities lay, at Northwestern Mutual Life Insurance they prioritized the microstrategies" in terms of desired application of resources" [10]. This not only kept the initiative pipeline in line with the goals of the company (thus making for an easier approval process), but it also kept the business units from pursuing as many dead-end ideas. Such early-stage prioritization of microstrategies forces the PMO and the business units into a real-time state of alignment.

Finally, mapped microstrategies can ensure that middle managers avoid strategic siloing. For example, few companies are successful at creating a portfolio of aligned projects. "Instead, projects are selected in a more-or-less political fashion, as the business units with the most influence win the budget dollars and the IT resources to pursue their pet initiatives" [11]. It is common for middle managers to take corporate goals "and transform them into little pieces of power" [12]. When, or if, messages of strategic importance even reach "the front line, it is less a datum of information and more a means of control" [12]. An IT PMO can enforce the *strategic architecture* through initiative reviews and project audits. Because of the potential for organizational backlash, the IT PMOs approach should not be via top-down direction; rather, it should be via "top-down communication" [3]. This is why a PMO needs to achieve absolute executive support from the beginning. Authority over projects, as well as accountability for the health of the portfolio, need to be core elements of the office. If microstrategies are well mapped up to the desires of the executives, then the IT PMO can educate middle management when they fail to act in the best interest of the company.

2.4   Reengineering Cumulative Digression

Considering that Joe's may have several projects ongoing, the aggregate digression of IT projects from their original goals can send companies in less than ideal directions. That is, projects that look like they are on track (program C) may have collateral deliverables that have nothing to do with the corporate strategy. This usually results from having more money than needed for the original business case and then taking the approach of "build it first, then sell it." The diagram in Figure 2.7 shows project A as part of a larger program and project B as an independent project. Many times there is a discontinuity between the organization's strategic direction and the organization expressed as the sum of its projects [8]. As more projects digress from the corporate strategy, the cumulative digression of the portfolio can be unwieldy. If such digressions from strategic goals are allowed to persist, balance and maximization of the portfolio will also spiral out of control.

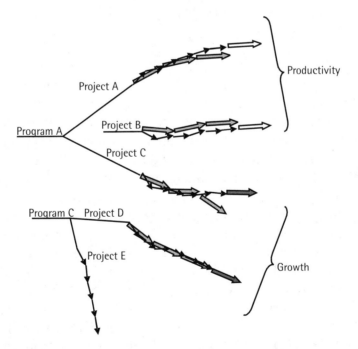

Figure 2.7 Results of cumulative digression of projects from corporate strategic directions.

With nonconcrete intermediates that software projects produce, it is easier for greater digressions from the strategy to occur. The result is that the company is led by the leash of rogue software projects rather than the other way around. Every once in a while, an unaligned initiative will prove so successful that upper management will alter the corporate strategy to accommodate the initiative deliverable (an optimist's view of project E). But this is rare. In most cases executives are left with one of three choices for undesirable initiative results:

1. Scuttle projects and start new ones that are realigned with the updated strategy.

2. Try to salvage IT solutions that are misaligned. This tends to force users to use IT in ways for which it wasn't developed. This, in turn, involves more overhead for the users (i.e., more inefficiencies and less productivity).

3. Change the corporate strategy to fit the capabilities of the delivered IT solution.

To save face on expenditures while still controlling the ever-changing marketplace strategy map, leaders will many times opt for the second choice. This approach usually rears it head under the guise of *reengineering business.* "Most management time is spent on restructuring and reengineering, which have more to do with shoring up today's businesses than creating tomorrow's industries" [13]. But if technical projects aren't tracked for their alignment with shifting strategies, then a company can get mired in this cycle of reengineering. In summary, this second choice will cause companies to be more focused on improving present problems rather than on achieving future opportunities.

As the executive teams become more nimble in their reaction speed to market changes, how confident are they that their ship will change course and speed quickly? Many times they'll just publish a new strategy, impose restructuring processes across the board, and require results from the business units. "In her book *The Seven Deadly Sins of Business*, Eileen Shapiro lists as one of the 'sins of strategy,' organizations that make the mistake of creating a vision but not giving any clear direction as to how that vision is to be achieved. The result is that the organization often develops in ways that the strategists hadn't intended" [8]. This chapter shows how aligning the corporate strategy needs to flex to forces from the top (the market) and the bottom (IT tactics). The next chapter will show how IT tactical implementations can flex to changing strategic forces. The combination of these two chapters provides a foundation from which an IT PMO can instill confidence in the executive staff that the IT project portfolio's direction is following the lead of the corporate strategy.

2.5 Summary

Before IT PPM can be effective, the executive team needs to first create a strategy that will flex to the changes in the marketplace and then communicate any strategic shifts as they occur. With this foundation, the business units can develop microstrategies and then business initiatives that will support the strategy. These lower levels of the strategy need to be just as flexible as the core strategy is to the marketplace. Otherwise, companies can end up being led not by their goals and desires, but by misaligned and costly IT projects. To combat this, IT PMOs can ensure that the projects in the portfolio are kept aware of any changes in the strategic layers. While business units ultimately decide how aligned their IT projects will be kept, IT PMOs can increase the risk ratings and thus lower the priority of those projects that don't change course with the strategy. Such prioritized lists of projects then help executive teams determine which projects to keep funding and which ones to drop. Where IT PMO authority over projects rests in how the executives leverage such prioritization lists, IT PMO accountability rests in how accurately their projections of project success match with reality. And, as will be shown, further accountability rests in how healthy the IT PMO can keep the portfolio of projects.

References

[1]   Michaelson, Gerald A., *The Art of War for Managers*, Avon, MA: Adams Media Corporation, 2000.

[2]   Harry, Mikel, and Richard Schroeder, *Six Sigma*, New York: Currency Doubleday, 2000.

[3]   Norton, David P., and Robert S. Kaplan, *The Strategy-Focused Organization*, Boston, MA: Harvard Business School Press, 2001.

[4]   Sommer, Renee, "Portfolio Management for Projects: A New Paradigm," in *Project Portfolio Management*, Lowell D. Dye and James S. Pennypacker, (eds.), West Chester, PA: Center for Business Practices, 2000, pp. 55–60.

[5]   Reifer, Donald J., *Making the Software Business Case: Improvement by the Numbers*, Reading, MA: Addison-Wesley, 2002.

[6]   Cleland, David, "The Strategic Context of Projects," in *Project Portfolio Management*, Lowell D. Dye and James S. Pennypacker, (eds.), West Chester, PA: Center for Business Practices, 1999, pp. 3–22.

[7]   Penker, Magnus, and Hans-Erik Eriksson, *Business Modeling with UML*, Needham, MA: OMG Press, 2000.

[8]   O'Connell, Fergus, *Successful High-Tech Project-Based Organizations*, Norwood, MA: Artech House, 2000.

[9]   McDavid, D. W., "A Standard for Business Architecture Description," *IBM Systems Journal*, October 7, 1998 (electronic version).

[10] Combe, Margaret W., "Project Prioritization in a Large Functional Organization," in *Project Portfolio Management*, Lowell D. Dye and James S. Pennypacker, (eds.), West Chester, PA: Center for Business Practices, 1999, pp. 363–370.

[11] Meta Group, "Centralizing Management of Project Portfolios," *Meta Group*, January 29, 2002, http://www.umt.com/site/Documents/IT_World_-_ Leading_Organisation_Centralize_Management_of_Project_Portfolios_-_ 29Jan02.pdf (last accessed on January 15, 2004).

[12] Larkin, T. J., and Sandar Larkin, *Communicating Change: Winning Employee Support for New Business Goals*, New York: McGraw-Hill, 1994.

[13] Englund, Randall, and Robert Graham, *Creating an Environment for Successful Projects*, San Francisco, CA: Jossey-Bass, 1998.

[14] Margulius, David L., "Overachiever—IT Payback," *CIO Magazine*, November 1, 2004, http://www.cio.com/archive/110102/overachiever.html (last accessed on January 15, 2004).

[15] Hughes, Laura Q., "Case Study: Royal Caribbean Cruises and Microstrategies," *CIO Insight*, January 1, 2002, http://www.cioinsight.com/ article2/0,1397,566231,00.asp (last accessed on January 15, 2004).

Appendix 2A: Case Study—Royal Caribbean Cruises—Microstrategies

In March 1999, Royal Caribbean Cruises Ltd. Chief Executive Officer (CEO) Richard Fain and President Jack Williams asked Tom Murphy to come on board as the new chief information officer (CIO). With a plan to expand the number of employees from 17,000 to 40,000 and the fleet from 17 ships to 29, the executives needed a well-planned IT strategy framework to support such growth. Tom Murphy went right to work developing several substrategies which, when grouped together, comprised the LeapFrog program. His plans included a new digital reservations network to replace 12 problematic systems, a new supply-chain management system to cut costs, and a new human resources system to better support the planned hiring of 23,000 new employees. Also, each additional $350-million vessel would carry $10 million in IT systems.

Unfortunately, the following day, 9/11 put a screeching halt to the corporate strategy and, thus, Tom Murphy's suite of substrategies. Royal Caribbean CEO Richard Fain asked all department heads to cut their budgets by 25% to account for the 50% reduction in passenger reservations. CIO Tom Murphy immediately saw his aggressive IT build-out plan get tabled. To accommodate this drastic shift in the corporate strategy, Murphy instituted a different series of microstrategies. Instead of leading the IT department down an inflexible path of cost reductions, Murphy maintained an open view on both long-term growth and short-term cost reduction. He did this by implementing a *survive and thrive* strategy followed by a *back to basics* strategy and ending with a *restart* strategy. With the survive and thrive microstrategy, only those projects that supported survivability were allowed to continue at first. Then, when the back to basics microstrategy was introduced, other projects that supported infrastructure, e-mail, Web sites, and telephony were given more attention. Finally, projects that were tabled in the beginning were reviewed for start-up potential in the restart phase. According to Murphy, "There are things that are optional and things that are not optional, and microstrategy helps to make the mandatory happen, one way or another, amid rapidly changing circumstances." Since the post-9/11 turmoil, Royal Caribbean has managed to maintain stability and then grow back to pre-9/11 levels [14, 15].

A company that has IT-oriented projects distributed around the organization and managed by the various business units would be able to react to such dramatic strategy shifts more efficiently if an IT PMO were in place. In this case, we see that the CIO had a firm grasp of the project portfolio under his wing. Did the other business units have the same control over their IT-oriented projects? Or did all IT-oriented projects fall under the management if the CIO? An IT PMO allows the IT department to stay in a support role, business units to have the freedom to manage their IT-oriented projects, and the IT project portfolio to react efficiently to quick strategy shifts.

3

Portfolio Flexibility

As the tides of the marketplace ebb and flow, the strategic piers need to bend and bob to them. And as these piers move, so too must the program of ships tied to them. Should we use iron bars or flexible nylon rope to tie the projects to the strategies? Or should we use string or steel cables? The methods we choose to keep projects linked with the shifting strategies need to be flexible yet firm enough to see any project through marketplace storms. On the same note, we need to make sure that our strategic piers can hold the ships we choose to tie to them. A project too large, too long, or too populated can rip a strategy to shreds even if the tie ropes are well strung. The last chapter showed how to develop proper piers for the marketplace and how to tie project ships to them. This chapter will first focus on how a company should choose which ships can tie to their strategies (initiative methodologies). Then, the rest of the chapter will show how to choose the proper methodology ropes for the projects (project methodologies) and how to monitor those methodologies and projects for strain.

3.1 Risk and Methodologies

As touched on earlier, a well-known general rule in the IT industry is that if a project doesn't provide a solution within six months, then it will fail. This mantra of IT projects is based on the well-developed know how that business rules change so dramatically over a six-month period that any IT project release will be based on requirements that are out of date. If a project doesn't deliver usable results in this time frame, the odds of entering into a downward spiral of scope creep increases dramatically. More recently, with the introduction of safer programming languages and COTS, business leaders now expect results in one to two months rather than the traditional six-month timeframe. These newer demands have added a level of risk that PMs have addressed by improving their release cycles.

Over the years, IT professionals have become very aware of the level of uncertainty inherent in almost all IT projects. This is why risk management is so deeply engrained into the project tasks of most IT PMs. A common tool used by IT PMs to mitigate risk is to split the project's deliverables into subdeliverables and thus create multiple functional releases—or iterations of the final release. They realize that business rules, or microstrategies, change so frequently in today's turbulent marketplace that they want to make sure projects don't fail as a result. Therefore, projects that iterate out their releases are providing project sponsors with options to change the course of the project rather than scrap it completely if the businesses strategic direction changes. Such options allow businesses to reduce the amount of loss attributed to cancelled projects and instead leverage the work of partially completed projects in a slightly new direction.

Notice how I wrote that project direction, or scope, should only be changed slightly. A fine line exists between disastrous scope creep and altering the direction of the project to match that of the corporate strategy. A project that changes too much from the original design risks failure. For example, IT projects tend to have a lot of time spent determining the best technical approach to problems before diving in and constructing. So if a project changes course too dramatically, then the new project deliverable may not make sense with the technology chosen for the original requirements. Scope management provides another well-documented set of project management tasks that most PMs follow. Change control systems, release signoffs, and time/functionality tradeoffs are just a few examples of how PMs keep projects pointed in a somewhat constant direction through scope management. The PMO, on the other hand, ensures that projects include flexible and frequent release schedules in their business cases before initiative approval and during project implementation. This provides companies with at least some slight wiggle room instead of being tied down to an entirely inflexible portfolio of projects.

3.2 Flexibility

What is meant by portfolio flexibility? Chapter 2 showed some examples of how changes in the marketplace can, through changes in the corporate strategy, put pressures on IT-based projects to change course. If the initiatives for project A and project B were designed to have just one release, then their project phases would have prevented them from being as flexible as they were. Figure 3.1 shows a comparison of two basic methodology types. The top figure shows the classic waterfall methodology, where each phase of the project follows the previous phase until the final project release is achieved. Newer methodologies have incorporated iterations of the phases and iterations of the releases to allow for higher quality, better mitigation of risks, and quicker reaction to changes in the environment (e.g., the corporate strategy). IT project portfolio flexibility is achieved when the IT-based *business initiative* methodologies incorporate iteration of the releases and when IT *project* methodologies incorporate iterations of the phases.

We will start by looking at how IT initiative methodologies can better design iterative releases into their business cases by using a powerful tool called Real Options Analysis. This tool shows how to bring together risks, project goal options, and cost/benefit analysis to lay a foundation for a flexible, auditable and sellable business case. Then, we will show how an IT PMO can leverage the power of established, iterative methodologies to create methods tailored to how a company prefers to audit their own portfolio. Flexibility applies not only to the methods used, but also to how they are chosen. As we review the various methods, it is

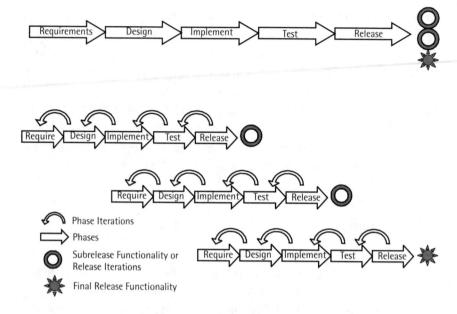

Figure 3.1 Single project release versus iterative project releases.

a central theme that the company provides its employees freedom in choosing from a core set of methods. Methodologies must never be overly constrictive and thus prevent the creative freedom required of IT-based project success.

3.3 Initiative Methodologies

A common cliché muttered by many IT PMs is that "if you do well on your midterms, then the finals will be that much easier." With IT-based business initiatives, project sponsors have the opportunity to plan out a project in sufficient detail to truly increase the chance of success. Consider the business case as the first midterm; if this is done well, the final project release will have a much better chance of success. Organizational effects, technical risks, cost analyses, resource requirements, and stakeholder lists are just a few of the elements of an IT-based business case that should be addressed. "There must be a balance between front-end planned activities and ongoing iteration during the project" [1].

While thorough planning is important, experienced PMs also live in constant fear of the analysis-paralysis beast that can delegitimize a cause. This is just one of many balancing acts that any PM will face during the project lifetime. The most inevitable is the famous chaos/order teeter totter toward the end of any IT-based project. But if a foundation of order and clarity is established well in the beginning and maintained deep into the project lifecycle, then a project has a better chance of tottering towards an orderly end.

Many IT-based initiative methodologies have been introduced by academics and implemented by businesses. Here, we will morph the concepts of several of these to come up with a process, a business-case template, a cost/option analysis approach, and a metric-mapping template. The first three are fairly standard for any business case. But the metric mapping is central to the needs of a successful PMO. Tracing project milestones back to the metrics, or hurdles, established in the project's business case is critical to being able to test for the health of a project. This, in turn, is necessary to prioritize projects and maintain an efficient IT project portfolio. However, because methodologies can be as constraining as they are guiding, PMOs should tailor methodologies to the custom realities of each organization.

One example of such a tailored methodology is shown in Table 3.1 and Figure 3.2. A company can have better control over the ideas generated by its business units if staff members are given structured guidelines. In this methodology, the person with an idea to improve the business can be considered to be in phase 1 of the business initiative methodology. The PMO acts as a reality check for the business case writer by providing a list of possible technical or organizational risks that the resulting IT-based project may encounter. In phase 2, the PMO provides guidance on standard risk, option, and cost/benefit analyses. The data that results from this phase is central to writing the business case in phase 3. The PMO can provide business case templates that writers can use to best sell their idea. After the business case is submitted, phase 3 continues with the project sponsor "preparing the battlefield" for project approval. In some cases, if the approval process is nothing more than a nod during the presentation, then the project preparation process will overlap into the project timeline. Once an initiative is

Table 3.1
Goals for the Phases of a Business Initiative Methodology

Phase 1	Understand the Problem and Its Context
	Specify Objective
	Identify Stakeholders
	Analyze Problem
Phase 2	Risk/Option/Costs Analysis
	Risk Analysis
	Options Analysis
	Cost/Benefits Analysis
Phase 3	Presentation and Project Prep
	Document the Case
	Make the Case
	Project Prep
Phase 4	Project Auditing
	Ongoing Reviews
	Metric Mapping

Source: [2–4].

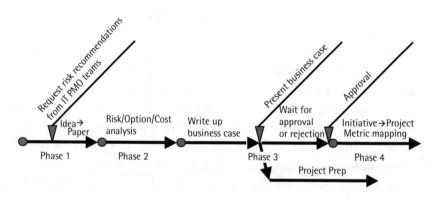

Figure 3.2 Phases of a business initiative methodology.

approved and funded, phase 4 of the initiative methodology kicks in. This last phase overlaps the chosen project methodology through the life of the project. Such overlapping ensures that future PMO audits correctly map business case hurdle points to milestones on the project.

3.3.1   Phase 1—Understand the Problem and Its Context

Most companies have staff members among their business units that are hungry to present new business improvement ideas. These ideas can only become fuel for the company if they are presented to and funded by those with the authority and the accountability for the success of the company. But what percentage of business initiatives ends up being a waste of the executives' time? How many sponsors of bad ideas block out the stream of good ideas just because they have louder voices? For good ideas to sprout from the current corporate strategy, the executives need to continually communicate the constant variations in its strategy. And for these ideas to be presented clearly, they need to follow a constant format set forth by the reviewing committee. To help ensure that early idea formation maps to what a company wants, the PMO can require that staff members use a template that also lists some of the current microstrategies of the various business units. An idea can evolve by first writing a preliminary initiative plan that addresses such things as [5]:

- What will be done;
- The project's sponsor;
- The link to organizational direction and business goals;
- A top-level description of the project's costs, benefits, and risks.

If the idea generator has any questions on organizational fit or technical feasibility, the IT PMO can provide two teams to offer advice (see Figure 3.3). This will help filter out any ideas before they are fed into the initiative pipeline as business cases.

3.3.2   Phase 2—Risk/Option/Cost Analysis

The job of the organizational gap and technical gap review teams at this stage isn't to reject ideas; rather, it is to offer the business case writer a list of risks. It would then be up to the writer to present her case with a complete review of these risks or to "filter" her own idea out. This review should present various options that the project can take if any of these risks become barriers to success. Then, costs should be tied to

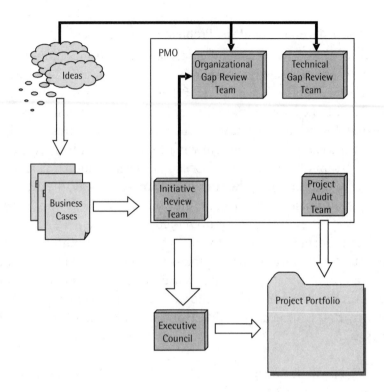

Figure 3.3 Initiative review process flow with PMO support.

these different options. Once cost analysis is included, the plan can start addressing "the issues that the seniors are most worried about. When the smoke clears, the thing that really matters to senior management is the numbers" [4]. But before the sponsor calculates the cost/benefits of the project, he needs to formalize the risks provided by the PMO teams and then develop a list of options.

3.3.2.1 Risk Identification

In Chapter 1 we showed how some risks gradually diminish, while others vary over the life of a project. Another way to categorize risks is by grouping the technical and organizational risks as unique risks and the market risks as commercial risks.

Unique risks, also called private risks, are those that are partially under the control of the PM. The level of control the manager has over these risks and the amount of damage the risks can incur on the project are both measured subjectively based on past experiences, gut feel, and probability equations. The higher these risks are, the lower the value of the project. Figure 1.5 shows how these risks gradually reduce in magnitude over the lifetime of the project.

Market risks are those that are not controllable by the PM. Examples include natural disasters, interest rate changes, and tax rate changes. While still subjectively calculated, their probabilities are based on statistics from other competitors, government, or academic research. Examples of approaches used to calculate the probabilities associated with market risks include the Black-Scholes formula, the binomial approximation, and risk-neutral methods. Though Figure 1.5 shows these types of risks as uncontrollable, financial markets take the approach that higher risk yields higher returns. While project sponsors would prefer to lower the incidence of unique risks, they may be more accepting of higher market risks.

As an example, let's look at project B from Joe's Telecommunications. Table 3.2 shows some of the tasks the sponsor would come up with and submit to the PMO for review. Once the PMO has "sanity checked" the project idea, the PMO can provide what it feels would be technical and organizational risks if the project were approved. Initiative sponsors would then map these risks and any others they felt should be included (e.g., market risks) to the initiative tasks. This mapping would then serve as a foundation for developing alternative options and cost/benefit analyses for the business case. Here, we will show how this can be done by evolving the business case for project B a bit further.

3.3.2.2 Cost/Benefit Techniques—Net Present Value, Profit Index, and Internal Rate of Return

Figure 3.2 shows how we mapped the technical and organizational risks (unique risks) and the market risks to the tasks. The figure also lists some high-level options the project can take at the end of each phase. If the PM is able to mitigate the unique risks sufficiently and avoid the downsides of the market risks, then the project has a good chance of ending successfully. However, if the project triad is adversely affected by any of the known or unknown risks, then the project can end in an unsuccessful state. At this point (either actual or planned phase

Table 3.2

Unique Risks Versus Market Risks on a Project

Goal	Make Field Reps More Independent/ Efficient			
	Tasks	Unique Risks	Market Risks	Options
Phase 1	Build up and train call center to handle new load		Minimum wage increases	
	Add dial-in number and configure phone switch	Technical problem with phone switch (tech)	Cost of 1-800 calls goes up	
	Train field reps	Field reps rebel over new training and responsibilities (org)		
				No problems
				Abandon project
				Fix problems, move forward
Phase 2	Develop mobile device software	Programmers' code too buggy (tech)	Programmers' union goes on strike	
	Purchase, test, and roll out mobile devices	Mobile devices are buggy (tech)		
	Integrate mobile software with call center databases		Radio frequency antennae company goes out of business	
	Train field reps	Reps are too busy for training (org)		
	Train IT help desk	IT help desk is understaffed (org)		
				No problems
				Abandon project
				Fix problems, move forward

completion date), the project sponsor has three choices: continue on with the next phase of the project, abandon the project, or fix the problems with the current phase and then move onto the next phase. These are options that need to be presented in the business case to enable the approval committee to make the best comparison with other proposed business initiatives. And they need to be presented in the context of the risks (mapped to the tasks) first and the cost/benefit analyses second.

When developing the business initiative methodology, there needs to be a requirement for financial audit points. That is, there needs to be a way for some auditing committee to track the progress of the approved project back to some original set of financial metrics in the business case. With such a standard set of metrics, auditors will then be able to compare apples to apples when balancing the health of the project portfolio. Different chief financial officers (CFOs) prefer different financial metrics when monitoring the progress or success of any project. The two most common are the net present value (NPV) method and the internal rate of return (IRR) method. Two other metrics that are used on IT projects are the profit index (PI) and the payback (PB) period.

NPV

To understand NPV, we must first understand the time value of money, or the present value (PV) concept. To receive $100 two years from now, the PV of that $100 is actually just $83 if we were able to get a 10% return on that money. In other words, if $83 is put in a bank today and earns 10% annually, we would end up with $100 in two years. Now, the NPV is defined as the PV of the expected future cash flow (e.g., $83) minus the initial cost of the project. "It represents the contribution of that investment to the value of the firm and, accordingly, to the wealth of the firm's shareholders" [6]. In general, a project should be accepted if its NPV is greater than or equal to zero and rejected if its NPV is less than zero. Or, in a portfolio of initiatives, if two or more mutually exclusive investments with equal risks have positive NPVs, the project having the largest NPV is the one selected. In short, "the NPV approach considers both the magnitude and the timing of cash flows over a project's entire expected life" and is a good measure for comparing project value [6].

IRR

Continuing with the example of the $83 invested, if we only got $96 in two years then the actual rate of return would be 8% instead of the expected 10%. The benefits, or the return from a project, can be measured in the same way using the IRR metric. The IRR is defined as the discount rate that evaluates the PV of the benefits (net cash flows) from a project with the PV of the total costs (net cash outflows). In a business case, obviously, the IRR is a projected value—it is the rate of return the project sponsor *expects* to get from the risky investment. The higher the perceived risk, the higher the expected IRR, in theory. This can be referred to as the risk premium, or the return investors expect over the risk free rate one would receive if they invested in U.S. Treasury bills [6].

When choosing metrics to monitor the progress of projects, a survey of 74 of the 100 largest firms in the *Fortune* 500 industrial firm listing indicated that 99% of the firms used IRR compared to 85% that used NPV [6]. However, the problem with using IRR to track project success is that, as we saw with Joe's Telecommunications, the projects can take several turns and deliver several different functional points. Each of these deliverables can provide different rates of return. Such multiple IRR calculations can end up being too complex to provide meaningful results. "Although several techniques have been proposed for dealing with the multiple internal rate of return problem, none provide a simple, complete, and generally satisfactory solution" [6]. The better metrics, therefore, for measuring the progress of a project are those that monitor real dollar values such as NPV rather than those that monitor dollar ratios such as IRR.

PI and PB

Two other metrics that could be incorporated into a business initiative methodology are the PI and PB measurements. The PI is similar to the NPV, but instead of subtracting the initial costs of the project from the PV of the future income, we divide the latter by the former. So if the PI is less than 1.0, then the project costs more than it returns. And if the PI is greater than 1.0, then the project is considered to be profitable. The PB is the time it takes for the project deliverables to earn enough money to pay off the costs of the project. This number, usually calculated in days, "gives some indication of a project's desirability from a liquidity perspective because it measures the time required for a firm to recover its initial investment in a project" [6]. Whichever metric is chosen for the initiative methodology, either one from the samples presented here or a more advanced one, it needs to be applied to all projects consistently so that project health can be normalized across the portfolio.

3.3.2.3 Real Options

With the different options the project can take and with the tools to conduct cost/benefit analysis, the business case writer can now draw up some decision trees. Figure 3.4 shows an example of a decision tree for phase 1 combined with a decision tree for phase 2 (Joe's Real Options

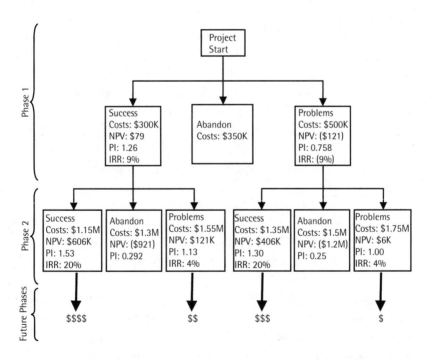

Figure 3.4 Real options analysis of a multiphased project. (M = millions, K = thousands.)

calculator used for this figure is on the accompanying CD-ROM). Most nodes on the tree show the NPV, the PI, and the IRR that would be realized if the project took the respective paths. With the different paths shown, an initiative reviewer can now see the costs that will result if any of the known risks affect the desired path of the project.

Because each phase has its own set of deliverables that produce their own returns, separate IRRs are shown for each phase. This is done because, as mentioned earlier, combined IRRs not only can become overly complex for multiphased projects, they are hard-won numbers (i.e., complex) that are still based on subjective estimates. Complexity that sits on a foundation of subjectivity can be more of an annoyance than a benefit for initiative review teams.

However, the NPV and the PI are shown as cumulative values for the whole project. For example, phase 2 NPV and PI numbers represent the return and costs for the functionality delivered in both phase 1 and 2. If the sponsor chooses to abandon the project, there will be some added costs associated with dismantling any hardware that was purchased, retasking idled resources, and paying off software or outsourcing contracts. Even more painful, the reviewer can see that there will be no NPV or PI because the product will never be delivered.

The combination of these two decision trees shows a set of real options that can help better decide whether this is a project worth financing. What makes this more than just a decision tree is how future benefits can still be realized in phase 2 even if the project is seeing negative returns from a problematic phase 1. As mentioned in Chapter 1, Real Options mapping is a way for the business case writer to conduct early mitigation of the identified risks. While the majority of risk management will be conducted during the project by the PM, Real Options analysis can provide early risk mitigation by showing the true value of the project. In this case, if the approval of the project was decided by the numbers presented for phase 1 only, the 50/50 risk of seeing negative NPV or a PI of only 1.26 might be enough to not approve it. But if the reviewing committee saw that if phase 1 completes, no matter the delays, they will then have options to realize projectwide PIs of 1.30–1.53. And if the Real Options analysis was carried further to future phases, the initiative may appear even more attractive.

NPV, as a tool for decision analysis, fails to take into consideration flexibility. By combining options and their respective NPVs, we can now see how the value of flexibility offers a more optimistic and realistic view to the decision maker. They can see that, even if the project is doing poorly, the additional options the project deliverable provides is more valuable than the intermediate project deliverables. "The appropriate mind-set is to recognize that the net present value technique systematically undervalues everything because it fails to capture the value of flexibility. NPV is only valuable as a tool because risk is assumed to be unchanging during the life of the project" [7].

Most projects are made up of *rainbow* options—phased projects that include design, construction, and rollout phases and that are subject to multiple sources of uncertainty [7]. With compound rainbow projects, one has the option to stop or defer the project at the end of each phase. Thus, each phase is an option that is contingent on the earlier exercise of other options—an option on an option (or options). For example, at the end of phase 1, the viability of the project could be reexamined based on project health up to that point. Either the project would be abandoned, fixed and continued, or continued without need for repair.

3.3.3   Phase 3—Presentation and Project Preparation

Once the general vision, objectives, risks, options, and cost/benefit analyses have been gathered, the business case can start to take shape. As the IT PMO provided guidance on risks and cost/benefit metrics, so can it also provide guidance on the business case by providing a common template—a template that is easy to follow "with clearly defined minimal acceptance criteria" [5]. Too much structure can inhibit the way a great idea can be best presented. On the other hand, certain elements of the proposal must be kept consistent to help with future auditing.

Phase 1 (of Figure 3.4) provided a means to develop a basic vision and set of objectives; the level that an executive summary should be written. From this, the business case can evolve by including a problem statement and a vision statement. Phase 2 went into far more detail by first developing a list of tasks, or work packages, from which a list of risks could be derived. Additional details could be added, such as

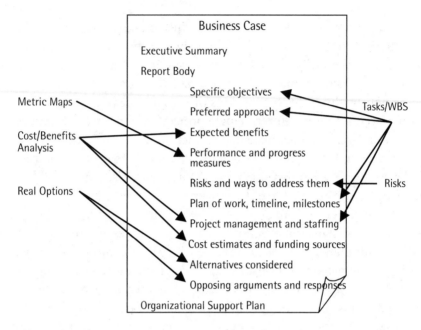

Figure 3.5 Linking elements of a business initiative to a business case. (*After:* [2, 4, 8].)

milestones, funding sources, and the risk mitigation plan. Figure 3.5 shows a business case template that can be used by all IT-based business initiatives.

Business case writers should not feel constrained to just the business case. They need to be able to sell their ideas using a whole host of communications approaches. The marketing of their ideas should include "a variety of presentations, both oral and written, with supporting media such as handouts, slides or demonstrations" [2]. But once the initiative is approved, the business case needs to explain how it will continue to garner organizational and executive support. An organizational support plan needs to be developed that explains how the stakeholders will enthusiastically embrace the final deliverable. Many times IT projects deliver some wondrous piece of technology, only to have it used as a doorstop because it wasn't marketed properly. While marketing to the stakeholders occurs throughout the project, marketing to the executives occurs before, during, and after the project timeline. "In order to retain support and funding beyond the initial approvals, state how and when you will give progress reports against the performance measures established in your business cases" [3].

Once the project is submitted for approval, the project sponsor has an opportunity to prepare the groundwork for a successful project kick-off. The following are some examples of long-lead activities that PMs can do while waiting for financing [4]:

- *Project planning.* Complete high-level Gantt charts and work breakdown structures.

- *Staffing.* Recruit key personnel and prepare transfer paperwork.

- *Stakeholder committee formation.* Have the sponsor lead this committee and then fill it with key stakeholders that will help ensure organizational embracement of the project deliverable.

- *Equipment and tool acquisition.* Submit requests for long-lead items, such as server racks and hard-to-find installers.

- *Facilities.* Search out and negotiate with the facilities department for space.

- *Operational concepts.* Develop communication plans for e-mail, phones, pagers, meetings, and escalation procedures.

3.3.4 Phase 4—Metric Mapping

The previous sections focused on auditing the project deliverables at the end of each phase for cost/benefit metrics. While these are important tools in the review process, many sponsors want to audit the project before a phase completes. Auditing of this kind can't focus on returns because the final product hasn't been released. Instead, the audit team will look more at elements of the project triad, such as percentage of functionality complete, percentage of budget used, and days left before the next milestone. Other metrics can look at the areas that the PMBOK brings up, such as number of risks eliminated and number of bugs found and fixed (quality). Because such metric tracing requires clear touch points between both the business case and the corresponding project, development of the initiative and choice of the project methodologies need to be in synch. As financial portfolios have basic metrics that monitor security risks [e.g., earnings per share (EPS), price/earnings (P/E) ratio], project portfolios have metrics to monitor project risks (NPV, IRR). But how can the PMO team ensure that each project in the portfolio is using the same metrics to verify that the projects are meeting their original goals? By adopting a suite of standard project methodologies, the PMO can make sure projects use consistent metrics to trace project cost, health, and risks back to the business case.

3.4 Project Methodologies

Before a project starts, it is critical to success that some method be established and communicated to the project stakeholders. Because IT projects involve so many nonconcrete work packages, milestones, and deliverables, some structure needs to be in place to hold everything together. For example, how can a PM know for certain that a developer has completed a coding module if no third party testing was done to verify it? How can the project sponsor know that a chosen technology will work if proof-of-concept documents weren't signed off? And why would end users use a delivered product if they were never trained on it? Testing processes, prototyping approaches, and training timelines are all examples of methods a PM needs to announce as part of the project methodology.

Industry has also learned over time that because projects vary so dramatically, different methods need to be used to ensure success on different projects. To support this, many methodologies have been invented for IT projects of various shapes and sizes. And because no two projects are ever the same, these methodologies act only as templates to support each project-specific methodology. One PM may look at an approved business initiative plan and see his battlefield. Another PM may look at the same plan and see her canvas. Each PM will then decide to mold a methodology template they feel will best ensure project success. The methodology template must fit not only with the mechanics of a project, but also with the psychology of the project microsociety. Because few PMs know how to play the methodology card game well, the IT PMO needs to establish a knowledge in and a support structure for some subset of these methodologies. This will, in turn, allow even the inexperienced PMs to leverage the right methodology for their projects.

Supporting all known IT project methodologies would be impractical for an IT PMO that is trying to keep a small footprint in the organization. Instead, a subset of methodologies needs to be chosen. Figure 3.6 shows the IT PMO in the center, supporting a larger virtual IT PMO (i.e., a PMO that appears larger than it actually is due to the organizationwide support from business units and PMs, to name a few). The details of the structure of a virtual IT PMO will be addressed further in the next chapter. The point to be made here is that the IT PMO should not decide on the set of methodologies to use behind closed doors. Rather, it should coordinate a sampling of PMs from the enterprise to come up with a short list of methodologies (step 1). Such an approach would reduce backlash from the project management staff because some self-appointed guru in the PMO office didn't create and

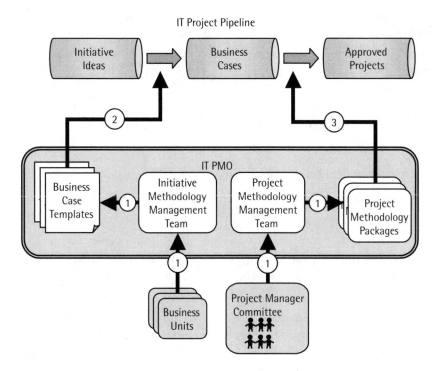

Figure 3.6 Virtual IT PMO—methodology management teams.

then impose a corporate-specific methodology. Instead, by allowing them to choose from methods voted on by those who will use them (step 3); the PMs will feel more confident as their projects progress. Furthermore, the PMO would be able to better compare the health of projects by placing an equal number of audit points in similar locations on each methodology.

The adopted project methodologies should be flexible to strategic long-term projects (e.g., ERP) and to tactical quick-implementation projects (e.g., eBusiness). To allow for such flexibility, high-level components that are common to most scenarios should be required in all audits. Tackle only the very basic standards and procedures, such as how to create a project plan, how to track issues, the use of a project charter, and so forth [9]. To support metric mapping in the methodology, these deliverables should associate with the phases of a project (i.e., the requirements gathering, design, and implementation phases). These end-of-phase deliverables will eventually act as audit touch points to monitor project metrics. As the organization learns, adopts, and gets comfortable with the basics, other elements of the methodologies can be added: document templates, instructions, and process guides. In short, any methodology should have [10]:

- *Breadth.* It must be transferable (flexible) across project types.
- *Depth.* It should show sufficient detail for each stage and phase.
- *Clarity.* It should be easily understandable.
- *Impact.* It must allow for measurable results.

3.4.1 Pitfalls

Understanding the need for project methodologies, we must, however, be wary of the pitfalls of spreading the religion of methodologies. One easy trap that PMOs can fall into is the overenforcement of project methodologies. A main reason so many projects run into problems is because of "too many procedures or too much methodology" [11]. The overt case for a methodology is "a long list of its supposed benefits, including standardization, documentary uniformity, managerial control, and state-of-the-art techniques" [12]. The covert case for methodologies, on the other hand, is that they can do "grievous damage [to a project] by trying to force the work into a fixed mold that guarantees a morass of paperwork, a paucity of methods, an absence of responsibility, a general loss of motivation" [12].

As many have pursued the golden fleece of project methodologies, many a project has failed because of its strained attempts to fit the mold of a methodology that was incorrectly dictated by a central office. Furthermore, "methodologies seek to force convergence through statue. Better ways to achieve convergence of method are: Training, Tools and Peer Review" [12]. By providing a source for training, a simple set of project tracking tools, and reliable audits, IT PMOs can effectively instill an enterprisewide project methodology. And any project methods training needs to be "more about behavior change and less about Gantt charts and PERT charts" [11].

Most new IT PMs who are allowed to run a project with little to no knowledge of proven project methodologies tend to fail. However, many seasoned PMs have shown success at managing projects from the seat of their pants. Once these managers are forced to follow a standard methodology, they become constrained and they falter. So how does a company introduce methodologies that mitigate the risk of new managers or new project types while still allowing for the freedom that have made experienced managers so efficient? PMOs need to have projects follow a method so that they can compare the health of projects side by side. If different methods are used, projects may unfairly be graded lower than others because the PMO would be comparing apples to oranges.

3.4.2 Audit Points

"Most PMs are preoccupied with bringing the project to a successful finish, and they cannot be expected to clearly see the project in an objective manner of supporting the enterprise mission" [13]. To continually ensure that a project's deliverable will end up supporting the enterprise mission, or strategy, the IT PMO's audit team can conduct audits at various key points of a project. In order for PMs to know when audits will occur, such audit points need to be added to each project methodology adopted by the organization. The following four figures show how a PMO can establish four audit points on each major phase of a project: initiation, execution start, testing start, and completion. In this case, the virtual IT PMO project committee decided to choose four methodologies that a PM could use and that the PMO audit committee would understand: a professional organization method—PMBOK by PMI, a private company method—Rational Unified Process (RUP) from IBM, a classic standard method—Spiral, and a new standard method—Extreme Programming (XP).

In the RUP, we see that the initial audit point is placed at the kick-off point of the project (see Figure 3.7). The second audit point is put at the end of the first elaboration phase but before the start of the second

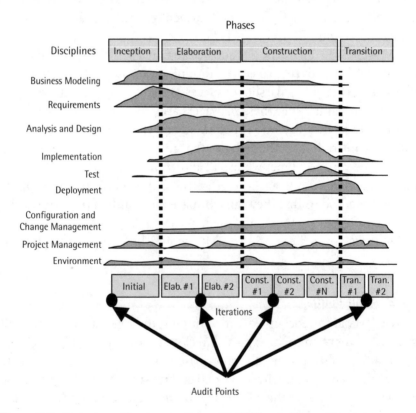

Figure 3.7 Project workloads over time with PMO-specific audit points. (*After:* 14].)

elaboration phase. This ensures that there are some tangible deliverables that the audit committee can review. Though the high-level diagram for this methodology doesn't show a test phase, we can deduce that it will more than likely start at the end of the first construction phase. So, we will put the audit point there. Keep in mind that each of these methodologies are defined to allow flexibility based on project management feedback. This same principle applies to how a PMO enforces audit points. As more and more projects are reviewed, the PMO should flex their audit points to the feedback from the audited projects.

The Spiral methodology (see Figure 3.8) was one of the first methodologies to introduce the concept of iteration. In this classic methodology, prototyping is used as a way to fine tune the final design

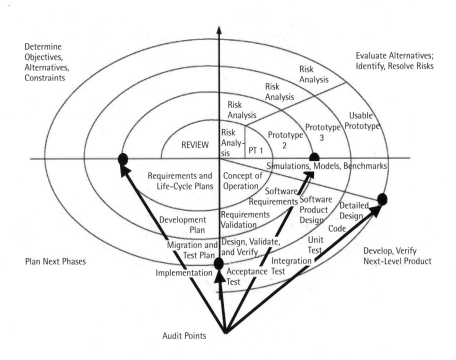

Figure 3.8 Spiral project methodology with PMO-specific audit points. (*After:* [15].)

while, at the same time, overcoming some high-risk proof-of-concept requirements. With the Spiral approach, a project starts in the center and spirals out through the four quadrants (objectives, risks, tests, and plans) over time. As the project reaches the outer rings of its lifecycle, its final product has been thoroughly tested and aligned with the end users' requirements through prototyping, risk assessment, testing and planning.

While it is easy to see which elements of an IT-based project are highlighted in this methodology, there are still some common elements that allow for the introduction of consistent audit points. Because prototyping is a merge between design and construction, the PMO took the midpoint and placed the second audit point after the completion of the second prototype. Because this methodology points out where the formal testing phase begins, it isn't too hard to place the third audit point.

XP is another highly iterative methodology that was introduced more recently. It calls for such processes as pairing developers together when writing software and *refactoring* (or revisiting and refining)

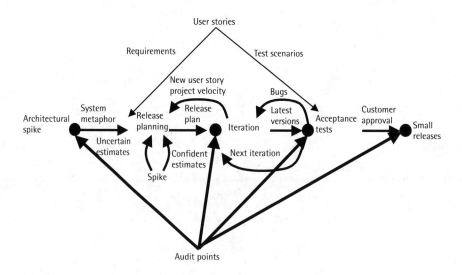

Figure 3.9 XP project methodology with PMO-specific audit points. (*After:* [16].)

previously approved software code. Figure 3.9 shows how the process flows of this methodology involve returning to previous phases as design reviews and tests require. Where the Spiral methodology diagram shows how a product evolves through development outward, the XP diagram shows how a product is iterated back on itself as it progresses forward.

Though Figure 3.9 is only the highest-level view, we can still see where the audit touch points can logically go. But, again, before the audit points are placed, the PMO needs to understand all layers and every deliverable of the methodology. Because the PMO will not only be enforcing the methodology, but also providing training on the methodology, a solid understanding is required. Here we see the construction start audit point is placed at the beginning of the iteration phase. Because there can be multiple iterations per release, it would need to be established at the beginning of the project that this touch point would be required at the beginning of the first iteration of each release. XP makes the placement of the other three touch points fairly clear.

The PMBOK is more of a generic methodology that was designed to support any project type, including non-IT projects. Nonetheless, by choosing only four audit points, the PMO can more easily see where to place them in even a high-level methodology diagram, as shown in Figure 3.10.

3.5 Summary

Before a program or project is funded, it goes through an approval process first as a technical idea and then as a business initiative. The sooner guidance can be provided to business initiatives, the better their chances of success. The IT PMO first provides assistance to an initiative by listing the potential risks for the business case writer. Then, after the IT PMO develops an initiative-submission methodology and a small set of business-case templates with a representative group of business unit leaders, initiative sponsors can write and then submit standardized business cases. While these business cases will have elements that are common among

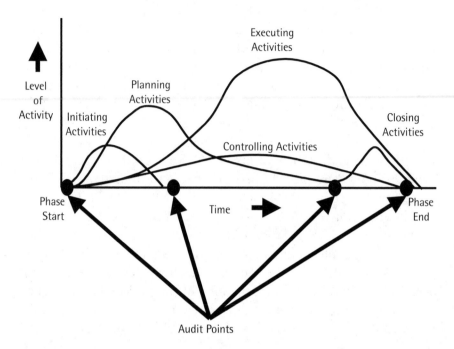

Figure 3.10   PMBOK project methodology with PMO-specific audit points. (*After:* [17].)

all other business cases, the sponsor should use other marketing approaches to win approval. Also, the IT PMO can support business case writers in understanding not only how to apply metrics such as NPV and IRR, but also how to use them to gauge the project's health during project audits.

Project methodologies, while critical to project success, should not be dictated by a central organization. Rather, a PM should be able to choose from a set of methodologies voted on by a committee of PMs. The chosen methodologies must adhere to highly iterative patterns. Projects that stretch iterations too long will face more scope-creep battles and produce more unaligned deliverables. Projects with shorter iterations will be able to react to changes in the layers of the strategy and stay aligned. Also, to ensure that IT PMO audit teams will be able to consistently map metric actuals back to initiative estimates, each methodology chosen should have auditable milestone points added to the end of each phase by the IT PMO. Ongoing initiative and project methodology training by the IT PMO will solidify their proper usage and the health of the portfolio.

References

[1]   Khurana, Anil, and Stephen R. Rosenthal, "Integrating the Fuzzy Front End of New Product Development," in *Project Portfolio Management*, Lowell D. Dye and James S. Pennypacker, (eds.), West Chester, PA: Center for Business Practices, 1999, pp. 339–362.

[2]   Dawes, Sharon S., et al., "Making Smart IT Choices: Understanding Value and Risk in Government IT Investments: Chapter 3," Center for Technology in Government, 2003, http://www.ctg.albany.edu/publications/guides/smartit2.

[3]   Pasko, Henry, et al., "Creating and Using a Business Case for Information Technology Projects," *Treasury Board of Canada Secretariat*, March 1, 1998, http://www.cio-dpi.gc.ca/emf-cag/bc-ar/bc-ar00_e.asp (last accessed on January 15, 2004).

[4]   Reifer, Donald J., *Making the Software Business Case: Improvement by the Numbers*, Reading, MA: Addison-Wesley, 2002.

[5]   Bridges, Dianne, "Project Portfolio Management: Ideas and Practices," in *Project Portfolio Management*, Lowell D. Dye and James S. Pennypacker, (eds.), West Chester, PA: Center for Business Practices, 1999, pp. 45–54.

[6]   Moyer, R. Charles, James R. McGuigan, and William J. Kretlow, *Contemporary Financial Management*, 9th ed., Cincinnati, OH: Thomson South-Western, 2004.

[7]   Copeland, Tom, and Vladimir Antikarov, *Real Options: A Practitioner's Guide*, New York: Monitor Group, 2001.

[8]   Pressman, Robert S., *Software Engineering: A Practitioner's Approach*, 3rd ed., New York: McGraw-Hill, 1992.

[9]   Young, D. Allen, "Project Office Start-Up," *PM Network*, February 1, 2001, http://www.pmi.org/info/PIR_PMNetworkOnline.asp (last accessed on January 15, 2004).

[10] Crawford, J. Kent, *The Strategic Project Office*, Monticello, NY: Marcel Dekker AG, 2002.

[11] O'Connell, Fergus, *Successful High-Tech Project-Based Organizations*, Norwood, MA: Artech House, 2001.

[12] Lister, Timothy, and Tom DeMarco, *Peopleware: Productive Projects and Teams*, New York: Dorset House, 1999.

[13] Cleland, David, "The Strategic Context of Projects," in *Project Portfolio Management*, Lowell D. Dye and James S. Pennypacker, (eds.), West Chester, PA: Center for Business Practices, 2000, pp. 3–22.

[14] Cantor, Murray, "Organizing RUP SE Projects," *The Rational Edge*, 2003, Rational Software, http://www.106.ibm.com/developerworks/rational/libr ary/content/03July/2500/2822/2822_MC.pdf (last accessed on September 28, 2004).

[15] Boehm, Barry, "Spiral Development: Experience, Principles, and Refinements," Carnegie Mellon Software Engineering Institute, February 9, 2000, http://www.sei.cmu.edu/cbs/spiral2000/february2000/SR08html/SR0 8.html (last accessed on September 28, 2004).

[16] Wells, Don, "Extreme Programming: A Gentle Introduction," http://www. extremeprogramming.com, 1/26/2003 (last accessed on September 28, 2004).

[17] PMI Standards Committee, *A Guide to the Project Management Body of Knowledge*, Newtown Square, PA: Project Management Institute, 2000 ed., p. 31.

[18] Sarkar, Pushpak, "Applying the Balanced Scorecard in the IT Organization," *DM Review*, http://www.dmreview.com/editorial/dmreview/print_action. cfm?articleId=7762 (last accessed on June 24, 2004).

[19] Zagarow, Herbert W., "Applying the Balanced Scorecard in Project Management," *allPM.com*, http://www.allpm.com/article.php?sid=879 (last accessed on June 24, 2004).

[20] Van den Eynde, Liesbeth, "Performance Measurement and Management in a Financial Sector Merger Case Study: ARTESIA Banking Corporation," http://www.pbviews.com/pdfs/articles/art0010.pdf (last accessed on June 24, 2004).

Appendix 3A: Case Study—Artesia BC—Flexible Balanced Scorecard

Traditionally, project sponsors have measured success levels of their IT-based projects using financial metrics. However, such metrics don't reveal the entire story. A more complete analysis of a project's success would include its impact on staff, customers, and the organization's function [18]. The Balanced Scorecard, developed by Robert S. Kaplan and David Norton, provides a means to choose metrics from four key performance areas that will help better align the various business units with the corporate strategy. In the case of IT-based projects, such metrics, or KPIs, can be invaluable in maintaining a well-balanced project portfolio. Some examples of KPIs that could be chosen include [19]:

1. Financial perspective—NPV, IRR, and payback;

2. Customer perspective—data from formal customer surveys, loyalty indexes, and market segment growth figures;

3. Internal business (organization function) perspective—process performance measures for requirements development, cost estimating, system design, or resource planning;

4. Growth and learning (staff) perspective—new skill and competency acquisition, employee morale, and process improvement.

At the end of 1999, the Artesia Banking Corporation decided to implement the Balanced Scorecard approach to achieve their strategic vision [20]. With 225 million EUR in net consolidated profit and with 1.2 million customers, this Belgian banking and insurance company's vision was to be in the top 25% of European banks in terms of return on equity by 2002. As their Balanced Scorecard initiative became embraced by executives and the grassroots, Rob Van Rensbergen, MIS/DSS manager and Balanced Scorecard lead, realized that they had accumulated far too many KPIs. Not only had these accumulated measures become out of alignment with the strategy, they had become unmanageable in his Excel spreadsheet.

To ensure the KPIs added true value, Van Rensbergen reviewed them and reselected a small set that represented each key performance area. He then purchased a software tool that specialized in gathering and reporting on KPIs. These efforts ended up paying off well when Artesia merged with Dexia in July 2001. As it turned out, because Dexia also had implemented a Balanced Scorecard, the two companies were better able to merge cultures and more quickly able to align on a common strategy. Today, Dexia continues to grow as a successful international banking and insurance conglomerate.

When rolling out a Balanced Scorecard or an IT PPM framework, organizational support is critical to success. The sponsor of such an initiative needs to gain executive and grassroots support through robust training and internal marketing efforts. And to ensure the long-term value of such frameworks, they need to be flexible to the changing marketplace. KPIs of a Balanced Scorecard, for example, need to change to support evolving corporate strategies. This means that a project that started six months ago may need to be reevaluated based on KPIs that have changed to support a new strategy.

4

The IT Portfolio Management Office

4.1 Defining IT PMO

4.1.1 Project Offices

When a project becomes large enough, the numerous and complex project management tasks can get overwhelming for a PM. So that the PM can keep a bird's eye view of the project, tasks such as risk management, scope management, resource support, and rollout management could be delegated to the staff of a project management office. Figure 3.1 showed an example of a project that has three release iterations delivering three different functional sets. If these three iterations of one project were, in fact, three separate projects with three different leaders, then the leader of this project set would be referred to as a program manager. In this case, the program manager would have the option to create and staff a program management office. The need for program and project management offices can depend on more than just the size of the related projects. For example, the strategic importance, integration needs, environmental complexity, resource instability, and budget/time constraints can all convince a project or program manager to establish a project or program management office. The higher the levels of any of these factors, the more an autonomous office would be needed to drive project or program success [1].

The IT PMO is the highest layer that provides support to all of the unrelated projects and programs. The IT PMO won't negate the need for program or project offices; rather, it simply helps these more focused offices be successful. Another way to refer to these is as level 1, 2, and 3 project offices [2]. Where a level 1 project office is focused more on individual project success, the level 3 project office is focused more on portfolio support and project prioritization. Others have referred to the PMO as the enterprise project management office (EPMO) [3]. This book will refer to the level 3 project office, or EPMO, as the IT PMO.

4.1.2 IT PMO Requirements

Three key categories of elements are necessary to allow an IT PMO to operate smoothly: people, process, and tools [2]. Figure 4.1 shows that within each of these categories, certain elements should be satisfied to guarantee IT PMO success.

We can then map these essential PMO elements to the building blocks of an IT PMO we introduced in Chapter 1 to get Figure 4.2. This

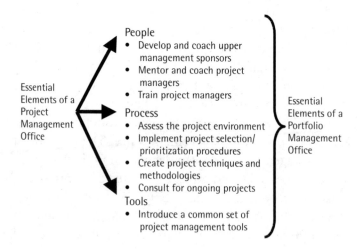

Figure 4.1 Mapping essential elements of a project management office to a PMO.

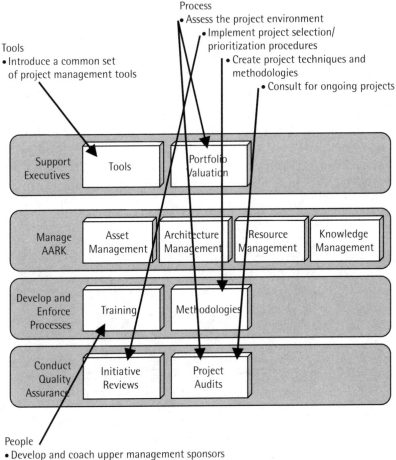

Figure 4.2   Mapping essential elements of a PMO to the PMO building blocks.

figure shows how support for the executives, development and enforcement of processes, and quality assurance all link to the key elements of the traditional PMO. But, because the IT PMO is in the unique position to provide support for the various project and program offices, AARK management provides an additional set of elements important for IT PMO success. Management of AARK is a core piece of an IT PMO that will be discussed further in Chapters 5 through 7.

4.1.3 Tailored PMOs

When times are good for a particular industry, companies tend to allow central control of IT projects to diminish—they disperse power across the business units. Such decentralization empowers middle and lower levels of management so that top managers can focus on strategic planning [1]. A side effect is that while executives are forming and then preaching corporate strategies, middle management has done the same with business unit–level strategies. Figure 4.3 (top) illustrates how different business units approve projects that best fit with their microstrategies. This isn't a problem as long as these microstrategies

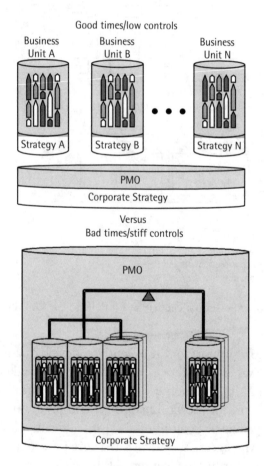

Figure 4.3 Distributed versus centralized IT PMOs.

stay in alignment with the central strategy. One way of ensuring continued digression of these microstrategies from the central strategy is for the IT PMO to become disengaged from the business units.

Once economic times take a turn for the worse, companies tend to centralize control of new business initiatives to better control expenses (see Figure 4.3, bottom). As the IT PMO tries to balance the project portfolio, it realizes that many initiatives are not just out of alignment with the central strategy, but the initiatives are being realized as out-of-control projects. They find out that business units have been implementing technical initiatives independently and without IT governance or support. And, because different business units were approving and running initiatives differently, there is no consistent way to measure initiative health between business units. So, without a way to compare initiatives, management has been forced to clean up the project chaos created by the IT spending and typified by good times and lax controls.

New market demands can require that the executives start slashing outlays for expensive technical initiatives. To do so without damaging the growth of the company, they need to prioritize all of the proposed and ongoing initiatives. Yet, it is difficult for upper management to discern which projects will potentially move the company in the desired direction more efficiently. Control of this chaos can be realized by centralizing control through an IT PMO. The IT PMO can ensure that when IT initiatives are cut, it is done so that there is a balanced portfolio of IT projects across the various business units (see Figure 4.3).

4.2 Virtual PMO

One fear that many companies have in creating a new central organization is that it will act as just another bureaucratic wall to efficiency. It is common for the IT PMO director "to be viewed as someone who is empire building" [2]. To diminish this perception, PMOs need to focus on building relationships and gaining early bang-for-the-buck successes rather than building large organizations. If a PMO is allowed to grow out of control, then it can become unresponsive and inflexible, and won't deliver the economic benefits to business units [4]. To combat this, companies that embrace the need to install a project support group, such as a PMO, use the virtual PMO or the PMO-light version.

Before a PMO initiative can start, the PMO team must realize that such an initiative is a type of corporate reorganization. Change-averse middle management in the business units will need to alter the way they propose business initiatives that require technical implementations, application designers will need to justify their designs to a central architect committee, and PMs will need to follow consistent methodologies when running their projects. As with any major organizational change, the PMO initiative needs to be driven and advocated from the top.

If executive management does not christen the PMO team, the sometimes-monumental task of getting top management to provide support for the effort calls for skillful articulation and great persistence [5], and none should be articulated to more persistently than the executive staff. Without their support, the business units will never jump in line. They will continue to develop siloed solutions that will, in turn, stop any portfolio valuation effort. The best way to tackle such an enormous marketing task with limited staff is to break the message up into subtasks and allow different groups in the organization to get involved in the PMO creation through special portfolio management committees. By getting stakeholders involved early, through portfolio management committees, a sense of PMO ownership will prevail over a sense that the PMO is dictating new policy.

4.2.1 Committees

When creating a PMO, "since the PMO will affect all parts of the organization, all parts of the organization should be represented" [1]. Therefore, the next step after establishing the executive committee is to establish a few cross-organizational teams to support the goals of the PMO. While an independent team will staff and build the core PMO, three committees need to be established early: the business unit committee, the PM committee, and the architect (EA review) committee. These three groups must be made up of representatives that are sponsored by upper management. For example, a good business unit committee would have middle to upper managers from the human resources, marketing, finance, operations, and manufacturing departments. The PM committee would have a random sampling of PMs from projects of varying cost and risk. And the architect committee would have architectural specialists such as senior systems administrators, database administrators, ERP architects, telephony managers, and eBusiness architects (see Figure 4.4). As AARK management is introduced in Chapters 5 through 7, specialized subteams in the IT PMO will be defined to better coordinate these committees.

As the IT PMO team guides these three groups in the development of the virtual PMO, organizational change inflexibility will become more apparent. Each of these groups wants to continue their current processes unhindered. The business units will want to continue to fund all business initiatives (regardless of strategic alignment), the PMs will want to continue to maintain autonomy (regardless of ROI), and the architects will want to continue to play with new toys (regardless of system redundancy). Such inflexibility can be diminished if these groups feel that they have a say in the development of the PMO.

There is a reason for having middle managers make up the team that represents the business units. The organizational support derived

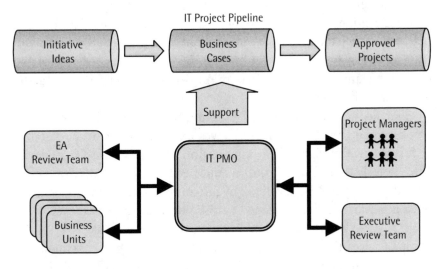

Figure 4.4 Virtual IT PMO—overall view.

from these middle managers will be the lynch pin to success. Middle managers are power sponges and are the root of most friction that a PMO will have when developing organizational acceptance. With so many initiatives clawing for money, it would be easy for the business unit leads to paint a bloated PMO as a good source of funds. This is why the PMO staff level should be kept as small as possible without sacrificing results. Though the business unit and PM teams will serve more advisory roles, the architecture team can provide support that will reduce the resources required to manage AARK. Not only does a virtual PMO team keep the size of the PMO small, and not only does it encourage corporatewide participation, it helps reduce business unit piracy. The case studies at the end of this chapter show how two companies use different approaches in making a central IT PMO-like organization appear larger than it seems. There is also a short PowerPoint presentation on the accompanying CD-ROM that reviews the basics of a virtual IT PMO.

4.3 PMO Structure

4.3.1 Large, Project-Centric Companies

Once the target audience of middle managers has been organized, a plan for rolling out the benefits of a PMO needs to be defined. But before the three PMO extension teams can be organized, the core PMO team needs to be formed. And, again, because of the support of the extension teams and the benefit of minimizing bureaucratic growth, the PMO team should be kept small.

Donald J. Reifer, author of "Making the Software Business Case, Improvement by the Numbers," gives an example of how to staff a group that is redesigning an organization's business and IT processes [6]. He feels that such a group would need a leader that is well connected and respected as a veteran by the company's upper management. Such a familiar leader is needed because business unit managers have spent a lot of effort on complying with the success-ranking system a company already has in place. If this system changes, business managers can risk losing any ground they've gained with the old system. Such upheaval, no doubt, will bring a severe backlash unless new process rollouts are treated with the utmost care. If the point man on such a rollout is not some outsourced newcomer and is instead someone who has a proven track record of making others successful, then middle management will have more early adopters. After establishing a core team of four, the leader can then recruit other veterans on a part-time basis. Academics can help the core team with methodology development and training and retired managers can help with interbusiness unit collaboration and PMO marketing.

Figure 4.5 shows how the resources would overlay some of the building blocks of a PMO. This figure illustrates how the core team members will each be responsible for one of four baseline building blocks. Other building blocks, which may require periodic support, would have resources cross-trained and rotating through them. For example, the bulk of the work required for tailoring methodologies and developing training material would be at the front end. These building blocks, supported by part timers, would get additional support from the various virtual PMO committees as the responsibilities of the PMO grew.

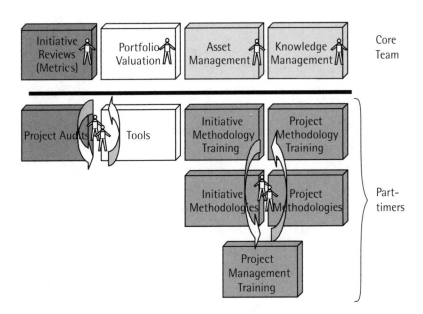

Figure 4.5 Staffing the IT PMO with rotating (cross-trained) duties.

Another way to look at this is to apply the IT PMO resourcing model in Figure 4.5 to the set of PMO building blocks we introduced in Chapter 1. Table 4.1 maps core PMO duties to the number of full-time people needed to implement and maintain these duties from scratch. The number of resources in Figure 4.5 is based on personal experience with a company that ran more than 220 concurrent IT-based projects. The accompanying CD-ROM has two staffing calculators that can help determine IT PMO staffing levels based on projects outstanding and initiatives in the pipeline.

Because the support needed by each building block varies independently over time, staff members will need to be able to support more than one building block (flow arrows in Figure 4.5). Initially, cross training can be focused on the PMO goals. As the PMO's work load increases, fresh faces will be rotated in and veterans will be trained to support other areas or be rolled back out to IT and the business units. Figure 4.6 shows how the resources listed in Table 4.1 would overlay the complete set of PMO building blocks. This figure also shows how, by implementing a virtual PMO approach, a large group of extreme part timers will exist to support PMO rollout. Extreme part timers are those

Table 4.1
Estimating Staff Requirements for an IT PMO in a Large Organization

PMO Goals	PMO Building Blocks	Resources
Executive support	Collaboration tools	
	Portfolio valuation	2
Manage AARK	Architecture management	
	Asset management	
	Resource management	
	Knowledge management	3
Quality assurance	Auditing—third party	
	Initiative reviews	2
Process	Methodology development	
	Training	2
	Total	9

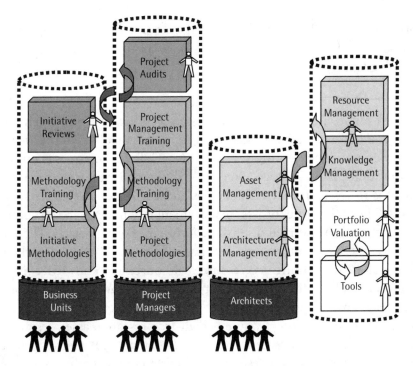

Figure 4.6 Virtual teams to support the IT PMO staff with rotating (cross-trained) duties.

resources who have very little time (and, initially, very little desire) to contribute to a new PMO. But if the PMO rollout is designed to show how it adds value with early wins, these part-timer committees can be quickly sold.

4.3.1.1 Executive Support

IT PMO support software exists that allows IT PMs to enter values for the health of their projects. After the IT PMO includes the prioritization of IT-based business initiatives and the results of project audits, executives can view prioritization lists. If no tool exists to monitor and update aggregate project health, then one to two resources will be needed to gather requirements, configure the system, and roll it out. Once it is released, one to two resources will need to stay on to ensure security, proper usage, and bug fixes. Such IT systems that support portfolio prioritization will be covered more thoroughly in Chapter 9. There is also a list of companies that sell such software systems on the accompanying CD-ROM.

4.3.1.2 AARK Management

The corporate architecture changes as projects propose new technologies. A dedicated staff will be needed to ensure that everything works together, nothing is left unused, and the overall design doesn't conflict with the corporate strategy. One of the duties of architecture management is to research new technologies and negotiate lowest cost solutions. One of the duties of asset management is to manage the inventory of purchased hardware and software licenses between projects. Though the architecture team will do the grunt work here, managing these duties alone will require two resources. Resource and knowledge management can be automated for the most part with Web-based utilities. But back-end support would take at least another resource. While architecture management requires high-tech research, asset, resource, and knowledge management can be automated. And as any of these become more automated, resources can shift to support other aspects of AARK management.

4.3.1.3 Quality Assurance

The amount of work required for both project audits and initiative reviews are directly related to the number of projects currently underway. By the time a dedicated auditor is staffed, there are usually more projects underway than one auditor is able to audit. Where all initiatives need to be reviewed before funding, project auditing can take an "IRS approach." This approach allows an auditor to review all high-risk and high-ROI projects and then take a random sampling of the rest. Two measures of when to add auditors depends on how many audits the PMO wants included in the random sampling and how detailed the audit should be. An audit by an expert PM should take no less than three days [7]. But because the average auditor will be one with less than an expert background, five days to complete an audit would be closer to reality. Table 4.2 shows how one can calculate how to staff for audits (column F) given other variables, such as number of ongoing projects and duration of audits.

Table 4.2
Calculating Staff Requirements for the IT PMO Audit Team

Number of High-Risk/R OI Projects	Number of Other Projects	Average Audit Duration (Man Days)	Average Project Iteration Time (Weeks)	Number of Auditors	Percentage of Projects Randomly Selected for Audit
B	C	D	E	F	
5	100	5	6	3	13%
5	50	5	6	3	26%
5	100	10	6	3	4%
5	100	5	4	3	7%
5	100	5	6	2	7%

A = Total man days = 5 days per week $\times$ E $\times$ F
Z = Man days for high-risk/ROI projects = B $\times$ D
% of projects randomly selected for audit = (A – Z / D) / C

For example, if there were five high-risk/high-ROI projects, 100 other ongoing projects, and three auditors, we would need to also look at the duration of each project iteration and the time it takes to conduct an audit. If project iterations are longer in duration, the audits can be spread out; if they are shorter in duration, then audits would need to occur more frequently. Given our current example scenario, if the average time between project iterations was four weeks, and it took the average auditor five days to conduct an audit, then the IT-PMO would only have enough manpower to conduct random audits on 7% of the projects in the portfolio. But, if the average time between project iterations were six weeks, then the IT PMO would be able to increase the number of auditable projects to 13%. (The staffing calculator on the accompanying CD-ROM helps automate this.)

This sort of calculation helps the IT PMO director understand the tradeoffs that need to be made when staffing the IT PMO audit team. For that matter, if either of the two IT PMO core teams (initiative review and project auditing) become understaffed and overburdened, the IT PMO can easily morph into just another bottlenecking nuisance for business initiatives. While the extended teams of the virtual IT PMO can support the IT PPM processes of AARK management (see Chapters 5 through 8), the core IT PMO teams need to be well maintained.

4.3.1.4 Process

Larger companies can have a large number of projects underway, each using some tailored version of the methodologies supported by the IT PMO. Because the IT PMO can only audit a set percentage of all projects when it reaches a methodology's audit points, there needs to be another way to ensure quality of projects. By developing and running methodology training sessions, the IT PMO can make sure that the PMs and the business case writers understand the core IT PMO methodologies. Then, as long as the predetermined audit points and metric requirements are unaltered, they can mold the methodology templates to the specific needs of the project or initiative proposal. As well as conducting methodology training, the IT PMO methodology team will also need to coordinate the PM committee and the business unit committee when reviewing new project and initiative methodology proposals, respectively. With such flexibility in methodology usage and involvement in methodology selection, the project stakeholders can move forward with confidence.

4.3.2 Smaller or Less Project-Centric Companies

Whether a company is simply small in size or has cut back on the number of running projects, the size of a PMO staff will vary over time. And because of the uncertain demand levels for IT projects, PMOs can be staffed by a rotating group of people. A core group of one to three people can be staffed by a permanent leader and a couple of retiree consultants (see Table 4.3). So, how would the goals of a PMO map to a limited PMO staff when few projects are underway and only a trickle of initiatives is being proposed?

4.3.2.1 Executive Support

Though fewer projects can minimize the workload of a PMO, it by no means eliminates the need to adhere to the goals of a PMO. Where larger companies would use enterprisewide project collaboration tools to valuate the project portfolio, smaller companies simply define and

Table 4.3
Estimating Staff Requirements for an IT PMO in a Small Organization

PMO Goals	PMO Building Blocks	Resources
Executive support	Collaboration tools	
	Portfolio valuation	~ 0.5
Manage AARK	Architecture management	
	Asset management	
	Resource management	
	Knowledge management	~ 1
Quality assurance	Auditing—third party	
	Initiative reviews	~ 0.5
Process	Methodology development	
	Training	~ 0.5
	Total	~ 2

adhere to structured communications such as weekly e-mail and status report updates. With so few projects, executive support tools may not be needed. However, upper management still wants to know the relative health of the one or two IT-supported projects that are underway. By focusing on regular, structured communications of these matters, the IT staff will be developing an early framework for advanced PMO executive support as the company grows.

4.3.2.2 Manage AARK

The IT department needs to manage assets and the corporate architecture very early to prevent problems. But because the IT staff may be small, resource management will show itself more as outsource management. Also, the need for a knowledge management database could be replaced with a file base of project postmortems or high-level business architectures (process flows and structures). If a standard format is defined for these postmortems and architectures early, then the IT department will be better prepared when the company grows and needs a more robust knowledge base.

4.3.2.3 Quality Assurance

With only a few projects and initiatives, the IT manager can usually audit them regularly. But as the pipeline grows, she will need to delegate this task. The person eventually in charge of this task will work with the growing need for executive support to come up with support tools.

4.3.2.4 Process

While methodologies are important for any IT project, training can be handled by the lead IT manager. With a small company, if one methodology is not chosen, then a methodology used by an outsourced company would be used.

4.4 Organizational Change

4.4.1 Impediments

There are nine main impediments to success that need to be addressed aggressively if the PMO initiative is to succeed. These barriers can be categorized as related to either lack of organizational support or lack of PMO deliverables.

As can be seen from Table 4.4, the organizational impediments to early PMO success can outweigh the deliverable impediments to success. These impediments (or risks) and the phased approach to eliminating them is the subject of Chapter 10. Phasing in the PMO will not only allow a small PMO team to build a solid foundation for future PMO functionality, it will also allow the team to manage expectations and nurture organizational support. Because an IT PMO requires a large effort in managing organizational change, results can be difficult to timeline. "A guaranteed no-win situation is when management sets a deadline for you to turn everything around" [8]. Early wins coupled with an ongoing effort to grow support will help overcome these barriers to success. Once the impediments to success are eliminated, PMO benefits can be realized in later phases of the PMO rollout.

4.4.2 Benefits

There are four keys to the successful rollout out of a new IT PMO:

Table 4.4
Impediments to Organizational Change During PMO Rollout

Organizational Support	*PMO Deliverables*
Lack of top-level support. Executive support needs to be gained at the very beginning by forming an enthusiastic executive committee.	*Lack of project methodology.* Chapter 3 showed how a set of methodologies is important to allow for healthier, more flexible projects that can be audited consistently. This is a deliverable that needs to be available early to see quick wins for the PMO marketing campaign.
Underestimation of the dimension of the change project. The introduction of a PMO can drastically change the way a company approves initiatives and maintains its health. If the PMO lead isn't aware of this, they may not apply the proper urgency to acquiring organizational support.	*Insufficient efforts to develop project professionals.* While methodologies can be restrictive for those who are experienced in project management, they can be confusing for those who are beginners. If the PMO ignores the opportunity to train new PMs, then a valuable support base will be lost.
Inadequate management of the change project. Once support is gained in the beginning, it must not only be maintained, it must grow. Others need to jump on the bandwagon once early benefits of the IT PMO are advertised.	*Lack of initiative methodology.* If business initiatives that don't include standard metric maps or iterated releases are allowed to be submitted, then the PMO will have no way to audit, and the company will be at the mercy of inflexible projects.
Bad timing. If the company is in the middle of a downsizing and all IT projects are on hold, then this would be an extreme example of when not to start an IT PMO initiative. Be sure the company is in a position to embrace this concept before diving in.	*No prioritization tool leverage plan.* An efficient way for executives to quickly see the health and the prioritization of their portfolio is essential early on. A release of such a system can gain rock-solid support from the executives who will now be able to see, in real time, how their company is reacting to the shifting marketplace.
Lack of corporate strategy. Without a strategy, the IT PMO will not have any way to prioritize or balance the portfolio to the goals of the company. Instead a chaotic portfolio will cause widespread dissention of the PMO concept.	

Source: [5].

1. *A good business case.* The PMO needs to practice what it preaches. As the central consolidator and reviewer of business cases for new initiatives, it has to also be accountable for its own success. A business case should be written with measurable ROI milestones. Meeting such milestones and proving ROI to the company will further validate the need for the PMO. And because PMOs are constantly under scrutiny, such winning hurdles are critical. Let the numbers do the talking. The organization will support any believable proposal that helps get its products out the door cheaper, quicker, and better [6].

2. *Organization's cultural readiness.* Are different organizations in the company willing to provide resources to the PMO? Can the management team support a redistribution of authority? These are just a couple of issues that should be listed in the risk assessment section of the PMO business plan. Mitigation steps should also be outlined for any organizational change barrier that may be expected.

3. *Sizing/tailoring of project office.* This flows directly from Dr. Markowitz's theories of proper portfolio management. That is, PMOs should be customized to particular companies. One cannot take the blueprint and rollout plans from the PMO of another company and use them for their own company. Even if the companies are the same size and are in the same industry, communication plans for executive or middle management can be drastically different between the two companies.

4. *Executive commitment.* Because there will be conflict when rolling out the PMO, clear and prompt executive support is mandatory. It will need to be made crystal clear to the troops that the PMO is central to the success of the company [2]. "To get their support and sponsorship, you must build a bulletproof business case that justifies your proposed investment of time, talent, and energy in terms of benefits to individual project (their projects). To win funding approval, you must generate near-term results" [6].

Overlaps can be clearly seen between the conclusions we reached from looking at the negative as well as the positive influences of PMO rollout. But what is most striking is the continued predominance of the need for organizational support.

4.4.3 Governance

4.4.3.1 IT PMO Governance

There are two main components of corporate governance [9]:

1. The decision-making mechanisms that are created (e.g., committees, review boards, and written policies);

2. The assignment of decision-making authority and accountability.

The PMO will create the written policies, and it will coordinate the virtual PMO committees and the initiative review board. But what sort of authority and accountability should be given to the PMO? First, it will be accountable for maintaining a healthy IT portfolio through the implementation of the PMO building blocks. How the PMO can prove that it has improved the health of the portfolio will be addressed in Chapter 9. Second, it will have the authority to grade initiatives and ongoing projects for the prioritization list presented to the executive review board. At any time, this board can institute a policy that cancels a bottom percentage of projects according to the initiative's or project's position on the prioritization list.

"Authority and accountability must be equivalent within an agency" [10]. Where an organization has little authority, there should be little accountability. Conversely, where an organization has significant authority, there should be significant accountability. If the executive committee is going to hold the PMO accountable for a healthy suite of projects that move the company in the chosen strategic direction, then the committee needs to also provide the PMO with a reasonable level of authority. And this authority should rest in the initiative and project review process.

It should be understood that the executive review board can override PMO recommendations at any time, but the more it does so, the more irrelevant the PMO will become. This is an area that the PMO organization needs to address to ensure legitimacy in the eyes of the business units. As time passes, the PMO needs to communicate clearly to the business units how the executive committee is using the prioritization list. This approach combines management of business unit IT projects by reward (those projects that are doing well will continue to be funded) and management by fear (those projects that are doing poorly can get cancelled). Then, by proving to the executive committee that the portfolio has improved, it will be less inclined to go around the recommendations of the PMO.

Sometimes, in the face of extreme strategic shifts, the PMO will need to split itself up in order to maintain continued organizational support. Keep in mind that centralization of corporate governance is more in line with company strategies focused more on improving productivity than those focused more on growth. One survey of 40 companies found that "companies that do well in terms of return on assets tend to have tight, centralized governance mechanisms, while companies looking to maximize their market caps tend to push IT decision making out to the local business unit or end users" [9]. To continue with an IT PPM concept in a company that is giving more IT project control to the business units, satellite IT PMOs should be set up for each business unit (see Figure 4.7). Then, if the company decides to switch back from a high-growth-oriented strategy, the PMO itself has been designed to be flexible enough to easily transition back to one that supports more of a productivity-oriented strategy.

4.4.3.2 IT Governance

Because the IT PMO relies so much on the IT department to be successful, the line of authority between these two organizations can be difficult to see. One way to view this is by including the other organizations with which the IT PMO shares responsibilities. Figure 4.8 shows the PMO as the central organization that not only has its own unique deliverables (review boards, training curricula, prioritization tools), but also binds elements from three other groups. The IT PMO relies on:

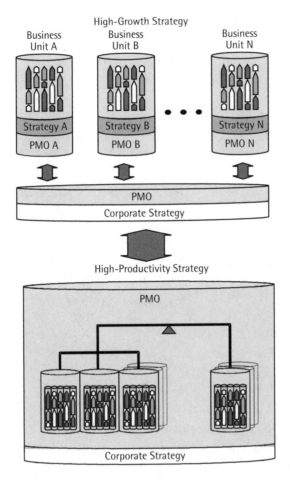

Figure 4.7 Types of corporate strategies applied to distributed and centralized IT PMOs.

1. The pool of PMs (who are drawn from all business units including IT) to help develop project methodologies and to ensure project audits run smoothly;

2. The business units to help develop IT-based initiative methodologies and to run initiative reviews;

3. The IT department to partner in the management of IT architecture, assets, resources, and knowledge.

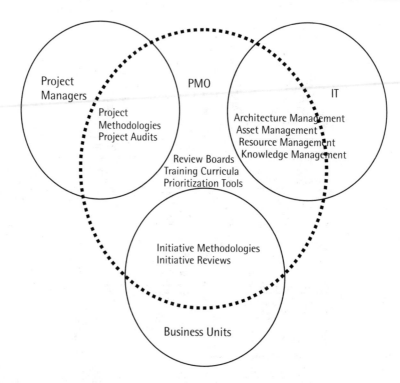

Figure 4.8 Distribution of virtual IT PMO deliverables.

Each group contributes its own strengths to the IT PMO to help ensure the overall health of the project portfolio. It just so happens that the IT organization contributes more to the IT PMO than do the other organizations.

IT governance drives decisions in three main areas: IT strategy, investments in IT projects, and IT architecture [9]. PMO governance drives decisions only in investments in IT-based business initiatives/projects. IT's footprint on the stream of these projects is seen when technical and organizational risks are solicited from the PMO by the business case writers. The IT PMO relies on the architecture committee, staffed completely by IT personnel, not only when presenting risks, but also when prioritizing initiatives and projects (see Chapter 5). But the biggest contribution by IT is in the form of its assets and resources.

Traditional IT governance uses various methods when making decisions on IT project investments. The most common methods are those that attempt to make IT less of a cost center [11]. The IT department can impose a "tax rate" on each department that uses IT services for projects or utilities. It can impose a fee for service, similar to a time-and-materials approach used by many IT outsourcing firms. Or, IT can use an allocation of costs approach, which varies the IT charge on departments based on their usage of IT resources. If the IT department already has sound programs in place that track where its assets and resources are distributed, then the IT PMO should leverage these. If such programs are nonexistent or substandard, the IT PMO should work with the IT department to make such tracking mechanisms robust (see Chapters 6 and 7).

To avoid any appearance of favoritism when prioritizing initiatives and projects, the IT PMO director needs to report directly to the executive committee. If the CIO is on the executive committee, then the IT PMO director can report to the CIO. If the CIO reports to the CFO, then the IT PMO director should report to the CEO. As soon as the IT PMO director reports up through a particular business unit lead (e.g., the CFO), then the image of objectivity in initiative and project prioritization will be sacrificed. If the CFO controls the prioritization process, a project on accounts payable automation, for example, could move up the priority list over an IT-based project on lead generation collaboration. It won't matter which is the better project for the company. If the former wins out over the latter, the resulting perception could demoralize the idea generators.

With prioritization being one side of the PMO accountability coin, project portfolio health is the other side. To accomplish this second major task requires seamless cooperation with the IT department. Because the IT PMO will need to effectively monitor IT assets and resources between projects [3], it would make little sense to create an organizational barrier between the CIO and the IT PMO director. The PMO needs to know when resources become available or unavailable and when assets are being fully used or are unused. Therefore, to create an IT PMO that most effectively supports projects with the fewest barriers with the IT department, the IT PMO director should report directly to the CIO.

Table 4.5 is a matrix that shows how the IT PMO can be affected by
who its director reports to in the company's organizational chart. The
optimal scenario would be if the director of IT PMO reported directly to
the CIO to reduce the barriers to resource and asset management, and
for the CIO to report directly to the CEO to eliminate perceptions of
favoritism when prioritizing the portfolio. This is shown in the upper
left quadrant of the table. Any other organizational approach will negatively affect the ability of the PMO to be successful in both of its primary
tasks: prioritization and project support.

4.5 Summary

Because rolling out an IT PMO results in enterprisewide organizational
change, its structure needs to be designed to ease this difficult rollout
and to ensure continued support. One approach is to keep the IT PMO
small and to leverage the skills and authorities of various senior employees. Such a virtual PMO will, in turn, require the IT PMO organization
to staff small teams to support various committees drawn from the
ranks. The executive committee will support the initiative/project
review process, the business unit committee will approve the EBA (discussed in next chapter) and the initiative methodology, the architecture
committee will approve the enterprise IT architecture (EIA) and review
project proposals for technical risk, and the PM committee will approve
the project methodologies. Then, based on the size and type of the company, the staffing of the IT PMO should be tailored accordingly.

Table 4.5
IT PMO Governance Matrix

	CIO Reports to CEO	CIO Reports to Business Unit Lead (e.g., CFO)
IT PMO director reports to CIO	Prioritization process = unbiased Project support = efficient	Prioritization process = biased Project support = efficient
IT PMO director reports to CEO	Prioritization process = unbiased Project support = inefficient	Prioritization process = biased Project support = inefficient

Specifically, to avoid initiative review bottlenecking, the core initiative review and project audit IT PMO teams need to be well monitored for proper staffing levels. Finally, it should be clear to the organization that the IT PMO is not infringing upon the "turf" of the IT department. Rather, the IT PMO is creating a support structure that will better market the strengths of IT and support a smoother flow of business initiative ideas to successful IT project deliverables.

References

[1] Englund, Randall, and Robert Graham, *Creating an Environment for Successful Projects*, San Francisco, CA: Jossey-Bass, 2000.

[2] Crawford, J. Kent, *The Strategic Project Office*, Monticello, NY: Marcel Dekker AG, 2003.

[3] Meta Group, "Centralizing Management of Project Portfolios," *Meta Group*, January 29, 2002, http://www.umt.com/site/Documents/IT_World_-_Leading_Organisation_Centralize_Management_of_Project_Portfolios_-_29Jan02.pdf (last accessed on January 15, 2004).

[4] Norton, David P., and Robert S. Kaplan, *The Strategy-Focused Organization*, Boston, MA: Harvard Business School Press, 2003.

[5] Dinsmore, Paul C., "Enterprise Project Management: Flavor of the Day or Here to Stay?" *PM Network*, February 1, 2001, http://www.dinsmore.com.br/artigos.htm (last accessed on January 15, 2004).

[6] Reifer, Donald J., *Making the Software Business Case: Improvement by the Numbers*, Boston, MA: Addison-Wesley, 2002.

[7] O'Connell, Fergus, *Successful High-Tech Project-Based Organizations*, Norwood, MA: Artech House, 2002.

[8] Young, D. Allen, "Project Office Start-Up," *PM Network*, February 1, 2001, http://www.pmi.org/info/PIR_PMNetworkOnline.asp (last accessed on January 15, 2004).

[9] Koch, Christopher, "The Powers That Should Be," *CIO Magazine*, October 15, 2002, http://www.cio.com/archive/091502/powers.html (last accessed on January 15, 2004).

[10] Bays, Michael E., *Software Release Methodology*, Upper Saddle River, NJ: Prentice Hall, 1999.

[11] Andriole, Steve, "Business-IT Strategies," *Cutter Consortium*, Vol. 2, No. 5, May 1, 1989.

[12] Melymuka, Kathleen, "Harrah's: Betting on IT Value," *Computerworld*, May 3, 2004, http://www.computerworld.com/managementtopics/manage ment/story/0,10801,92759,00.html (last accessed on June 24, 2004).

[13] Chase, Victor, "How HCA Brought Business, IT Together," *CIO Insight*, June 1, 2002, http://www.cioinsight.com/print_article/0,1406,a=28591,00.asp (last accessed on June 24, 2004).

Appendix 4A: Case Studies—HCA and Harrah's—Virtual IT PMOs

4A.1 Harrah's

It took Harrah's seven years to develop a system and an IT PPM culture within its various business units. They approached the problem in classic IT PPM style by creating a core IT PMO staff backed up by *governance* teams from the various business units. These governance teams met monthly and quarterly to approve funding for small projects and to review the health, alignment, and balance of the project portfolio. The governance teams were an extension of the IT PMO and staffed by IT personnel, business leaders, and accountants. Any projects with a budget greater than $250,000 would be forwarded for approval by a corporate capital committee made up of the CEO, chief operations officer (COO), CFO, CIO, and other senior vice presidents. This layered approach to project funding reduced executive bottlenecking and helped streamline the project approval process.

Before initiatives are proposed, their IT PMO's "business office" provides support to business case writers on how to choose metrics that can be used to audit the eventual project's health and ultimate ROI. The chosen metrics are then used in a software tool to keep track of the project portfolio. This portfolio management tool allows management to segment the ongoing projects and the IT-based initiatives by business unit, product, life cycle stage, revenue growth, cost reduction, or marketing channels. According to Heath Daughtrey, vice president of IT services, this IT project portfolio tool "provides one integrated version of the truth."

With a heavy reliance on business cases, organizationwide IT PMO support, and an embraced IT project portfolio tool, Harrah's has created an environment of structured flexibility. According to CIO Tim Stanley, such an approach to their IT project portfolio allows them to "have crisp operating procedures and structures" while at the same time maintaining "flexibility to constantly align with the business" [12].

4A.2 HCA

As the largest provider of health care in the United States, HCA has a constant need to improve its use of technology to cut costs and grow beyond its 200 hospitals and 80 outpatient surgery centers. Unfortunately, CIO Noel Brown Williams saw that many of the ongoing IT-based projects weren't aligned with the direction of the corporate strategy. To resolve this misalignment, Williams created five new "solution leader" positions (called relationship managers by research firm Gartner, Inc.) that would become closely involved with the day-to-day activities of the various business units.

These solutions leaders work for IT but attend business unit meetings. In this way, new IT-based initiative ideas are created that are aligned with not only the business but the IT architecture as well. A collateral duty includes helping out other idea generators with the technical metrics written into their business cases. Not only does this help IT get involved earlier in the project design, it allows IT to become part of the build versus buy decision. Williams even includes a way to rate their performance by including the business leaders in the performance evaluations. According to Jim Gabler, research director at Garner, Inc., these relationship managers are "a very powerful way for IT to be very responsive to the business" [13].

These two approaches to extending the IT PMO are equally valid. Where Harrah's created explicit business unit committees to prioritize and recommend projects for financing, HCA created implicit business unit committees by sending solution leaders out to business unit meetings. The former had authority to make portfolio decisions, while the latter acted only as a means of aligning IT with the businesses. Neither of these approaches, however, addressed some of the extended elements of IT PPM, such as formal resource management, architecture management, asset management, or knowledge management. To do so, Harrah's and HCA would need to create committees out of the PMs and the architects. They may also need to implement some software tools that would aid in asset, resource, and knowledge management.

5

Architecture Management

If a company has a large suite of IT projects, it needs to develop a strategically aligned blueprint from which all IT-based initiatives can draw. Such a blueprint starts with modeling the goals, rules, structure, and processes of the microstrategies as a cross-business unit architecture. This business architecture is a way of communicating the various microstrategies of the business units to not only business case writers but also to the IT architecture team. While IT-based business cases will be able to include more detailed process flows and structural diagrams of their proposed solution, the IT architecture committee will be able to anticipate new directions and develop training programs, design updates, and vendor reviews. Then, when business case writers request early risk analyses of their ideas from the IT department, there will be a level of alignment already established that will speed the process.

The IT PMO is a well-positioned organization to coordinate the business units, the business case writers, and the IT architecture teams to help create the various pieces of what is known as the enterprise architecture (EA). This architecture can be split into two main categories: the enterprise business architecture (EBA) and the EIA. While a

117

simple version of the EBA would include organizational charts and job descriptions, an advanced version would include state charts and process flow diagrams developed in the early stages of other IT-based projects. The EIA can be a high-level set of diagrams drawn up by the IT architecture team, or it can be real-time infrastructure dispositions maintained by an auto detection software package. Combined, they define "the direction and priorities of IT in an organization, linked to business goals" [1]. Where the IT department will develop the EIA, the IT PMO will support a committee of business units to verify the EBA. By then guiding business case writers in how to write more detailed business views, the IT PMO can become the heart of a much larger virtual IT PMO that helps to continually evolve IT's EIA. Other benefits of a comprehensive EA include [1–4]:

1. Long-term savings in support;

2. Better alignment with business strategy;

3. More consistent IT processes;

4. Best practices in software reuse;

5. Common look and feel that makes all systems using the new architecture seem more familiar and therefore easier to use;

6. Lower costs of integration.

To illustrate the various layers of a business blueprint, let's break the organization down into different architectural models [3, 5]. Figure 5.1 shows how we would develop the EBA components at the bottom and then work our way up to the EIA.

- *Layer 1*, the EBA, details the company's processes (behavior view) and structures (structural view). Figure 5.1 shows some example designs for these two sublayers. In the structural view, we see that a company could have payroll under the vice president of human resources and investment management under the CFO for each sub-CEO executive. Or the company could place both of these responsibilities under the CFO, as seen on the right. Each of these

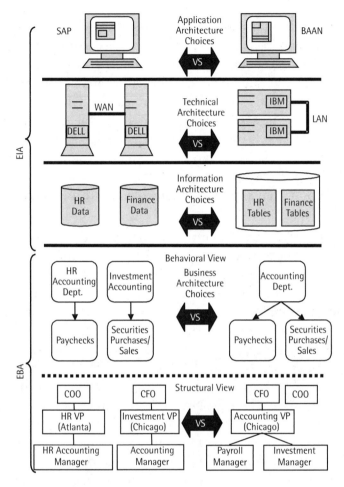

Figure 5.1   Choices to be made when developing an EA. (*After:* [2, 3].)

is an example of the choices a company can make when designing its organizational structure. The company can also make some tradeoffs when designing its processes. On the left side we see simple process diagrams where the human resources department dispenses paychecks and the accounting department purchases or sells securities. Another option, on the right side, would be to have a central accounting department handle both of these tasks.

- *Layer 2,* the information architecture, determines what data, processes, and integrations need to be defined to implement layer 1 (EBA or strategy map) through technology. Figure 5.1 shows that a company can design its information architecture to allow each business unit to store its own data in its database (left) or to store it in a central database (right). This central database can be designed to keep the business data separated at the table level, if the business initiative requires it. A common guiding principle in designing the information architecture is to ask "Can we get information from anywhere in our company to anywhere in our Value Chain?" [4].

- *Layer 3,* the technical (or infrastructure) architecture, scrutinizes the underlying technologies that are required to run the applications. A typical example would be choosing between having a company's servers geographically separated or having them in the same building. In the former case, the technology architecture would need to show how a wide area network (WAN) was designed to support communications between the servers. In the latter case, only the local area network (LAN) specifications would be needed when explaining the interserver communications. While the technical architecture serves as the foundation on which applications and information sit, it can also be defined by the designs of the various IT project needs. Examples of other technical (or infrastructure) components could include security, telephony, satellite communications, or personal computers.

- *Layer 4,* the application architecture, builds upon the business architecture and the information architecture. Here we see the company choosing between two enterprise resource planning software packages (SAP and BAAN). Such a choice, many times, is but one of many a company makes in developing its comprehensive application architecture. The applications chosen can either depend on the technical architecture that the company has built or it can necessitate a change in the technical architecture.

5.1 The EBA

Chapter 2 showed that after an executive committee develops its corporate strategy, the business units could build on it with mapped microstrategies. As these strategy maps stay aligned with shifting marketplaces, the company is, in effect, maintaining a road map of strategies. Once these road maps are developed and distributed, business units can then start presenting business cases for technical and nontechnical initiatives. These business cases need to prove their alignment by drawing up high-level versions of the business processes and structures that the project will be affecting. These views will then need to show how they link to and support the microstrategies of the affected business units.

One major flaw in all of this detailed strategizing is that business units will very rarely find the time to document their processes and goals. The only time they will drill down to such details is when they are required to do so while developing requirements and design collateral for IT-based projects. IT PMs, in their drive to deliver the exact expectations of the stakeholders, can become quite meticulous in documenting the inner workings of a business. Such documentation, when gathered in a project knowledge base and then saved by the IT PMO in a central repository, tends to be the only way a business will find the time to evolve an EBA beyond simple organizational charts and job descriptions. Sure, executives sometimes launch a large drive to map out Balanced Scorecards or process flows, but more times than naught, such initiatives wither under the bureaucratic steam roller. The IT PMO can ensure that the evolution of the EBA occurs when it is necessary and thus prevent organizational backlash to companywide strategy trends. In this section, we will present a few modeling approaches that an IT PMO can advertise to business case writers and PMs when establishing common modeling techniques for a central EBA repository.

5.1.1 Supply and Demand

One place we can start in explaining business architectures is in the basic concept of supply and demand. Figure 5.2 shows how the corporate strategy is first developed to supply the demands of the marketplace

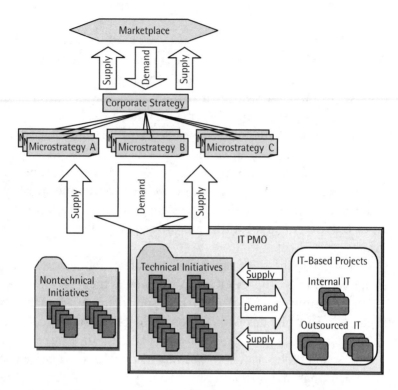

Figure 5.2 Linking the supplies of an IT project portfolio to the demands of the marketplace.

with profitable solutions. A foundation of microstrategies, in turn, supplies the demands laid out by the higher level corporate strategy. Then, to provide for the demands of this next level of strategy, business initiatives are supplied to the various review committees. Finally, to provide the approved initiatives with their demands, a supply of well-managed projects are added to the IT project portfolio. This final supply can be provided by internal IT resources, outsourced IT resources, or a combination of both. If the available supplies don't meet the achievable demands well in any part of this flow, then either the demand or the supply aren't aligned to the same goals—or there are too many constraints to the supply/demand flow.

Figure 5.3 shows that after developing a business architecture from the microstrategies, a set of IT architectures can be developed that help

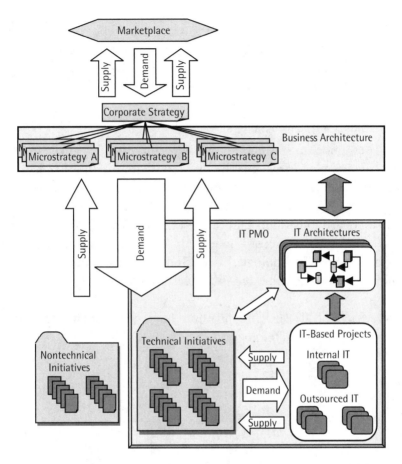

Figure 5.3 Leveraging the enterprise architecture in the project portfolio supply/demand chain.

keep the lower end of the supply and demand flow properly aligned. (The accompanying CD-ROM provides an animated version of Figures 5.2 and 5.3 in the AARK Management PowerPoint presentation.) While the IT department is best qualified to develop these architectures, the IT PMO is better positioned to ensure all IT-based initiatives and projects maintain alignment with these architectures through their history. As the IT department keeps their architectures up to date with the changing business architecture, they are, in essence, anticipating the types of initiatives that will be going before the review committees. The IT department can then preemptively research the types of technologies that may be needed to satisfy the business architecture. Also, the IT PMO will have a more detailed map to review when prioritizing initiatives and projects.

5.1.2 Constraints and Enablers

When designing the business architecture, it is often beneficial to know what constrains and what enables the smooth flow of internal demands and supplies. Figure 5.4 looks specifically at the pipeline between the initiative portfolio and the project portfolio. The figure illustrates that while there are constraints that can restrict the flow of initiatives, there can also be enablers. According to Nate Whaley, senior practice manager at Excelon Technologies, two kinds of constraints can tend to inhibit the success of financed initiatives:

1. Facts of life (FOL) constraints (e.g., government regulations, geography, technology);

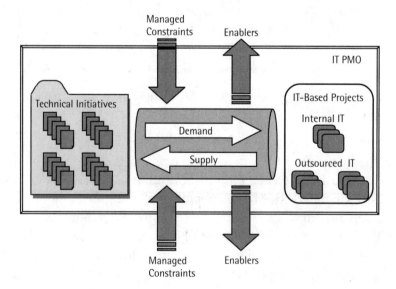

Figure 5.4 Constraints and enablers in satisfying the demands of technical initiatives.

2. Manageable constraints (e.g., capital allocation, organizational structure and forces, IT architecture).

FOL constraints are those that an IT department can't avoid in the short term. Government regulations capping access to mobile carrier frequencies, countries with no telephony infrastructure to access remote geographies, and software companies developing "must-have" software only for specialized operating systems are all examples of FOL constraints. Business case writers need to realize the existence of risks and adapt their ideas accordingly. However, if they think certain FOL constraints will disappear in the long term, then they should provide evidence of this probability when presenting a case that depends on the elimination of the FOL constraint.

Where FOL constraints permanently restrict the flow of acceptable initiatives, there are two other mechanisms that the initiative sponsor can use to alter the flow—both positively and negatively. All risks that can be mitigated fall into the category of manageable constraints. As these risks get more insurmountable, the IT supply pipe becomes tighter. On the other hand, if the results of another IT project that is expected to complete shortly increases the speed of the network, it can act as an enabler that causes the IT supply pipe to become wider. The business case needs to list those constraints that could be mitigated and those potential enablers that could improve the success of the project. Moreover, the central IT PMO is in a perfect position to know which constraints and enablers have been added to the project portfolio and which new initiatives they will affect the most.

5.1.3 Business System Modeling

An enterprise IT architecture "is a business/operational thing first and foremost" [6]. Once an enterprisewide business architecture is developed, only then can the technical architectures be correctly mapped to the goals of the company. Enterprise architects must first establish a foundation that describes an understanding of the business. Such a foundation should "list the required parts of a business, show how the parts are structured and interact, and show how the architecture should evolve" [6]. As the PMO monitors and supports the project portfolio, it will then be in a position to ensure that these business and IT architectures continue their evolutions.

There are many traditional ways to model businesses (e.g., CIMOSA, PERA), but some methods may be more suited to bridge gaps between business goals and IT implementations. D. W. McDavid's 1999 *IBM Systems Journal* paper, "A Standard for Business Architecture Description" [7], introduced a model that helps map out the details of the microstrategies into a high-level business system architecture. McDavid, himself, explains that another modeling technique that can help bridge this gap is business object modeling such as the Penker-Erikson extensions of the Universal Modeling Language (UML). A third technique, Kaplan's Business Scorecard approach (introduced in Chapter 2), makes sure that the output of the chosen business modeling paradigm stays aligned with the corporate strategy. These three approaches are just a few examples of modeling paradigms that can be used. Each one should be used for different situations and for different levels of abstraction.

5.1.3.1 McDavid Subdomains

Of these business modeling techniques, McDavid's approach merges best with the business supply and demand model just introduced. Table 5.1 shows how his business subdomains would map to our model of constrained and enabled supply and demand flows [7].

On the demand side, McDavid defines the drivers of business as business situations, purposes, and outcomes. McDavid argues that by first modeling around situations, the business architects will be able to reason about and predict "the external factors that are driving the business." Business situations are made up of those situations that the

Table 5.1
McDavid Subdomains Mapped to the Supply/Demand/Constraint Model

Demand	Drivers of the business = business situation, business purpose, business outcome
Constraints	Business boundaries = business roleplayer, business commitment
Supply	Business delivery system = business function, business behavior

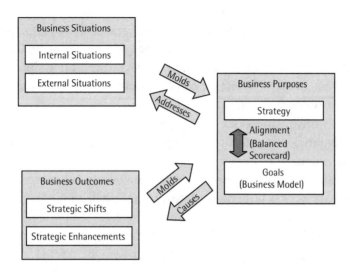

Figure 5.5 Applying McDavid subdomains to EBA evolution.

marketplace presents (external) and those situations that the company itself presents (internal). That is, McDavid asserts that the corporate strategy can't be written to accommodate just the marketplace movements, but that it should also be written to accommodate internal changes. Both of these fluid environments create situations that mold the strategy (see Figure 5.5).

Business outcomes are another source that molds the strategy. We saw this with how Joe's Telecommunications had to alter its desired strategic direction to satisfy the results (or the technical limitations) of some of its IT projects. Many think that the goals of the business result in initiatives that, in turn, are the only causes of business outcomes. But, as seen at Joe's, the undesirable results of IT projects can also cause business outcomes. We found that if the goals of the microstrategies of the company are kept aligned, then the frequency of misguided IT outcomes will be lessened.

The boundaries (or constraints) to business are, according to McDavid, made up of business role players and business commitments. Role players can be people, organizations, or devices that either bind initiatives to certain prerequisites or open them to more opportunities. For example, if a new CIO required all new projects to use a certain hardware vendor, then this could be a form of constraint. But, if that hardware vendor was too expensive for the previous CIO, even though it offered much more functionality, the new CIO could actually be an enabler. Business commitments such as customer and supplier contracts also act as boundaries that can constrain or free initiatives.

Finally, we have the supply side of the business flows referred to by McDavid as the business delivery system. This system of supplying the various demands of the business is made up of business functions and behaviors. Figure 5.1 showed behaviors (or processes) as one layer of the EBA and business structures (or functions) as the other layer. In our example, we saw how both the structure and the behavior of accounting and human resources controlled how paychecks are supplied.

By combining McDavid's modeling approach with some others, we can recategorize business concepts into four basic buckets [7, 8]:

1. Resources and their associated context diagrams (e.g., organizational charts);

2. Rules (e.g., constraints);

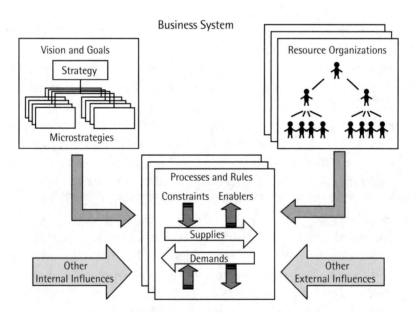

Figure 5.6 Combining advanced EBA paradigms into a business system model.

3. Processes (e.g., supply/demand flows, flow diagrams);

4. Vision and goals (e.g., strategies and microstrategies) (see Figure 5.6).

Using these four concepts, Figure 5.6 illustrates how the vision and goals (4) and the organization of the resources (1) make demands on, and thus mold, the lower level aspects of the business system [the processes (3) and the rules (2)]. This figure also takes into consideration that there might be other demands from both inside and outside the company that can mold the inner workings of a company. Sometimes a company might have to react to internal or external forces that the strategy or the organizational charts didn't anticipate. The influences of a natural disaster (external) or of an accounting/budget miscalculation (internal) are both examples of forces that can make a company react immediately rather than wait for the strategy to change.

5.1.3.2 Penker-Erikson Extensions

When computers were introduced to businesses in the 1960s and 1970s, the common modeling technique was the flow diagram. This paradigm served as a means to translate *business speak* into *IT systems speak*. As we entered the 1980s and 1990s, systems started being designed around things called objects. Instead of having central data stores and several applications that presented and built the data, we started seeing a distribution of the data in business objects. Systems designers felt that the IT architectures of the future would better represent the real world by combining data with functionality in these objects. Since then, new business modeling techniques have evolved that better map *business speak* to this new form of *IT business object speak*.

Many IT consulting companies have developed process-modeling techniques that allow them to map the flow of the business to an abstraction understandable by IT systems architects. A common theme among these process modelers is that they don't restrict themselves to the constraints of organizational charts. Many of the processes they model are horizontal to the organization and affect many functions across the business. "Object-oriented techniques can easily show these processes, as well as the traditional organizational structure" [8]. One

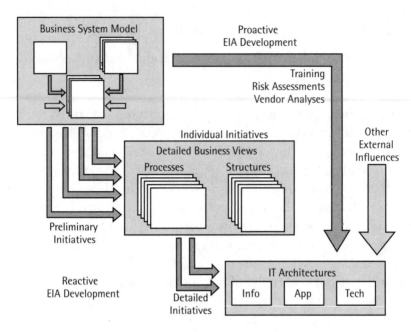

Figure 5.7 Leveraging prepared EBAs to reactively and proactively modify the EIA.

example of such a modeling technique is the Penker-Erikson extensions to the UML. UML sequence or collaboration diagrams can represent the interactions among different resources. Sequence (or process-oriented) and collaboration (or structure-oriented) diagrams can represent the interaction among a number of objects. (Figure 5.7 shows these two as process and structure diagrams.) The architecture review committee sees a business case that models its proposal at this level of detail as being very clear on what it wants. Such detailed modeling avoids the communication-tag delays that occur between the project sponsor and the architecture review committee.

Because business strategies and goals are constantly shifting to meet the demands of the market place, business modelers should be careful not to overmodel. That is, diagrams that don't aid in aligning any IT initiatives, don't aid in making strategic decisions, or may become obsolete quickly should be minimized. Figure 5.7 shows that the IT architecture committee can leverage the higher-level business system model to plan training, assess risks for prebusiness case ideas, develop improved system designs, and conduct vendor reviews. Business-case writers, on the other hand, should take the business system model to one more level of detail whenever necessary (i.e., detailed business views). Such an approach helps to keep the IT architecture aligned with the business strategy without being mired in analysis paralysis.

Appendix 5A shows how Safeco Corporation put a priority on aligning the business architecture with the IT architecture. This was so central to the corporate strategy that the company made the CIO head of strategic development. Getting IT involved with strategy development is good. But because many proposed and ongoing IT-based projects can be out of IT's view, a portfolio-aware IT PMO may have a better feel for the technical heartbeat of the company.

5.2 The EIA

Where an EBA helps guide the business initiative stream, the EIA helps guide the acquisition and deployment of technology [2, 3]. But before any purchases can be made, they need to be associated with a business need. These needs come in the form of approved business initiatives. When a business idea is presented to the IT architectural committee, the EIA is used to help establish the risks that might be involved if the initiative is allowed to proceed. Then, as the business case is presented and the project proceeds, the IT PMO leverages the EIA for better prioritization. This is how the EIA influences the architectures of the various projects as they get approved. How then could initiatives continue to evolve the EIA in new directions?

An overriding principle when evolving an enterprise architecture should be to constantly ensure it is flexible to changing business needs. For example, architectures shouldn't be so rigid that they slow down projects or prevent companies from capitalizing on new technologies quickly. Standardization should only occur in areas where it would lower costs, provide greater efficiencies, or fuel competitive advantage [1]. For example, if every business unit was allowed to choose its own ERP system, the help desk staff would end up spending most of their time training on each of these systems. But if the IT PMO was able to negotiate a good deal on an enterprisewide system, help desk, licensing, integration, and training costs would all be reduced. In other areas, however, it might be more efficient to not standardize. An example would be personal computer purchases. If the business unit was allowed to shop around for the best deal, the IT help desk should have no problem supporting them as long as they had the same core operating systems. That is, the business units would save money, but not at the expense of increased costs with the IT help desk. Such flexibility paired with firm standardization creates an architecture that both reacts well to market changes and takes advantage of cost reduction opportunities.

Earlier we showed how the EIA could be split into three layers: the information architecture, the application architecture, and the technology architecture. These layers are influenced by technical trends, the constant flow of IT-based initiatives, and the IT strategy. However, as we determined, the central influencer to the EIA is the fourth layer: the EBA. Once all four of these layers have been defined, the PMO is in a great position to maintain the architecture as the business changes. Every time a technical business initiative is proposed, the PMO will need to ensure that it doesn't conflict with any of the architecture layers. If new technology is proposed, it will need to be reviewed as an update to the existing architecture. Such a review should determine [5]:

1. How the new technology will fit with each of the four layers;

2. How it will be deployed;

3. The timeline for help desk training;

4. What external support will be available;

5. Whether the technology will be migratable to future technologies.

The EIA is made up of several subarchitectures that show how IT assets are dispersed and used throughout the enterprise. These subarchitectures can include configuration, process flow, integration timeline, and user interface diagrams. Network, telephony, client, server, protocol (e.g., Internet protocol), wireless, and security architectures can all be a part of the EIA. Because these can change so frequently, focus should be on creating architectural documents that can be altered easily. If the document can be autogenerated from some inventory automation tool, all the better. Too much time spent on creating pretty documents can hamstring the productivity of an architecture team. Therefore, be sure to document only those elements that will help quickly determine risk levels for proposed business initiatives.

5.3 Implementing EIA

5.3.1 The EAM Team

It is very easy to establish a committee of cross-business unit representatives who crawl into a closet for six months and come out with a blueprint that represented the company to a T six months ago. It's an entirely more complex task to get the same committee to stand firm in the glare of the entire company and develop a blueprint that flexes quickly to changing market demands but that also clearly underscores

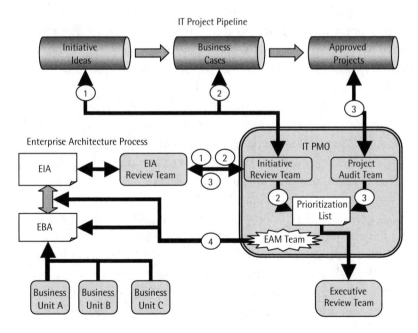

Figure 5.8 Virtual IT PMO–EAM team.

the company's core, unchanging values. If a committee can accomplish this task, that's great for the company for about a week after it is released. The real value returned to the company is if the PMO continues the duties of the committee. The duties associated with maintaining the business' blueprint is known as enterprise architecture management (EAM).

Figure 5.8 shows how an EAM team can help expand the boundaries of the IT PMO to become a more effective (and larger) virtual IT PMO. We know that the IT PMO supports the IT project stream by (1) providing early technical risk assessments, (2) reviewing the viability of initiatives and prioritizing them, and (3) auditing ongoing projects for health and prioritizing them. These tasks are supported by the initiative review and the project review teams within the IT PMO. The EAM team is another group within the IT PMO that coordinates the various business units and the IT architecture team to develop and evolve the EBA and the EIA (4).

When the EAM team coordinates the EIA review team, "there is a tendency to lose track of product priorities and developer concerns" [9]. The architecture team will not only have to overcome resentments that they are a select group off doing interesting things, but they also have to overcome overt or covert opposition to what they release to the developer community [9]. An organizational management priority is in how the EIA review team is organized and maintained. A single leader should be permanently assigned, with subject matter experts coming and going as component elements of the EIA get designed [9]. This approach allows the lead architect to focus on the big picture while providing fresh designers from the field to contribute designs that reflect the true needs of ongoing and future projects.

The case study on Toyota Motor Sales in Appendix 5B shows how this company developed the equivalent of an EAM team. The company not only staffed people to baseline the architecture, rather than pull architects part time for committee meetings, but they also hired someone for the task of monitoring architecture shifts. Such awareness of the dynamics of IT and business architectures is important if the IT PMO hopes to accurately compare initiative proposals to current-state systems.

5.3.2 Technical Process Reengineerings

Most of the time, if there is no prior EIA, then the company will have a chaotic environment that will need to be migrated to a supportable architecture. Many enterprise architecture initiatives just come up with a large model and then start major migration projects. However, "most successful architecture implementations occur in four overlapping phases: 1) planning, 2) initial migration [quick hits], 3) major application migration and 4) post-migration" [2]. That is, to maintain ongoing support for the technical equivalent of a business process reengineering—known as a technical process reengineering (TPR)—effort, be sure to split out those migrations that will show early success. Table 5.2 lists some other critical elements for EIA migration success. The most common element here is the strong focus on maintaining

Table 5.2
List of Organizational Change Tasks for TPR Initiatives

Organizational Change	*Planning*
Be opportunistic (to help with selling the architecture).	Reorganize the work and the people to save money.
Build a sense of urgency.	Ensure a strong IT and business skill set representation.
Build a strong executive sponsorship.	Ensure architecture is business driven.
Gain commitment at the grassroots level.	Develop a good understanding of business drivers and form a vision.
Build a strong team dynamic.	Establish a framework and a methodology.
Communicate plans and benefits.	Establish baselines and performance metrics. There is an axiom that the perceived value of a service diminishes exponentially after the service is rendered. That phenomenon can derail any initiative.
Empower others to act on the vision.	Combine technical and financial planning.
Publicize shared architecture values.	
Regularly publish progress updates.	
Unify the enterprise architecture efforts.	
Remain flexible.	

Source: [2, 10].

continued organizational support when creating an EIA or when over-hauling an existing EIA.

5.4 Summary

When IT-based business initiatives get submitted for review, the EAM team of the IT PMO acts as middle man between the business case writer and IT's architecture review team. The business case writer understands that the technical risks returned from such a review are based on architectures developed by representatives from business units and from IT. The EBA and the EIA both comprise the overall EA. We showed that Balanced Scorecards, McDavid subdomains, and the Penker-Erikson UML extensions allow for progressively more detailed modeling to bridge the business/IT strategy gap. Many organizations develop such EBAs and EIAs only to see them collect dust as weighty architectural documents ignored by developers [2, 11]. To prevent this, the architectures need to be flexible in some areas and firm in others. Create a plan that outlines goals, standards, and policies; post it to solicit ongoing input; and then update it annually [1]. To ensure that the architecture is understandable, as well as implementable, develop training curricula that are updated with the architecture [9, 12]. The IT PMO will be responsible not only for coordinating the architecture teams, but also in gathering the architecture collateral from each project.

References

[1]   Schneider, Polly, "Blueprint for Harmony," *CIO Magazine*, September 1, 1999, http://www.cio.com/archive/090199_acrimony.html (last accessed on January 15, 2004).

[2]   Cecere, Marc, "Architecting Architecture," *CIO Magazine*, April 15, 1998, http://www.cio.com/archive/041598/view.html (last accessed on January 15, 2004).

[3]   Sims, David, "Enterprise Architecture: The Executive Advantage," http://www.eacommunity.com/articles/art10.asp (last accessed on January 15, 2004).

[4]   Slater, Derek, "The Whole... Is More Than Its Parts," *CIO Magazine*, May 15, 2000, http://www.cio.com (last accessed on January 15, 2004).

[5]   Miner, Clyde, "IT Architecture—Where, What, Why?" http://www. eacommunity.com/articles/art1.asp (last accessed on January 15, 2004).

[6]   Genovese, David, "CIO Q&A," *CIO Magazine*, November 17, 1998, http://www2.cio.com/ask/date.cfm?DATE=1998&Go=Go (last accessed on January 15, 2004).

[7]   McDavid, D. W., "A Standard for Business Architecture Description," *IBM Systems Journal*, October 7, 1998 (electronic version).

[8]   Penker, Magnus, and Hans-Erik Eriksson, *Business Modeling with UML*, Needham, MA: OMG Press, 2001.

[9]   Bredemeyer, Dana, and Ruth Malan, "Architecture Teams," *Bredemeyer Consulting*, January 26, 2001, http://www.bredemeyer.com/Architecture_ Teams.htm (last accessed on January 15, 2004).

[10]   Foroozesh, Mehrdad, "The Making of a Successful Enterprise Technical Architecture," http://www.eacommunity.com/articles/art3.asp (last accessed on January 15, 2004).

[11]   Meta Group, "Centralizing Management of Project Portfolios," *Meta Group*, January 29, 2002, http://www.umt.com/site/Documents/IT_World_-_ Leading_Organisation_Centralize_Management_of_Project_Portfolios_-_ 29Jan02.pdf (last accessed on January 15, 2004).

[12]   Bredemeyer, Dana, and Ruth Malan, "The Role of the Architect," http://www.eacommunity.com/articles/art14.asp (last accessed on January 15, 2004).

[13]   Banham, Russ, "Safeco's Alignment Strategy," *CIO Insight*, July 1, 2002, http://www.cioinsight.com/article2/0,1397,334057,00.asp (last accessed on June 24, 2004).

Appendix 5A: Case Study—Safeco—Aligning IT and Business Architectures

In January 2001, Safeco hired Roger Eigsti as the new CEO to turn around the insurance company. With net income at half of what it was the previous year, Eigsti decided to take a radical approach by driving a new business strategy with a new IT strategy. Rather than have the different business units first define their substrategies and then ask IT for support, Eigsti asked the new CIO, Yom Senegor, to act as the chief strategist. This way, the new corporate strategy had no choice but to evolve through the eyes of a technologist.

Realizing that Safeco's core products of automobile and small commercial lines insurance were commodities, they focused on a strategy of improving the two differentiators in their market: price and service. To help guide the business in improving both of these while also improving corporate growth, Senegor showed how the relationship between business and technical strategies were so codependent. By obtaining credit histories of policy applicants through more efficient interfaces with motor vehicle records, Safeco was able to both refine price segmentation and improve response time to the customer. And by improving the systems in customer support centers, complaints and field agent inquiries were able to be handled quickly. For the chief strategist to have such a clear understanding of how technology could be applied in achieving the corporate strategy, IT project alignment became a nonissue.

Senegor explains that "Technology doesn't run the business, but the business cannot run without technology; it is part and parcel of the enterprise. Once you integrate technology with business strategy, you learn immediately that it can drive enormous value" [13].

Appendix 5B: Case Study—Toyota Motor Sales USA—Flexible IT Architecture

When CIO Barbara Cooper joined Toyota, she found that the technology was 10 years behind current trends and that the IT organization was not aligned with the sales, distribution, and marketing businesses. One of her reorganization efforts involved creating an eight-person architecture committee headed by Architecture Manager Karen Nocket. Understanding that the new architecture manager position would involve a lot of negotiation and relationship building with the various business and IT units, she placed someone who had strong communication skills and strategic vision.

5B.1 The Architecture Committee

While the architecture committee was pulled from different areas in the IT organization to provide direction, Nocket hired three more employees to work solely as architecture experts. With Nocket, the three architects' first job was to market the concept of a standardized architecture to the right people, solicit additional volunteers for the architecture committee, and then spend four weeks taking inventory of the current-state architecture. While the next phase of developing the architecture should take no more than six months, Nocket realized that architectural needs could shift in this timeframe. As a result, she hired a fourth person to keep track of such shifts and manage the review process.

5B.2 Flexible IT Architecture

Once the business architecture is completed, Nocket understands the need to market the final plan as an added value to the businesses. By explaining that the business can flex much easier if it isn't tied down by a web of complex and nonstandard technologies, business units would be more willing to have IT dictate what software goes on their desktops. On the other hand, while Nocket understands that a standard IT architecture would improve IT-market flexibility, she also knows that tech-savvy "users will learn to get around your standards" [1]. Therefore, the architecture should dictate core, necessary systems but also allow some flexibility with the end users. That is, let them request secure, nonstandard software for their desktops that make them more productive as individuals but that don't conflict with the backbone architecture.

6

Asset Management

As business units diverge from central governance and into their own governance silos, problems other than strategic misalignments and IT initiative explosions can occur. One such problem arises when independent business units create their own IT inventory and control process. Ultimately, as business unit silos solidify even more with such inventories, organizations as a whole become less able to react to changing marketplace dynamics. For example, imagine if the marketing department implemented a campaign management system with a UNIX/Oracle-based CRM system and the sales department implemented a lead-generation system with an NT/Sybase CRM system. Now if the company wanted to best sell products uniquely to different demographics, the campaign management system would be a critical tool. Integrating the less critical, but necessary for success, lead-generation system will take as long as replacing it with an extended campaign management system: six to nine months. If a central asset management process was in place, CRM project leads would have been aware of the existence of another CRM system that could have been leveraged. The result would have been an integrated system that allows a shift in corporate strategy without the six-to-nine-month wait for IT to catch up.

Without a centralized purchasing process, business units could find themselves with duplicate assets. With a lack of communication between units, the company could also find itself with unnecessary costs, poor alignment, and decreasing morale [1]. Many times, the IT department will control the inventory of all IT assets in a company. Usually, however, assets are purchased without IT knowledge during the span of IT-based projects. Because an IT PMO is an organization that is in touch with the progress of such projects, it is well positioned to aid IT in controlling a company's IT assets. With such a centralized asset inventory control, the IT PMO could support interproject communications and, thus, reduce the frequency of redundant system purchases.

6.1   Inventories

The first step in controlling such redundancy is to get a handle on the current inventory of IT assets. While stronger communications between disparate projects is a good selling point for centralized asset inventory, many times executives include two additional goals to make up the three core purposes of IT asset management.

1. *Financial.* To ensure an accurate balance sheet, upper management is first interested in understanding the total cost of ownership (TCO) of its IT assets.

2. *Operational.* Business units and IT are constantly looking for ways to improve the efficiency of the IT help desk. It can be a never-ending drag on productivity if IT is slow to respond to problems with business-critical IT systems. If a centralized IT asset management system was in place and monitored, the IT help desk would be able to respond more quickly to problems and solve them.

3. *Project support.* Here the PMO can ensure that not only does the asset procurement workflow follow guidelines, but that the

project portfolio reduces redundancy with training, licensing, and help desks.

6.1.1 Static Inventories

"The baseline inventory of IT assets is the most expensive, most visible and, therefore, most intimidating step required to implement an asset management program" [2]. Such a project is visible because every employee that is assigned IT hardware or software will be involved. First, surveys are distributed and filled out by field employees. Then, the inventory team enters the surveys into a database. To verify the data, the inventory team needs to see the equipment listed in various inventories and log onto the equipment and inventory all software. Finally, the IT PMO can support ongoing inventory efforts by requiring all new project hardware to be "viewable" by some central inventory tracking system. Compiling surveys, reconciling different inventories, and configuring autotrackers will end up taking the most time [3].

If, for example, a company has telecommuters and traveling laptops to consider, "an inventory of 900 computers can take between 60 and 120 worker days" [2]. To eat such an elephant of a task, first "understand how people use their assets and leverage the resources within those groups to get the data in the form you need it." You can start on the operational side by understanding how the help desk gathers inventory data to "distribute software more rapidly or provide technical support to resources more readily." Or you can begin on the financial side by keeping track of all leased and purchased assets to provide accurate financial statement numbers (see Figure 6.1) [4]. If a methodical initial inventory is conducted, and dependable tracking processes are put in place, then long, future inventory durations can be eliminated.

6.1.2 Dynamic Inventories

Most companies understand the value of keeping an updated inventory. Finance can get real-time IT valuation figures, IT operations can manage efficient help desks, IT PMOs can leverage assets across projects, EIA teams can ensure architecture alignment, and the legal department can enforce lease and license compliance. So to ensure such an

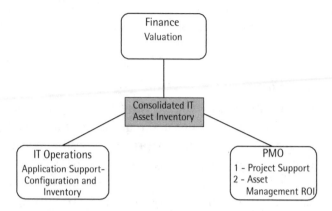

Figure 6.1 Benefactors of a consolidated IT asset inventory.

inventory exists, IT departments launch expensive inventory initiatives. However, what many of these initiatives fail to consider is that while this inventory is underway, new assets continue to come in and supply ongoing projects. Even worse, while their inventory project is under-way, distributed business units will continue purchasing assets to sup-port their own technical initiatives [4]. More times than not, these purchases are nothing more than unrecorded ad hoc purchases written off as project expenses. Basing corporatewide inventory projects on such a chaotic, distributed environment can first lead to inaccurate data and, second, cause an endless cycle of yearly inventory projects. There-fore, before an inventory can take place, the organization needs to gain control of these silo-like processes. "You have to track assets every time they move and capture every hardware or software change" [2]. Gain-ing such control is the first step in creating an asset management system.

After gaining control of the distributed IT asset purchasing processes, the asset inventory team can start meeting the goals of a con-solidated inventory project. They can learn:

- What assets exist in each division;
- What their costs were;
- How they are used;
- Why they were purchased (see Figure 6.2).

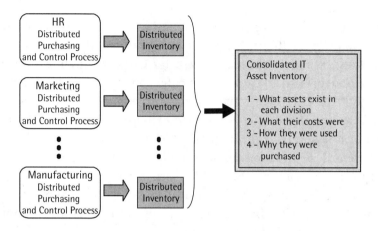

Figure 6.2 Benefits of consolidating distributed asset inventories.

6.1.2.1 Project Inventories

Many times, an IT-based project will accumulate more hardware and software than is necessary for a successful production rollout. Some projects resolve the problem of excessive hardware by converting it to production use; others use lease arrangements; still others just give it to operations for future product upgrade development. However, it's the hardware and software licenses that go unused that creates the biggest missed opportunities for the project portfolio. For example, the normal course of events for a software project is to first create a development environment, then a Q/A environment, followed by a production environment. In larger, more methodology-strict projects, integration and training environments may also be created. All of these environments can mean a lot of money spent on hardware, software, and networking. A central inventory needs to include such assets when conducting asset inventory initiatives. If such nonproduction environments aren't tracked, then they can fall into the black hole of untracked IT assets.

What happens to all these assets when a project is deemed completed or cancelled? If 30 personal computers are made available from the training and Q/A staff of a completed, enterprisewide project, will the personal computers go to another project in need or will they be used to upgrade a business unit's desktops? If a 20-server NT system is made available from a cancelled project, will the central architecture team be notified before signing a long-term lease agreement with a UNIX vendor? In the first case, IT is losing departmental valuation opportunities, and, in the second case, the corporate architecture team is marching forward as a loose cost-center cannon. To prevent such lost valuation and EAM chaos, the less visible management of assets needs to be kept strong. And the best way to manage such a process between siloed business units is through an IT PMO. By reconciling new asset purchase orders that are submitted by projects with what IT spits out from their autotrackers, the IT PMO will be able to provide a much clearer, cross–business unit picture of all IT assets. Establishing a central inventory is one thing, but managing the dynamic inventory is another task that requires due diligence.

6.2   Enterprise Asset Management

Not only can assets get abandoned upon project completion or cancellation, but assets can get purchased that don't align with the corporate architecture. Economists refer to the assets that result from the combination of these scenarios as *stranded assets*. Such assets both fail to contribute (they were abandoned) and fail to easily convert (they were unaligned). Chapter 5 shows through the creation and maintenance of an EIA team that new asset purchases can be screened before commitments are made. Such centralized screening allows the EIA team to recommend abandoned asset conversions over new purchases. It also helps the EIA team ensure that assets continue to contribute in the face of project cancellations. For example, with more than one inventory system, too many personal computers can end up being purchased, duplicate licenses can be acquired, and old systems can end up collecting dust [4]. Multiple inventory systems can also prevent efficient policing of vendor leases and maintenance commitments to signed contracts. All of this ultimately can lead to a major loss of cost control. Regaining this control is an ideal opportunity for a central, independent group that has close ties to the creation and maintenance of the EIA.

While the organization is gaining control of its asset costs, it also needs to become aware of the dependencies between its enterprise architecture, its consolidated asset inventory, and any other asset procurement and control processes. Figure 6.3 shows how the asset inventory is molded by both the EA (ideal) and siloed business units (nonideal) as well as how the EIA is restricted by existing assets and by decisions made by out-of-touch business units. So, to increase the freedom of the EIA team to influence the flexibility of the EIA-to-market dynamics (3), restrictions need to be reduced (2). And by reducing the authority of business units through a centralized asset management system, an organization can help eliminate those restrictions. (An animated version of Figure 6.3 appears in the AARK Management PowerPoint presentation in the accompanying CD-ROM.)

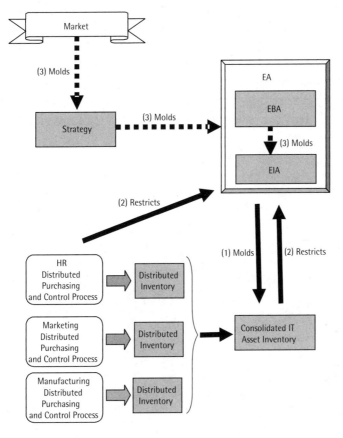

Figure 6.3 Effects of distributed and consolidated asset inventories on the enterprise architecture.

A consolidated inventory system allows for improved EIA control and flexibility by reducing the imposed restrictions and the influences of distributed inventories. As Chapter 4 showed, EIA flexibility ensures EBA flexibility and, in turn, strategic flexibility. This IT flexibility chain not only allows the company to more quickly adapt to market changes, it also supports the operational and financial goals of the various business units (see Appendix 6A for an example). While an IT PMO can prove it achieved these goals through before and after snapshots, how can it show real reductions in cost?

There are two ways an asset management team can prove that its efforts add monetary value to the company: by realizing stranded assets (short term) and by increasing asset reuse (long term) (see Figure 6.4). With stranded assets tracked, more accurate balance sheet numbers can be calculated. The asset management team needs to make sure that snapshots of before and after values are made to best illustrate its impact on the bottom line. Long-term asset management return can be attempted by converting stranded assets to reduce future and ongoing project costs. This cost savings will only be realized in the long term,

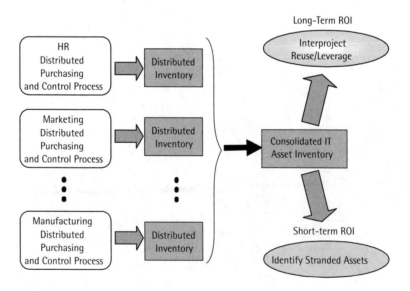

Figure 6.4 Long-term and short-term benefits of a consolidated IT asset inventory.

after the architecture team has been given access to a well-maintained asset inventory system.

However, such long-term benefits, though attractive and possible, can be elusive. "It is hard to share assets across projects because of the way work is budgeted and people are rewarded" [5]. For example, assets are difficult to reuse with COTS software environments due to support agreements. That is, vendors of COTS products will drop support for an installation if an unapproved third-party software is installed on the COTS servers. Also, the ability to reuse assets varies widely among business units in the same company. For example, defense contractors may be unable to use the same hardware on different projects because project timelines don't allow for revalidation of security. As another example, shrink-wrap software houses may find that the reuse of a common class library across products increases productivity (i.e., there are no security concerns). With an almost fanatical focus on time to market, these types of companies sometimes specifically design or purchase software and hardware for their reusability. A good general rule when going down this path is the three-strikes rule: don't develop or purchase an asset to be reusable unless three or more projects in the company agree to use it within a specified time period [5].

6.2.1 Financial Asset Management

Financial departments are always interested in ways to improve the IT valuation information they get. Many times their zealousness causes IT to conduct reactionary IT asset inventory projects. But without an understanding of all aspects of asset lifecycles and without an existing asset management system, any valuation numbers that result from such inventories will be inaccurate.

There are several phases to the lifecycle of an IT asset. Before any asset can even be requested it should go through an EIA assessment. The tasks for such an assessment include [6]:

- Is the asset already in the enterprise's inventory?
- Is the request for a standard product listed in the enterprise's approved product catalog?
- Is the asset compatible with your environment?

- Do you need to review the pricing and negotiate with the vendor?
- Should the asset be added to the standard catalog?

Many times, because IT capital needs to be acquired quickly, such reviews can tend to just add bureaucratic slow downs to a project with tight deadlines. Here, an IT PMO can ensure rapid review by applying risk levels rather than outright rejections to an asset request. Then, as this process is proven to be speedy, the IT PMO can be given some teeth to reject only the most ludicrous of requests.

Once an asset passes such a review, it enters a life cycle of tasks that are traditionally managed by the PM and IT operations:

- Requisition—request for an asset by the PM;
- Approval—approval by the project sponsor and notification to IT support;
- Procurement—purchase order sent to vendor and notification to IT support;
- Receipt—shipment received and turned over to IT support;
- Deployment—installed by IT support and tested by the project team;
- Tracking—viewable by autotracking tools, status sent to asset management;
- Disposal—shut-down status sent to asset management.

But many IT departments lose control of their IT inventories because they don't get wind of new assets until the last three steps. An asset management system that resolves this chaos must "not only track hardware and software assets, but must also manage software licenses, equipment contracts and leases, and networks from cradle to grave" [4]. Otherwise, independent business unit purchases will force a never-ending cycle of costly reinventory projects.

6.2.1.1 Autotracking Tools

Many software tools on the market can drastically ease the gathering and tracking of an organization's IT asset inventory. Such tools can link into internal financial software for purchase order generation, external vendors for license reconciliation, operations for asset health alerts, and the PMO for interproject communications. They can also track the status of an asset anywhere in its workflow through natural integration points with other departments. For example, such a tool can print expenditure reports, interface with accounting, link with facilities support software, and even track vendor compliance with lease and licensing terms. With such a tool, a more aware IT help desk will be quicker in providing solutions to problems.

While the cost of setting up an asset management system can be high and therefore difficult to sell, the long-term costs of an asset management system can be easier to sell. For starters, ongoing asset management of up to 10,000 assets, including about 1,000 personal computers and several workstations, can require the equivalent of one-and-a-half full-time employees with about another nine people using the asset management tool off and on. In addition, annual reconciliation inventories can end up costing up to $30 per personal computer [3]. When combining such personnel costs with the costs of installation and maintenance of the asset management tool, the asset management team needs to provide ROI numbers as soon as possible.

Reconciliation inventories are those that compare a random sampling of field assets to those that are recorded in the asset management database. As these smaller inventory endeavors show more and more errors between actual and recorded numbers, a full-scale, item-by-item inventory becomes more necessary. With a solid inventory management system supported by a robust autotracking tool, however, such reconciliation errors will increase at a slower pace over time. With real-time asset valuation reports, the asset management team can show that running a complete inventory can be a lot more costly than maintaining ongoing measurements [7]. As well as continually monitoring the autotracking software over the network, the asset management team will need to update the system as computers are installed or moved, as software is updated, as hardware is added or replaced, and as users are connected to the network [2]. With the rigid asset workflow process that an automation tool provides, the asset management team should be able to show before and after snapshots that prove reduced stranded costs and increased balance sheet accuracy.

Before such tools can be effective, the asset management team needs to gather support—not just for the initial financial cost, but also for the continued organizational costs. As a company shifts between siloed and centralized forms of governance, asset management, like the IT PMO organization, must shift its strategy to best maintain effectiveness. "IT asset management is an iterative process that needs to be reevaluated as business objectives evolve" [6]. Quicker help desk response via auto-tracking tools, supported by effective reconciliation inventory teams, will establish a flexible asset management foundation. Then, by showing ongoing financial ROI and organizational flexibility, support for the asset management wing of the IT PMO continues regardless of the governance shifts.

6.2.1.2 Centralization

Centralized monitoring of business unit (or project) asset purchases not only reduces the need for full inventory projects, it also supports tighter cost controls for projects. For example, budgets for assets "tend to be approved at the project, not enterprise, level. That's why they are expensed rather than depreciated" [5]. A central asset management team would allow for software purchases for these environments to be capitalized and for hardware purchases to follow Internal Revenue Service–mandated depreciation models (e.g., five years for computers and three for printers using the straight-line method under the assumption of no salvage value) [5]. With a PMO in place, projects will benefit from a clearer understanding of the corporation's accounting standards so that new equipment purchases don't end up being an unnecessary drain on project budgets. This could "free up millions of dollars in firms that do their licensing on a project-by-project basis" [5]. Other benefits of changing to a centralized asset management system include:

- Vendors would be more responsive because you became a larger client.
- You could simplify procurement by negotiating some form of centralized ordering.

◆ You could ask your legal department to negotiate improved license terms and conditions.

Centralized management of project-level asset purchases provides particularly noticeable legal support. While the IT PMO asset managers focus on how to purchase and leverage licenses, the legal department can focus on improving license contracts and vendors' accountability to those licenses. The legal wing will also be able to more clearly prevent vendors from dictating unneeded upgrades and new technologies. They'll be able to monitor for pirated software and be able to ensure vendor compliance to maintenance caps and renewal dates [4]. This added clarity of the asset inventory will allow the legal department to become a cost-reducing member of the extended virtual IT PMO.

6.2.1.3 TCO

Who controls the costs of services for and the value of the IT asset inventory? Most of the time, business units will own the IT assets they acquire to support their IT projects. The IT department will then provide support for those assets on a time and material cost basis. That is, the IT department will charge the various business units for support of their installed IT assets. This may handle the cost of services, but how would a company value the accumulation of IT assets in the company? Sometimes the IT department is asked to value the entire corporate IT asset inventory, and other times the business units just include the cost of new IT assets in independent profit and expense statements. The IT PMO can support the IT department in the former scenario and the business units in the latter scenario. With the awareness of the state of every project in the portfolio, the IT PMO's asset management team provides an additional view into what assets have become abandoned and which assets are about to be acquired.

Once the inventory is developed and managed, how can the asset management team attach a cost value to it? A common way to get cost numbers on IT assets is by implementing a TCO formula. Keep in mind that this is not a valuation approach because it doesn't include revenue figures in its calculation. The lack of revenue in determining TCO is one of the reasons many don't use it as a valuation tool [8]. Nonetheless,

TCO can be based on the narrower, technology-based sticker price of hardware and software, or it can be based on the broader people-based definition [7]. When determining the costs of IT assets based on this latter definition, more factors need to be included. These can include "the direct costs of user support, hardware maintenance, software updates, training, lost productivity while users try to fix a problem, security, downtime, [and] administrative costs" [7]. The Gartner Group's TCO model tends to be the standard definition many follow. This model takes the elements described here and categorizes them into four quadrants: capital costs, administrative costs, technical support, and end-user operations. The accounting numbers provided by splitting the costs of the IT asset inventory into such categories will allow IT and finance to better manage how assets are distributed.

This model provides just a framework on which a company can base its own customized TCO definition. For example, different companies allow for different levels of complexity on their desktops. The more freedom given to end users to configure their personal computers, the more costly the support requirements. So, a TCO model must, in turn, put more weight on support variables when end users have greater control over the content of their personal computers [7]. Also, to communicate the subjectivity of these measurements more clearly, probability distributions can be used. Probability distributions are used in statistics to show the probability that a value is between two other values (i.e., as illustrated in a bell curve). "Companies can then calculate confidence intervals for TCO numbers, which basically pair a range of numbers with a confidence rating" [8]. For example, a company could be 99% confident that its server TCO is between $10,000 and $20,000 and 89% confident that the TCO is between $12,000 and $18,000 [8]. Complete inclusion of such *soft costs* in TCO measurements can be rather subjective. Because these subjective costs are difficult to measure and can add up quickly [4], there needs to be a way to communicate them effectively within each company.

Dependable TCO numbers rely just as heavily on accurate auto-tracking tool results as they do on the people who verify these results. This is another reason why many don't agree that TCO is a good valuation approach. While many IT departments use tools to proactively *ping* for existing hardware and software assets, these assets won't be seen if the IT help desk isn't notified of their installation. For example, a misconfigured switch is all that would be needed to hide a project's entire development lab. But, with an IT PMO aware of which assets will be purchased throughout the life cycle of every project, the IT help desk will have one more level of insurance that some IT asset won't pop up for support unannounced. "Three-quarters of a typical business's desktop TCO results from management issues [e.g, integrating into help desk support] rather than technology problems [e.g., hard disk failure]. It's about the management of people [e.g., help desk training] as much as it's about the management of IT" [7].

6.2.2 Operational Asset Management

By keeping the IT asset inventory current, an asset management group essentially reduces the restrictions on the EIA group. If the EIA needs to shift to some new corporate strategy, a well-managed IT asset inventory will allow for more flexibility. This link of asset data to organizational, strategic, and technical changes improves the quality and agility of the IT operations staff. To give IT operations a real boost, however, real-time asset data needs to also be linked to IT problem management (e.g., service level, service request, and disaster recovery) [4, 9].

As with TCO initiatives, tools exist to help IT operations streamline their problem management duties. The most common are the autodiscovery tools such as Hewlett-Packard's HP OpenView and Microsoft's Systems Management Server. As explained earlier, because such automatic inventory tools can be unreliable, they need to be complemented with continual field audits and workflow processes dictated by an IT project PMO [3].

Such asset awareness can lead to quicker help desk call resolutions, which is a continual cost reduction focus of IT management. More advanced systems integrate the asset base with other systems, such as human resources. For example, by typing in an employee's name or identification code, a help desk employee can see a profile of all equipment and training that an employee has. This "reduces call time because help desk staffers don't have to ask as many questions" [4].

Other advanced asset management systems can include electronic software distribution and automated backups. Such control of desktop configurations just adds to the benefits of asset management for IT operations.

6.3 Organizational Support

According to Carl Wilson, CIO of Bethesda, Maryland–based Marriott International, "We've been actively involved in asset management now for almost two years, and one of the biggest lessons we've learned is that support from senior management to implement and monitor the program is a must. For us, it's been a top-down directive to proceed with asset management; without that, we wouldn't be as successful as we are" [4]. That is, the process can only be enforced if it is supported by all levels of management. And to get support, "Early, clear and complete communication with managers and end users is crucial" [2]. To ensure complete organizational support for the new centralized approach, the inventory team needs to first understand and control duplicate asset procurement and management processes and then be aware of any other software and hardware surveys that other business units may be undertaking. Once this is done, a *moving* inventory can begin that logs incoming assets while it is tracking existing assets.

6.4 Summary

As business units become more autonomous, they also tend to develop their own asset management procedures. These individual IT asset inventories, supported by custom IT architectures, can make a company less flexible to market changes. Centralized IT asset management, via an IT PMO, allows a company greater contract negotiation power over IT vendors. Figure 6.5 shows how the IT PMO fits into such a centralized IT asset management system.

1. *Architecture alignment.* As initiative ideas form and business cases get reviewed, the asset management team of the IT PMO

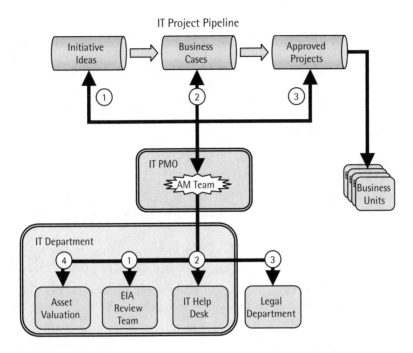

Figure 6.5 Virtual IT PMO—asset management team view.

leverages the EIA committee for support. The EIA committee will analyze architectures and the supporting asset proposals for risks and deliver their findings to the initiative proposer.

2. *Rapid asset change notification.* An inventory that is connected to an asset autotracker and that is verified by a field inventory team will allow the IT help desk to respond to requests quickly. The asset management team has the opportunity to ensure that the help desk is promptly notified of any changes to the asset landscape anywhere in the project portfolio pipeline.

3. *Contract centralization.* As business cases are approved and asset purchases begin, the legal department can play a key role. By keeping a clear communication pipeline between individual projects and the legal team, the asset management team allows for a consistent vendor-relationship plan. Furthermore, redundant purchases and varying contract terms can be reduced.

4. *Stranded assets.* While the IT department will continue to be responsible for overall valuation of the IT asset inventory, the asset management team needs to validate their results. Too often an inventory initiative will overlook nonproduction IT assets. This leads to stranded assets that could have been used by future projects to cut costs.

References

[1]   Ferranti, Marc, "Gartner—Align Thyself," *CIO Magazine*, November 15, 2001, http://www.cio.com/archive/111501/align.html (last accessed on January 15, 2004).

[2]   Caston, Joe, "Watch Your Assets," *CIO Magazine*, June 15, 1996, http://www.cio.com/archive/061596/ins.html (last accessed on January 15, 2004).

[3]   Essex, David, "Cover Your Assets," *Computerworld*, June 21, 1999, http://www.computerworld.com/news/1999/story/0,11280,36078,00.html (last accessed on January 15, 2004).

[4]   Schwartz, Karen, "Controlled Substances," *CIO Magazine*, June 1, 2000, http://www.cio.com/archive/060100_controlled.html?printversion=yes (last accessed on January 15, 2004).

[5]   Reifer, Donald J., *Making the Software Business Case: Improvement by the Numbers*, Reading, MA: Addison-Wesley, 2003.

[6]   Adams, Patricia, "Optimize Workflow Processes to Gain Efficiencies in IT Asset Management," *TechRepublic*, September 20, 2001, http://www.techrepublic.com (last accessed on January 15, 2004).

[7]   Wheatley, Malcolm, "Every Last Dime," *CIO Magazine*, November 15, 2000, http://www.cio.com/archive/111500_dime.html (last accessed on January 15, 2004).

[8]   Hildebrand, Carol, "The PC Price Tag," *CIO Magazine*, October 15, 1997, http://www.cio.com/archive/enterprise/101597_price.html (last accessed on January 15, 2004).

[9]   Brittain, K., and P. Adams, "Make Asset Management Part of your Consolidated Service Desk," *TechRepublic*, August 23, 2001, http://www.techrepublic.com (last accessed on January 15, 2004).

[10] Lawson, Loraine, "Three Questions: Moving Beyond Strategic Business Alignment," *TechRepublic*, December 9, 2003, http://techrepublic.com.com/5102-6298-5099413.html (last accessed on June 24, 2004).

Appendix 6A: Case Study—BMC Software—Aligning Asset Management

Establishing a good asset tracking system is just one step in effectively managing IT assets across the portfolio of IT projects. Many times, after conducting an initial hand audit, IT help desks will be provided a list of assets to monitor. According to Atwell Williams, director of Enterprise Service Management at BMC Software, "We'd gotten really good at managing and monitoring our infrastructure" [10]. However, as Williams became more familiar with the workings of the other business units, he found that certain parts of the business architecture were more vital to the success of the company than were other parts. For example, he found out that if a currency conversion system became unavailable during a deal, the company could lose tens of millions of dollars.

From these types of lessons, Williams realized that while the asset tracking system was strategically aligned with the goals of the company, it wasn't tactically aligned with the substrategies (or macrotactics) of the various business units. To resolve this, he simply created a prioritization of assets to be monitored. Similar to levels of customer support, this new system would involve higher levels of escalation in shorter amounts of time for problems with those systems deemed critical.

As initiatives get funneled through the IT PMO approval process, an architecture review committee needs to work with the business case writer to understand where in the priority list the project's assets will need to fall. Sure, most project sponsors will try to place their assets at the top of the list. However, by putting new initiatives in the perspective of other project's assets and other in-place system assets, the architects will be better able to negotiate a reasonable monitoring priority for any particular asset.

7

Resource Management

Resource management is a rather broad category that can cover everything from product inventory to staff expertise to liquid assets such as cash. Resources can be broken down into five general categories: "physical things, energy, monetary value, information resources and various kinds of capabilities" [1]. While other chapters focus on IT asset resources and IT knowledge resources, this chapter will focus specifically on human resources assigned to projects. Project stakeholders are those individuals that have a stake in the success of the project. While the PM and the sponsor are the two most obvious ones, other stakeholders make up the project's human resource pool. This pool could include the end users, the programmers, the vendors, the architects, the testers, and various other support personnel.

Traditionally, when one thinks of human resource management in an IT project context, they think of how to best leverage various skill sets, over time, on a single project. Elements such as team acquisition, scheduling, morale, motivation, training, productivity, and success are all things that a PM needs to consider when managing the human resources on a project. These same elements also serve as part of the foundation for how an IT PMO will need to manage resources across multiple projects. If resources are continually pulled from one project and placed on another, the focus on their personal growth and training will get lost in the shuffle. Low morale will lead to unmotivated and unproductive project team members. While PMs now focus on maintaining the motivation of the resources on their own projects, will they also need to understand how past and potential future projects affect them? This is where the IT PMO can provide cross-project support and growth opportunities for project resources, and thus allow the PMs to keep their focus where it should be—on supporting project resources on their own project.

Supporting the morale of IT project resources across projects is a task required of IT PMOs in highly project-centric organizations such as IT consulting companies. In less project-centric organizations, this task is left to the resource's interproject, or functional, manager. Another resource management task that is common among IT PMOs in any organization is resource leveling. "Portfolio management is about resource allocation." If you squander scarce resources on the wrong projects, you can starve the truly meritorious ones [2]. In other words, as the IT PMO manages the aggregate project portfolio to satisfy the corporate strategy, it also needs to balance the company's finite project resources. With the IT PMO leveling the project resources across the portfolio, projects in the pipeline won't have to spend as much time competing for resources throughout the project's lifecycle [3, 4]. Ignoring political wrangling, PMs will more clearly understand whether they are worthy of a high-demand resource based upon the priority and the progress of their project.

The last two chapters showed how a PMO can centralize and help manage the more technical aspects of the portfolio through architecture and asset management processes. While these management tasks are embraced by leaders with technical backgrounds, it can be easy for an IT organization to mistakenly focus only on a portfolio's technical hurdles and goals. "The main reason we tend to focus on the technical rather than the human side of the work is not because it's more crucial, but because it's easier to do" [5]. This chapter will show that risks to the success of a portfolio reside in the management of project resources, as well. The IT PMO can help projects acquire, support, and schedule internal resources to ensure a healthy portfolio. Also, when outsourcing is necessary, the IT PMO can apply some of the same concepts it uses in asset management to outsourced vendor management. Finally, we will review how the resource management team best fits into the project pipeline.

7.1 Acquiring Resources

As a project goes through the approval process, the sponsor (or the project proposer) should start building the project team (phase four of the initiative approval process). Starting with the project or program manager, the sponsors will usually seek out people they know have been successful in the past. But before the candidate can be assigned to a sponsor's proposed project, the candidate needs to be either free of project or departmental duties or have sufficient spare time to make part-time contributions. The sponsor will need to work with the project candidate's functional managers, whether they are other PMs or other functional business unit managers. Before approaching the functional managers, the sponsor should prepare or have answered the following questions for each candidate.

1. Are they available?
2. What is the relative priority of their current projects?
3. Are their best skills not being leveraged fully?
4. Do their matrixed managers want them to return quickly?
5. Who is lined up to grab them next?

7.1.1 Functional Managers

Typical project-oriented organizations follow a *matrixed* structure, where each resource reports to the project or program manager and to their assigned interproject matrixed manager (or functional manager). For example, a systems administrator (SA) or a database administrator

(DBA) may report to the director of infrastructure and the director of data support, respectively, for reviews and compensation. While a company's project list has a set of priorities, a functional manager has his or her own independent priorities that can prevent critical resources from being freed up. Therefore, when acquiring a resource, a PM needs to contend with not only the priorities of the project portfolio (via a portfolio resource manager), but also with the priorities of individual business managers that are responsible for the resources (see Figure 7.1). As projects come and go, resources may or may not become available, depending on the needs and the priorities of other higher priority projects and functional managers.

The IT PMO can make the functional manager's job easier by keeping the prioritized list of projects and initiatives up to date and visible not only to the executive committee but also to the business unit community. This allows the functional manager to make more informed decisions when agreeing to provide her resources to IT-based projects [6]. A more extreme approach as to how the functional manager fits into a highly project-centric organization would be "to alter the role of

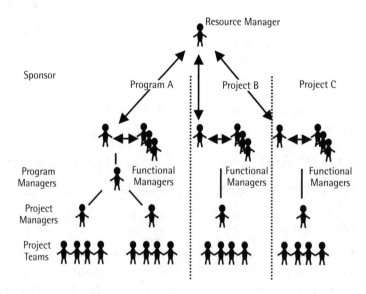

Figure 7.1 IT PMO resource manager with a clearer view of the portfolio than other managers.

functional managers from resource owners to project resource suppliers" [7]. PMs may successfully lobby to impose such organizational change on functional managers if they see a particularly negative trend, such as functional managers only providing those resources they don't want in their department anyway [8]. If this latter approach were taken,

then the IT PMO would need to take on more of the responsibility in supporting the career growth of the project resources. Whether the IT PMO acts as surrogate to or an enabler of the functional manager, strong communications need to be established with the business units to ensure smooth resource allocation.

Without smooth resource allocation, the project pipeline can get clogged. Many initiative selection committees don't "consider the time-dependent resource requirements of projects, and most implicitly assume that all projects selected will start immediately" [9]. This is why phase four of the initiative approval process is so critical. Project sponsors need to understand the disposition of resources before the project is even approved. The IT PMO, with its awareness of this disposition across the entire portfolio, helps manage the uninterrupted flow of the approval pipeline [10]. For example, by not allowing projects to be added to the pipeline until resources are available to staff them adequately, the IT PMO has ensured that prepared projects won't get denied access to asset, architecture, or knowledge management resources of the IT PMO.

Another way that the IT PMO can more efficiently clear up approved initiative traffic jams is through the use of resource management tools. IT tools exist that help show how IT resources are distributed by skills, across projects (see Appendix 7A for an example). If the IT PMO leverages such tools, it can remove itself as the default middleman for resource negotiations and be just a provider of up-to-date knowledge on resource disposition. However, there would be some cases where "two or more managers may be bidding for a potential project team member at the same time." In this case, the IT PMO would need to have the authority "to say which manager requested a given person first or decide which project should get priority in staffing the desired person" [8]. To prevent business case writers from prematurely flagging the resources they may eventually need, the initiative review committee should establish an initiative hurdle gate. For example, those initiatives that pass early review checks such as fundability, feasibility, and desirability can be allowed to flag, but not acquire, resources. Then, as the initiative gets closer to approval, the project sponsor will be closer to getting the resources needed for kicking off the project efficiently.

A common way to staff a project is to bring on few people in the beginning, then add the bulk of the staff in the second quarter of the project, and finally reduce the staff size as the project rolls out. There are several reasons why a PM follows this traditional bell curve of resource staffing on a project:

- They'd like to keep their turf wars over resources low until they can prove success with early pilots.
- Most skill sets aren't needed until later in the project.
- They'd rather wait for the best talent until it becomes available.

However, it may be better to focus on staffing the project well in its early phases and put less energy in staffing the project in its later phases. If battles for resources have to be fought, the PM should focus on negotiating for resources needed early in the project rather than later. These fights will be become easier later in the project as future successes help validate the project's cause. Also, "even if that early staff allocation turns out to be wasted, your political situation may be safer with all those people on-board early then if you were to proceed leanly staffed through the first six months" [5]. This isn't to say that you should staff up the project to where many team members are sitting idly or, worse, slowing the progress of the project (e.g., the mythical man month). Rather, if certain critical resources aren't needed for several weeks, but are difficult to acquire, get them now rather than risk a last-minute, doomed-to-failure political battle.

Once a resource is acquired, the PM should stick with his allotted time for that resource. The reason for this is "if one project requires a resource more than expected, it affects other projects requiring that resource" [10]. The only way to audit this would be to validate that the resource is applying their core, highest demand skills to the project. The IT PMO audit team could include just such a check when conducting audits of ongoing projects (see Chapter 10). If the PM has held onto a resource beyond the required need, the IT PMO will need to have the authority (and accountability) to distribute resources to mitigate the overall risk of the portfolio.

7.2 Supporting Resources

PMs who are beginning their careers will apply the project management knowledge they've learned in courses and from books. Following such project management standards helps guide the manager toward successful project completion. But the daily battles will rely just as much on the manager's leadership skills (e.g., team building, inspiration, vision). Such skills will help keep the team continuously glued together as a focused force. When applying such principles to interproject resource management, an IT PMO needs to ensure that resources and their functional managers feel comfortable about the direction their careers and their departments are moving, respectively. Just as a PM coordinates the team to move in the direction of project success, an IT PMO coordinates the organization to move cohesively in the direction of strategic success. Part of this coordination involves ensuring that resources receive fair and ongoing career support between projects. Such cross-project attention helps resources feel that contributions to any project, as well as to their departmental manager, carry just as much weight on their performance reviews.

To ensure that a project-oriented organization gets the utmost output from its personnel on projects, employees' performance evaluations need to also be tied to their work on projects. This means that project sponsors will need to also participate in a project member's career growth and not rely on their functional managers to fulfill all of these tasks. Sure, human resources lays out guidelines for peer reviews, management reviews, and career path templates. But, to support such long-term (usually annual) goals, PMs need to ensure that the resource will be a good asset to the project (i.e., happy, focused, motivated, and productive). The IT PMO can support the functional manager by ensuring the projects to which the resource is assigned map to the goals of the individual's career, as well as the goals of the company. Then, with such multidirectional support from the organization, the resource can be held fairly accountable during their performance review.

7.3 Scheduling Resources

Scheduling resources on a project has always been one of the key challenges of a PM. Even when the PM has a good bead on a resource that they have worked with several times in the past, a personal crisis or an unforeseen technical hurdle can throw schedule estimates out the window. To account for such unknowns, the PM can use the common technique of adding buffers to the end of each major work package. For example, if the resource feels that it will take three days to complete a task, the PM will add it as a four-day task to the project plan. The extra day is an *implicit* buffer, or an increase in the duration of a task just to account for risk. Another method of adding time buffers to a project is shown in Figure 7.2. Here, a program of dependent projects has *explicit* time buffers added to the end of some critical release iterations in each project. These buffers, which are a part of the project plan, act as a secondary level of schedule risk mitigation. Combined, both types of scheduling buffers can help keep projects on a planned schedule and, thus, reduce the overall risk for failure.

The challenge in leveraging the buffer management style of project scheduling is in where to best place the buffers and in deciding how big to make them. Most PMs introduce time buffers using three different

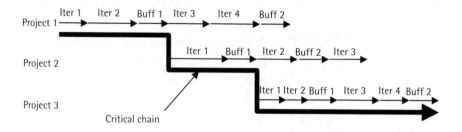

Figure 7.2 Critical path example using three projects, each with multiple iterations.

mechanisms. The first one is that estimates should be based on pessimistic views of past experiences. The second is that total estimation should increase in direct proportion to the number of management levels involved. Management layers are the roots of bureaucratic slowdowns for any project. And the third is that estimators also protect their estimations from a global cut made by executives. For example, many times upper management will request a cut in schedules by 20% across the board. To anticipate this, estimators will add an additional set of buffers that increase the project duration by 20% [11]. As with corporate earnings, project duration estimates are judged by how accurately they match reality. Estimators can be just as scrutinized for overestimation as they would be for underestimation. This desire for accuracy helps keep project sponsors from requesting drastically more time than is needed in business cases.

Another method PMs use when scheduling projects is the critical path approach. Projects can have bottlenecks when certain tasks in a project cannot begin until other tasks have completed. If not scheduled properly, this can lead to idle resources and delayed releases. Critical paths can also exist in a larger scale scenario such as a program of dependent projects. For example, Figure 7.2 illustrates a critical path scenario where project 2 can't begin until iteration 2 of project 1 has completed and where project 3 can't begin until iteration 1 of project 2 has completed. The PMs will not eliminate all unforeseen timeline problems through buffer management and critical path awareness, but they can reduce them.

7.3.1 Drum Resources

When multiple projects share a constraint resource, such a resource is referred to as a *drum resource* (because the projects tend to go by the beat of the drum of that resource). Drum resources are usually identified as those resources where demand for a particular skill outstrips supply. Seasoned IT PMs are experienced with the bottlenecks that certain drum resources can create: SAs, DBAs, and IT operations are all well-known examples. The ideal position for such an organization is to have the supply of drum resources slightly in excess of the demand. "This then gives the organization some contingency to deal with the unexpected" [12]. By better scheduling and staffing these drum resources between projects, the IT PMO, the PMs, and the functional managers can ensure that less time is wasted on lead or warm-up time.

Many PMs handle drum resources' time by requesting that they distribute their workload across projects and document the percentage of time they are spending on each project. "Firms in shorter-term projects and dynamic markets" lean more toward this flexible resource model of allowing resources to multitask [2]. Unfortunately, such fragmented time "is guaranteed to waste the individual's time" and results in long delays in product launch, which can lead to lost revenues [13]. A worker with multiple cross-project assignments will spend a large amount of time each day readjusting to each new task on different projects [5, 11]. Instead, the resource should be scheduled to complete one full task on one project before shifting to another task on another project. Generally, companies with a longer term perspective tend to take this latter approach.

Once initiatives and projects are prioritized by the IT PMO and once the resource manager understands which drum resources will be needed by which projects, a central drum resource schedule can be developed and maintained. Before a PM develops his project schedule, he should be aware of when the drum resources are being used by other projects. To help reduce resource contention, project schedules must be synchronized to this central drum resource schedule. In essence, the project pipeline "becomes a pull system because the drum schedule determines the sequencing of projects" [14]. Projects get pulled into the pipeline if drum resources complete tasks on other projects early. For this reason, projects add buffers to guard against another type of risk: drum resource availability. Such buffers need to overflow before and after the desired start time of the drum resource. This allows for flexibility in the usage of drum resources that may become available early or late [14].

An estimator should not buffer the end of each task on a project; rather, she should buffer the beginning of those tasks that require the drum resource [11]. Transferring the buffers in this way not only increases pressure for noncritical task completion, but also mitigates the risk of other projects not releasing a drum resource when scheduled.

Such buffers are called *capacity buffers*. In reality, the noncritical path buffers shouldn't really be removed from the project. Rather, they should be tacked onto the projectwide buffer at the end of a project. As unforeseen events cause tasks to take longer than scheduled, corresponding blocks of time should be removed from the project buffer. This allows the PM to focus his stress on those tasks that reduce the project buffer. Secondary focus should then be placed on those tasks that are not yet affecting the project buffer but are consuming part of the capacity buffers [11] (i.e., other projects that might affect the PM's project schedule).

7.3.2 Critical Chain

Figure 7.3 shows the critical paths of three projects that have been prioritized and scheduled without the guidance of a central drum resource

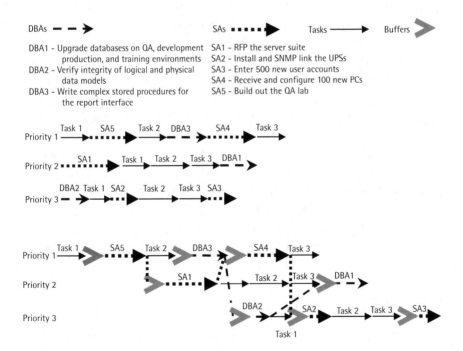

Figure 7.3 Critical chain example using one SA and one DBA as drum resources.

schedule. This example shows two types of tasks that need to be completed by drum resources: DBA tasks and SA tasks. If these schedules were allowed to stand, then PMs would be spending much of their time battling for use of the resources. In order to remove a contention for a resource, the project sponsor will need to consider postponing one of the tasks [11]. To help decide how to best delay project tasks or alter the project kick-off dates, the IT PMO will need to work with the functional managers of these drum resources to develop drum-dependent schedules (the third box in Figure 7.3). The second box shows how a project schedule can then be altered by showing how drum resources are scheduled on other projects and how projects are prioritized by the IT PMO.

The critical paths of the first box in Figure 7.3 are bridged by what Eli Goldratt, author of "Critical Chain," refers to as the drum usage, the buffer protections, and the interproject ropes (drum-buffer-rope for short). By eliminating fragmented drum resource allocation, a PM can feel more confident that when given a drum resource for a given amount of time, the PM will have 100% of that resource's attention until the scheduled task is completed. The path the drum resource takes between projects is the rope that shows the interdependence of each seemingly decoupled project. These drum resource ropes between project critical paths are referred to as the critical chains of the project portfolio. By managing these ropes, the corporate drum resources, and the project buffers, an IT PMO can help prevent projects from stumbling over each other after they are approved and financed. (The AARK Management PowerPoint presentation in the accompanying CD-ROM provides an animated version of Figure 7.3. There is also a listing for a company that provides critical chain project management software in the PPM software section of the CD-ROM.)

7.4 Outsourcing

One reason companies can get disenchanted with out-of-control and unwanted IT deliverables can be a lack of control over IT and strategic outsourcing. Companies may hire management consultants to help develop corporate strategies and business initiatives, and they may hire

IT services companies to run IT projects. While this is necessary in many cases due to a lack of resources and experience, many companies use these tactics more than they should. Because outsourcers are under extreme pressure to complete a project, they tend to recycle past successes into new projects to help in reaching deadlines on time. To tip the balance of risk mitigation more in their favor, outsourcers prefer to install the same "canned" solution they did for your competitors. "The more a company uses outsourcing as a competitive thrust, the more likely it is that its competitors will copy its strategies and move to an equitable market position" [15]. If a company wants a custom solution, it better be prepared to spend quite a bit more money on deliverables and a lot more time on contractual details.

Chapter 5 showed that to meet the demand of the technical initiative portfolio, internal IT departments and external IT companies had to provide a supply of technical solutions. The main test that would determine which of these two IT groups supplied what percentage of the solutions is known as the *yellow pages test*. This test states that "when shared service units cannot outperform external competitors, companies should outsource these functions" [16]. Where Figure 7.4 illustrates a majority of business units "going it on their own" with their technical initiatives, Figure 7.5 shows a diminished reliance on

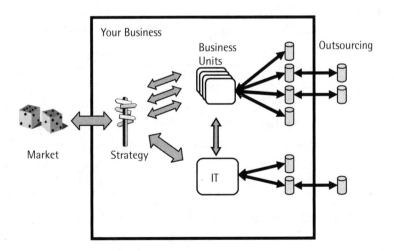

Figure 7.4 Business units that bypass IT resources for outsourced resources.

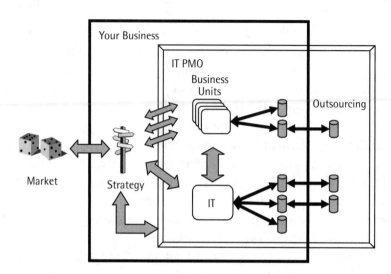

Figure 7.5 IT PMOs can draw attention to and better manage resources to avoid unnecessary and expensive outsourcing.

outsourced companies with the added support of an IT PMO. That is, the IT PMO helps replace the company's reliance on the yellow pages.

While the IT PMO not only provides better visibility into the health of the portfolio, it also helps improve and maintain the health of the portfolio. Moreover, the IT PMO acts as a marketing wing for the IT department. Too often a business unit will bypass valuable IT department resources for less-than-qualified outsourcers. While many outsourcers are experts, project sponsors can save considerable costs if they first sought and then found equitable expertise in the IT ranks. For example, outsourced IT companies are known for the motto "We get IT done"—the notion being that they are sure your IT department isn't living up to its potential. "Hundreds of millions of dollars" are being invested by outsourcing companies to shake the confidence in IT departments among business units [17]. The IT PMO won't discredit outsourcing, but would instead act as a broker of outsourcing vendors and IT resources. Even IT resources may, in turn, outsource some tasks required of them by business units. In this way, project sponsors will be more aware of which resources are available from within the company before they go shopping for resources outside the company.

There has been a recent upsurge in the desires of executive staffs to outsource IT projects to eastern European, Indian, and South American companies. Lured by the bait of lower wages, business units can overlook the many layers of risk (i.e., unforeseen costs) inherent in IT-based outsourced projects. But do the new risks associated with remote development outweigh the benefits of reduced costs of wages? Where costs can add up in travel, cultural training, project monitoring, and avenues for litigation, can companies break even with the lower costs of wages? However the costs balance out, the IT PMO is in a perfect position not only to communicate all risks and costs posed by remote outsourcing vendors, but also to require adherence to the same hurdle gates (audit points) imposed on in-house projects.

7.5 Summary

When a project sponsor wants a particular resource for his project, he needs to understand (1) whether that resource is being used in another project, (2) whether the resource's functional manager is willing to let the resource go, and (3) whether the resource will be satisfied and productive on the project. The IT PMO can help each IT-based project resolve all three of these preconditions. With the aid of the IT PMO's resource manager, a project sponsor will be able to more easily acquire and schedule resources that are used across projects. The resource manager will also help ensure that the resources are supported in their career development between projects. Figure 7.6 shows that as the business case goes through the approval process, the project sponsor can negotiate and then acquire resources from other projects or from functional managers (path 1). Resources (e.g., drum resources) can also be acquired in the middle of a project (path 2). We can see from the figure that both business units and the IT department provide the supply of drum resources. Then, as a task ends, drum resources are returned to the central pool to be used by other projects (path 3). Drum resources are those that are in high demand and require a central schedule maintained by the IT PMO. Using drum-buffer-rope scheduling techniques, the PMs can get a better handle on the critical chains of their projects.

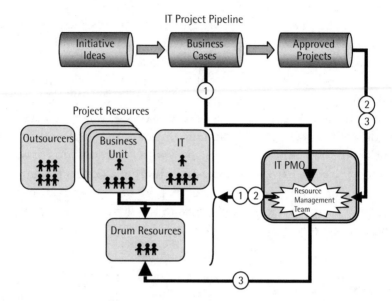

Figure 7.6 Virtual IT PMO—resource management team view.

This in turn leads to efficient resource leveling (usage) and to reduced initiative bottlenecking across the portfolio.

References

[1]   McDavid, D. W., "A Standard for Business Architecture Description," *IBM Systems Journal*, October 7, 1998 (electronic version).

[2]   Edgett, Scott, Elko Kleinschmidt, and Robert Cooper, "Portfolio Management in New Product Development: Lessons from the Leaders, Phase II," in *Project Portfolio Management*, Lowell D. Dye and James S. Pennypacker, (eds.), West Chester, PA: Center for Business Practices, 1999, pp. 97–116.

[3]   Spring, Steve, Beebe Nelson, and Bob Gill, "Building on the Stage/Gate: An Enterprise-Wide Architecture for New Product Development," in *Project Portfolio Management*, Lowell D. Dye and James S. Pennypacker, (eds.), West Chester, PA: Center for Business Practices, 1999, pp. 87–96.

[4]   Elkins, Tony, "Resource Management on an E-Commerce Project," 2002, http://www.gantthead.com (last accessed on January 15, 2004).

[5]   Lister, Timothy, and Tom DeMarco, *Peopleware: Productive Projects and Teams*, New York: Dorset House, 2000.

[6]   Kutoloski, David M., and C. Thomas Spradlin, "Action-Oriented Portfolio Management," in *Project Portfolio Management*, Lowell D. Dye and James S. Pennypacker, (eds.), West Chester, PA: Center for Business Practices, 1999, pp. 261–270.

[7]   Crawford, J. Kent, *The Strategic Project Office*, Monticello, NY: Marcel Dekker AG, 2004.

[8]   Abramson, Gary, "Matchmaker, Matchmaker," *CIO Magazine*, October 15, 1999, http://www.cio.com/archive/enterprise/101599_hr.html (last accessed on January 15, 2004).

[9]   Ghasemzadeh, Fereidoun, and Norman Archer, "An Integrated Framework for Project Portfolio Selection," in *Project Portfolio Management*, Lowell D. Dye and James S. Pennypacker, (eds.), West Chester, PA: Center for Business Practices, 1999, pp. 117–134.

[10] Englund, Randall, and Robert Graham, *Creating an Environment for Successful Projects*, San Francisco, CA: Jossey-Bass, 2001.

[11] Goldratt, Eliyahu, *Critical Chain*, Great Barrington, MA: The North River Press, 1998.

[12] O'Connell, Fergus, *Successful High-Tech Project-Based Organizations*, Norwood, MA: Artech House, 2003.

[13] Khurana, Anil, and Stephen R. Rosenthal, "Integrating the Fuzzy Front End of New Product Development," in *Project Portfolio Management*, Lowell D. Dye and James S. Pennypacker, (eds.), West Chester, PA: Center for Business Practices, 2000, pp. 339–362.

[14] Leach, Lawrence, *Critical Chain Project Management*, Norwood, MA: Artech House, 2000.

[15] Cleland, David, "The Strategic Context of Projects," in *Project Portfolio Management*, Lowell D. Dye and James S. Pennypacker, (eds.), West Chester, PA: Center for Business Practices, 2001, pp. 3–22.

[16] Norton, David P., and Robert S. Kaplan, *The Strategy-Focused Organization*, Boston, MA: Harvard Business School Press, 2004.

[17] Low, Lafe, and Sarah D. Scalet, "Come Together," *CIO Magazine*, December 15, 2000, http://www.cio.com/archive/010101/together.html (last accessed on January 15, 2004).

Appendix 7A: Case Study—Siemens Building Technologies, Inc.—Automating Resource Management

Siemens Building Technologies, Inc., a subsidiary of German conglomerate Siemens, Inc., was seeing the majority of its projects come in late. Some even took six times longer than the original estimates. Combining this with a large number of employee complaints of being overworked, management realized that they weren't managing their resources well. The most valuable experts in the company were being split between so many concurrent projects that the company risked not only project failure, but also diminished returns from the embittered employees. To resolve the problem, IT manager John Braun installed a new application called Business Engine to better manage human resources across the project portfolio.

Employees and managers can update skill sets and availabilities into Business Engine so project sponsors will be better aware of the internal resources they can use. Such knowledge allows the business case writer to better understand whether she will need to outsource certain skill sets for different phases of the project. Another valuable feature of Business Engine is that it allows prospective project sponsors to view the resource bottleneck in real time. Before initiatives are approved, project sponsors can place tentative bids on resources to help streamline project launch upon financing. As long as such flagging of resources has imposed time limits, proactive resource management can reduce confusion and conflict between projects over resources.

So far, Business Engine is managing over 400 subject experts between 300 projects across 22 departments. Because these experts come from four different subject areas, the central project management body (e.g., IT PMO) needs to coordinate resource availability entries with the functional managers as well as with the PMs. Without such a tool, communication between all of these managers would end up becoming a tangled web of voice messages and e-mails. For large, international companies like Siemens Building Technologies, automated resource management tools such as Business Engine are essential to a smooth-running project pipeline [8].

8

Knowledge Management

In this age of information, knowledge is one of the most powerful tools for success. Those companies who know how to get it, manipulate it, and use it the fastest stand to win their market races. The path of knowledge management (KM) runs from how a company gathers its knowledge to how a company learns from this knowledge to how a company implements its new wisdom in business initiatives. From gathering knowledge to changing the course of the company, KM serves as a guiding compass of any company. A break anywhere in this path can cause this important tool to guide the company in fatal directions.

Many experts have defined KM differently: some feel that protecting patentable secrets is the most critical form of KM (e.g., biotech and chip manufacturing companies), while others feel that maintaining strong personal knowledge through training is the backbone of the company (e.g., business and IT consulting companies). Both of these examples can be considered forms of KM in the business IT field. Depending on market conditions or industry verticals, some forms may be higher in priority than others. Not only is it important to manage to the highest level of KM success, it is also important to leverage the forms

179

of KM that best fit your company. First, identify the different business competencies that can be enhanced by KM and then develop different knowledge strategies to fit them [1].

An IT PMO is an organization within the company that focuses primarily on ensuring the good health and direction of the company's portfolio of IT-based projects. So, which forms of KM best support the goals of the IT PMO, and how should they be managed? We will first look at what many consider the different levels of successful KM. Then, we will briefly review some of the forms of KM that have been proposed. Finally, we will develop an approach that allows an IT PMO to better manage the flow of knowledge among the portfolio of IT-based projects.

8.1   Success Levels

There are many ways that an idea can sprout from the mind of someone wanting to improve a business. Awareness of the market, personal experiences, emotional intelligence, and sporadic opportunity are just a few of the factors that can cause the light bulb to pop up over someone's head. To help guide the creation of good ideas that can eventually lead to financed projects, a company needs to ensure that the various sources of data entering a company are well presented to its employees. Such data can come from external sources such as customers, suppliers, or competitors, or it can come from internal sources such as the company's own employees. Figure 8.1 illustrates that gathering this data is just the first level of success in supporting idea generation. As a company adequately builds the various levels of an enterprise KM system, its initiative pipeline will become a solid push for the company rather than the cumulative digression presented in Chapter 2.

Jonathan Wu of DMReview designed five levels of success when creating an enterprise KM system [2]. In level one, data is gathered from external and internal sources to be placed in various databases throughout the company. The company's design of its databases determines the form of its data. While most of these databases are meant to support only certain solutions (or products), others act as gathering points (or warehouses) of data that can be shared across the enterprise. The

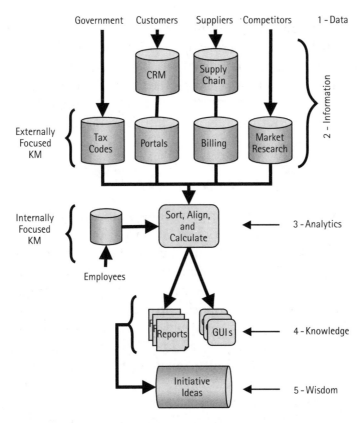

Figure 8.1 The layers of external and internal corporate knowledge.

accumulation and cursory presentation of this corporate data makes up the second level of success, called information. Level three KM success is reached when the company leverages the power of data analytics. This is achieved by presenting the information in a separated or regrouped form that allows "relationships, patterns, trends and exceptions" to be identified [2]. Then, what can be considered advanced analytics can be applied to allow users to discover "knowledge in their data," or level four success. Level five success (or wisdom) is achieved when knowledge is realized as the IT-based business initiative pipeline.

Even if the requirements for success are met and rolled out smoothly in phases (or levels), and even if it is embraced as part of the corporate process base, how would KM prove its value to the corporate bottom line? A company can't measure knowledge itself, "only its indirect effects can. That's because knowledge exists in the context of its use" [3]. Michael Schrage, a research associate with the MIT Media Lab, believes "that knowledge is only important to the extent that we act on it" [1]. The next sections will show some examples of the forms of KM that a company can implement. Then, we will see how an IT PMO can take one of these forms and prove the value that KM adds to the organization.

8.2   Externally Focused KM

Many companies operate more efficiently on their knowledge of how their customers and suppliers best interact with the company. For example, the late 1990s saw the introduction of technology that improved the efficiency of gathering customer wants. From CRM systems to GIS/census demographic data sets, companies were given the opportunities to react more quickly to the needs of their customers. Such initiatives, along with supply chain and B2B systems, have provided opportunities to acquire real-time customer and supplier needs. Managing this knowledge, in turn, can make the interfaces with the customers and suppliers more efficient.

However, stockpiles of siloed data can result with this increase in the volume of knowledge from external IT interfaces. KM systems that focus on gathering data from these disparate systems into central repositories such as data warehouses can help better organize and present information on customers and suppliers. True value from such externally focused KM systems is then realized when focus is centered "on high-transaction, high-customer touch points" such as customer service, inside sales, or accounts payable [3]. These types of systems provide constant feeds of very current information that a company can flex to in real time. Without a KM architecture that centralizes the data from these systems, opportunity knowledge can be too distributed to analyze.

8.3   Internally Focused KM

Where externally focused KM relies more on data collection and presentation, internally focused KM relies more on creating systems that will support knowledge evolution and control. For example, *intellectual asset KM* is used to support the creation and security of a company's suite of patents, copyrights, and other intellectual assets. *Innovation and knowledge creation KM* is used to support the research and development of new products and procedures for the company. *Personal KM* provides employees with support for personal growth and training that will further the goals of the individual and the company. *Expert systems KM* is a way to store the collective knowledge of a company's employees. All four of these KM forms are more than just data stores; they are also a set of processes that should be supported by the organization.

The KM system that an IT PMO will create and support draws from each of these internal forms of KM. It will provide guidance on how to submit IT innovations for patents; it will direct independent developers to IT labs for IT research and development; it will create training curricula for PMs and business case writers; and it will develop databases of project-specific lessons learned. The most consuming of all four of these tasks will be the last one: the task most similar to expert system KM.

Expert systems involve extracting specialized knowledge from the workforce and then making it available to the company through software applications. While these systems have been highly successful in medical, field service, auto repair, and military environments, they continue to run into resistance in other fields. In jobs that require a level of creativity, there comes a point when people become reluctant to part with hard-earned knowledge. Their acquired skills are their tickets to career growth, if not job security. Examples of such job positions include AIDS researchers, machinists, artists, and athletes. The more that creativity and innovation are a part of a job, the more difficult it is to extract knowledge (or the "human" element of the decision-making processes). Secret tricks of the trade and veiled training plans are common among craftsmen and athletes to maintain positions in their fields. And these workers have legitimate reasons to worry. "In the past, some companies have solicited workers' expert advice in the name of making their plants more competitive, only to turn around and move jobs to lower-wage locations" [4].

In many ways, this problem doesn't exist in the IT field. With constant changes in technology, an IT employee is forced to constantly train in the latest methods for success. While a machinist may be safe maintaining expertise on a few processes, an IT specialist needs to keep up with rapidly changing technology. Such technical-expertise devaluation causes IT employees to be more willing to submit postmortems, reusable code, and software patents. Furthermore, because PMs are aware that project risks and cost/time estimates vary so much between projects, they will also be willing to contribute these items to the central knowledge bases. That is, with variability in the details between projects and with the continual obsolescence of technical know how, job security shouldn't be an inhibitor to IT knowledge-base contributions. So, with all this out-of-date data, what value can come from an IT project knowledge base?

Many IT consulting companies built centralized IT project knowledge-base systems by combining example information from past projects with frameworks for best practices [5]. These frameworks are made up of templates for documentation deliverables, timelines, audit procedures, and processes. For example, a PM that needs to gather requirements for his project and then design a hardware architecture can go to the knowledge base, download some templates, view some examples from previous projects, and then create a requirements database or a hardware architecture document. Or, if project completion estimates are needed, the PM could access estimation equations in the knowledge database without reinventing the wheel.

8.4 PMO-Supported KM

Two areas in which an IT PMO can apply KM to support the project portfolio are project knowledge bases and personal training. These specialized forms of KM focus on providing support for IT-based initiatives and projects from their beginning to their completion. As the central resource manager for projects, the IT PMO builds the strength of the resource base by providing training opportunities. This is, in fact, a way to manage the knowledge in the organization so that the odds of project success improve. Such risk mitigation can be further enhanced for projects if stakeholders have access to collateral and tools from other successfully completed IT-based projects. This central project knowledge base, combined with ongoing training of the project team members, provides structure and organization to the unending flow of knowledge between projects.

8.4.1 Personal KM

While such knowledge is ultimately the responsibility of the individual employees, PMs could use the help of the IT PMO here. Project team members can more efficiently acquire knowledge that is beneficial to the project if training options are more proactive to pending projects. Because the IT PMO has an ear to the initiatives proposed, training can be altered early to prepare for the demands of projects. Though the IT PMO prepares and conducts training in project and business case methodologies, it needs only to provide direction for all other project-specific training. Preferred vendors of training in hardware maintenance, programming languages, or stakeholder interview skills can be compiled and used when the needs arise. Costs can be saved, flexibility can be ensured, and a more competent project team can be provided with such planning by the IT PMO.

8.4.2 Project KM

Project KM, like expert systems KM, requires people to enter data reflective of their expertise. As the IT PMO evolves, it can "develop a repository of knowledge about technology and business relationships, corporate needs, best practices, and individuals with particular skills within the IT organization" to improve project design and management [6]. The PM can enter timeline estimates and actuals, staffing plans, cost calculators, vendor analyses, and change management techniques; the developer can add source code, design documents, and test plans; and the sponsor can add the business case, funding sources, and resource reviews. Whether the project was a success or a failure, lessons can be learned from such real-time gathering of information. They can then codify their findings in this IT project knowledge base (see Table 8.1) [7]. With guidelines set forth by the IT PMO, data entered by

Table 8.1
Knowledge Base Metadata Used to Codify (or Categorize) Saved Data

Project Management	Deliverables	Business Unit
Resource mapping	Supply chain	Executive support
Plans	CRM	Marketing
Timelines	ERP	Cross business unit
Configuration management (CM) systems	Portals	Manufacturing
Requirements systems	Databases	Core product A
Design systems	Infrastructure	Accounting
	Network	Research and development
	Servers	
	Clients	

project team members can provide a structured, well-organized source of knowledge for the project portfolio.

Portfolio KM shouldn't stop with just one central knowledge base, it should continue with smaller project-specific knowledge bases that act as sources of communication and information specific to the ongoing project. At the end of each workday, project teams can meet to examine the gap between their to-do lists and what was actually accomplished. These smaller knowledge centers can be made up of project-specific Web sites, Lotus Notes applications, version control software, or just a combination of e-mail attachments. Sometimes, these can form and then break apart once an issue is resolved—a natural cycle [7]. Figure 8.2 shows how the IT PMO fits into the project life cycles not only by managing the central project knowledge base, but also by supporting the creation of each project's knowledge center.

When describing the process of developing a company's EBA, we showed that business units have little to no time to spend on drawing up detailed diagrams of how their businesses operate. Instead, after creating organizational charts and job descriptions, they develop ad hoc processes that solve the problems of the moment. This can be seen very

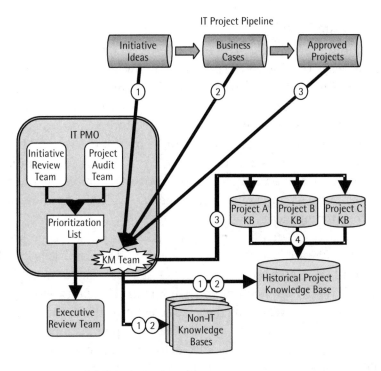

Figure 8.2 Virtual IT PMO–KM team view.

clearly in the early stages of an IT project, where detailed business process flows and structures are diagramed to best understand the needs of the stakeholders. This same seat-of-the-pants approach is taken by IT projects when asked to develop project postmortems. While many organizations require them, little effort is applied by project staff when writing them. Project members are usually already too focused on their next projects to be worried about more detailed documentation. As with EBAs, project postmortem collateral can be gathered dynamically or as projects require (and acquire) the knowledge to support them. Then, at the end of a project, the project team will need only to draw up brief lists of lessons learned and key collateral already stored in the project's knowledge base. By providing structured, project-specific, real-time communication centers that only take codified data (metadata plus collateral), the IT PMO can ensure that the EBA and the central project knowledge base continue to evolve.

8.4.3 The KM Team

Throughout the life cycle of an initiative/project, knowledge is used in different ways (see Figure 8.2). Various knowledge bases in the company can be used to help sprout new business initiative ideas or further refine the business case. As initiatives get approved, therefore, there are certain forms of knowledge that can be used more effectively by projects. The KM team can act as the suborganization of the IT PMO that ensures projects don't get overwhelmed by irrelevant data. Moreover, such a team can also act as a central source of information; the KM team can show business units how to leverage other sources of information when researching ideas.

The leader of such a team is referred to as a knowledge broker, knowledge steward, facilitator, or champion. This knowledge broker would lead the KM team in such duties as retrieving knowledge and entering it into the system, interviewing internal experts, writing KM success stories, and validating that examples entered into the system are accurate and kept up to date [7]. These last two points support the dual goals of mapping historical knowledge to new project successes and of marketing the knowledge base to the rest of the organization. The more the KM team and its leader maintain a support base of successful users, the more the company can grow from past successes and lessons learned from failures.

8.4.4 Organizational Support and Rollout

Just as was the case with other PMO-driven initiatives, so it is with KM: it will not succeed without clear executive support and end-user buy in. Assuming that the labor-intensive task of acquiring and keeping executive support is handled, how can a PMO acquire and keep end-user embracement of a PMO's KM approach? Are there systematic processes for capturing knowledge (both external and internal), organizing it, and sharing it throughout the organization? Is the contribution of knowledge measured [5]? The KM team can take on these challenges, effectively, if it addresses the following requirements for KM success.

1. *The money trail.* By keeping track of what knowledge data is used to support which projects, the KM team will be able to link

the ROI back to the knowledge base. Eventually, value may be realized if the dollars returned exceeds the dollars invested in KM. Arjan van Unnik, head of knowledge management and virtual teamworking for Royal Dutch/Shell E&P, estimates the annual cost of his KM system at about $5 million, with the majority of that sum going toward engaging community members. "The cost is man power," he says, including two to three full-time employees per major online project (of which Shell has 12) just to support KM. The key to KM's continued support and usage at Shell is how the company maps dollar figures to its KM efforts. They've been able to calculate that leveraging saved knowledge has created an estimated annual return of more than $200 million [7].

2. *More out than in.* If the users put more into the knowledge base than what they receive from it, they will stop using it. The interface needs to be easy to use, and the information needs to be easily retrievable. As data is stored, users should be prompted to attach a certain set of key words to each chunk of data. Such keywords, which can be used to categorize and then search for information, are referred to as metadata. Table 8.1 shows a list of keyword categories that can be used for each of three main groups. For example, a document from a finished project can be saved under the project management group category of "Timeline," and the deliverable group category of "ERP," and the business unit category of "Manufacturing." So, when some future user of the knowledgebase needs information on examples of timelines for ERP projects serving the needs of the manufacturing unit, the system will retrieve this document.

3. *Recognition.* Those users who input data need to be recognized for doing so. Bear in mind that you shouldn't pay people for sharing knowledge, but you must recognize those who do. "The most powerful incentive for sharing is peer recognition" [7]. One approach to recognition would be to require all data entered to have the author's name attached so that those who use the data can recognize that person as a source of their successes.

Another example would be to provide incentives for those who enter the most data *approved* by the KM team.

4. *Reliability*. Project collateral such as auditable documentation, timeline estimation tools, and personnel reviews all need to be accurate and dependable. The more such data has been used on successful projects, the more reliable it will be for future projects. For example, cost-estimation spreadsheets can be considered reliable if repetitions of a measurement produce results that vary between projects by less than a certain amount [8]. If the costs of parts of a project result in being fairly close to those calculated at the beginning of the project, then such a cost-estimating tool needs to be made available to other projects. Also, risks will be mitigated on future projects if an organization captures its experiences from similar successfully completed projects [9].

8.5 Summary

For a company to launch forward into its industry fueled by a constant flow of great ideas, initiatives, and projects, it needs a way to capture information and present it to the employees. External knowledge from customers, suppliers, and government entities can keep the idea-generating machine of the company focused on the needs of its industry. Internal knowledge such as strategies, initiative and project methodologies, and IT project lessons learned keep those ideas aligned with the goals of the company and then ensure smooth project pipelines. While there are many forms of corporate KM, the IT PMO builds on the concepts of personal KM and expert systems KM. With personal KM, the IT PMO can proactively set up training programs with third parties to support the near-term needs of recently approved initiatives. Such involvement with the training of project resources helps keep training costs down by negotiating with one provider. The IT PMO also provides KM support to the portfolio by implementing a central knowledge base of material from past projects. Similar to expert systems, the data is entered using metadata tags so that project collateral can be retrieved easily. Easy retrieval and reward systems help ensure that data is entered into the system. Then by mapping project successes back to information retrieved from the knowledge base, the IT PMO can show how KM contributed real value to the organization. Another way to provide KM support to the portfolio is to help new projects set up project-specific knowledge bases. These act as a means of communicating data between project members. At the end of the project, a cleansed subset of these knowledge bases can be added to the central knowledge base as a project postmortem.

References

[1]   Manasco, Britton, "Knowledge Strategies—Generating Lasting Value," *Quantera,* http://webcom.com/quantera/KI019901.html (last accessed on January 15, 2004).

[2]   Wu, Jonathan, "Business Intelligence: The Transition of Data into Wisdom," *DM Review,* November 1, 2000, http://www.dmreview.com/master.cfm?NavID=55&EdID=2524.

[3]   Sviokla, John, "Knowledge Pays," *CIO Magazine,* February 15, 2001, http://www.cio.com/archives/021501/new.html (last accessed on January 15, 2004).

[4]   Aeppel, Timothy, "On Factory Floors, Top Workers Hide Know-How From Managers," *Wall Street Journal,* July 1, 2002.

[5]   Skyrme, David, "Developing a Knowledge Strategy," David Skyrme Associates, January 1, 1998, http://www.skyrme.com/pubs/knwstrat.htm (last accessed on January 15, 2004).

[6]   Meta Group, "Centralizing Management of Project Portfolios," *Meta Group,* January 29, 2002, http://www.umt.com/site/Documents/IT_World_-_Leading_Organisation_Centralize_Management_of_Project_Portfolios_-_29Jan02.pdf.

[7]   Paul, Laura Gibbons, "Why Three Heads Are Better Than One," *CIO Magazine,* December 1, 2003, http://www.cio.com/archives/120103/km.html (last accessed on January 15, 2004).

[8]   Mantel, Samual, and Jack Meredith, "Project Selection," in *Project Portfolio Management,* Lowell D. Dye and James S. Pennypacker, (eds.), West Chester, PA: Center for Business Practices, 2000, pp. 135–168.

[9]   Ghasemzadeh, Fereidoun, and Norman Archer, "Project Portfolio Selection Techniques: A Review and a Suggested Integrated Approach," in *Project Portfolio Management*, Lowell D. Dye and James S. Pennypacker, (eds.), West Chester, PA: Center for Business Practices, 1999, pp. 207–238.

[10] Berkman, Eric, "When Bad Things Happen to Good Ideas," *Darwin Magazine*, April 2001, http://www.darwinmag.com/read/040101/badthings. html (last accessed on June 25, 2004).

[11] Santosus, Megan, "How Siemens Keeps KM Blooming," *CIO Magazine*, February 10, 2003, http://www.cio.com/research/knowledge/edit/k021003_ bloom.html (last accessed on June 25, 2004).

[12] Lamont, Judith, "Behind the Scenes at Wipro: How a KM Vision Became a Reality," *KMWorld*, Vol. 12, No. 7, August 2003, http://www.kmworld. com/publications/magazine/index.cfm?action=readarticle&Article_ID=15 58&Publication_ID=94 (last accessed on June 25, 2004).

Appendix 8A: Case Study—KM at Five Companies

After KM became popular in the early 1990s, many software companies developed products to help manage growing knowledge bases and expert systems. But when many companies started seeing little or no ROIs with these expensive software solutions, executives became more skeptical of KM. The lessons many took from the failed quick-fix solutions offered by software vendors was that KM is best realized first through organizational change and then through technological support. If the organization hadn't adopted KM as a part of its normal workflow, then no software package would prove successful. As KM evolves in an organization, certain methods should be used to roll out technical solutions. The following five companies show the various stages of how this can be done.

Some of the most successful KM solutions can be very simple and effective. For example, *Ritz Carlton*, three-time winner of the Malcolm Baldridge national quality award, doesn't even use technology in its most successful KM initiative. CIO Pam Angelucci has a "green book" of best practices updated and distributed annually. The contents of the green book are staff experiences that get reviewed based on quality scoring techniques [10]. German conglomerate *Siemens* uses a similar approach with their KM implementation guide. According to Chief Knowledge Officer Guenther Klementz, their implementation guide acts as "something of a best practices sharing bible that helps with implementation" [11].

Creating simple KM solutions rather than overly complex, time-consuming software systems is a good way to get initial grassroots attention. Long-term buy in, however, requires continued internal marketing of KM and the introduction of structured systems. While such systems may require more effort to input information, the additional structure allows for easier data retrieval. Siemens' Klementz has created a small corporate team to help preach the gospel of KM while creating over 300 virtual communities of practice. These online communities act as a way to categorize experiences and documentation around topics rather than around experts. Siemens shows the community administrators how to build effective communities through the use of incentive programs. As another example, public relations agency Hill &

Knowlton provides incentives by having a "best-seller" list. Employees get recognition if their KM data is highly popular across the company. Employees also receive random prizes from Web-enabled pop ups when using the KM system [10].

While grassroots embracement of KM processes can be quite a hurdle, the KM champions also need to sell the executives on the concept. One way to do this is to show measurable business impacts from KM. Pharmaceutical giant Johnson and Johnson showed that by reviewing saved information from previous Federal Drug Administration (FDA) applications, they were able to reduce the number of FDA rejection questions. This decreased the time required for drug approval and thus increased time to market. The KM team was able to translate this into $30 million worth of business on one product alone [10]. Wipro Technologies, an IT outsourcing company in Bangalore, India, attributes its 90% on-time project completion rate to a combination of KM processes and Six Sigma quality improvement techniques. They require a highly structured post-mortem process that gathers project collateral, lessons learned, risks encountered, and mid-project direction changes [12].

A simple grassroots approach, followed with incentives and structure, coupled with clear benefits for executive buy in has led many companies to organizationwide embracement of KM. Don't hope that some technological band-aid will allow a company to bypass the hard work of organizational KM change. As with dieting to avoid working out, such short cuts can lead to an endless cycle of lost business intelligence and market advantage.

9

Portfolio Prioritization

In Chapter 1, the core goals of the PMO were defined as maximization, balance, and alignment [1, 2]. The portfolio should be maximized against some corporate goal such as profitability, it should be balanced across several dimensions (most commonly across risk versus reward), and it should be aligned with the business unit's and ultimately the company's strategy. Most methods for prioritizing initiatives have focused on maximization and strategic alignment. These methods rank initiatives and projects against each other by assigning scores. Balancing the portfolio, on the other hand, may require some initiatives with lower ranks to be approved for funding. With financial systems, the portfolio analysis begins with weighting individual securities for risk and return. It ends with conclusions concerning portfolio balance as a whole [3]. The conclusions that an IT PMO needs to provide to the executive committee are that the balance of chosen projects provides the optimal vector (time and scope) of growth the committee desires.

9.1 The Prioritization Process

In previous chapters, we showed how a company can promote new ideas by effectively capturing and then presenting both externally and internally generated knowledge. We also showed how the IT PMO provides support to the idea creators in the form of early risk assessments and business case templates. Yet, how can idea creators feel confident that their ultimate business cases will be reviewed fairly and consistently against other proposals? The IT PMO, along with the executive team, needs to first create a review process and then communicate it to the staff. They need to balance between a culture in the enterprise that encourages innovative ideas and an environment that ensures rigorous strategic assessments [4]. With visibility into how initiatives are prioritized and then approved as projects, business case writers will feel safe that their hard work will get the due diligence it deserves.

But before a review process can be effective, it needs a solid initiative methodology that serves as the incoming pipeline of new business cases. If such a methodology isn't clearly defined, then the review committee will be spending most of its time wading through worthless ideas and indecipherable template formats. The following elements were presented in previous chapters as necessary components to build the pipeline that will allow the review committee to spend time where it is most needed: prioritizing initiatives and projects. The IT PMO will need to make sure that [5]:

1. The strategy, the EBA, and the EIA were developed.

2. An IT initiative review methodology was created and communicated.

3. Minimal acceptance criteria (early hurdles or gates) were established.

4. Business case templates were posted.

Two different review teams will be established by the IT PMO to run two ongoing prioritization review processes: the IT initiative review and the IT project audit processes. Where initiative reviews are held to determine the selection and resourcing of a project, project audits are held in terms of the project's timetable and milestones to determine ongoing health and alignment [6, 7]. In both cases, each team will compile, as a group, the results of its reviews into a central project prioritization list to be presented to the executive review committee. Such group decision processes have been found to work best in top-performing businesses when creating prioritization lists [8]. Sometimes, referred to as the *murder boards* [9], these teams' powers are similar to those of a congressional subcommittee: if they "prioritize out" an initiative, then the central floor (executive review committee) will never see it.

When developing the prioritization criteria, it is widely accepted that the selection process should be based on multiple criteria [3]. Initiatives should be evaluated against a standard set of criteria that include both quantitative measures, such as value-creation potential, sales cycle time, and human resource requirements, and qualitative measures, such as consistency with the company's strategy [10]. Because both the quantitative and the qualitative measures are based on speculation, initiative reviews can only be graded on the return the business case expects to see by a certain future date. Once the project begins, however, quantitative measures can become more objective and less subjective. Therefore, when presenting an initiative for selection, it would be best to calculate the measurement criteria as ranges, or small bell curves of uncertainty, rather than as single point forecasts to describe future possibilities. "Using ranges enhances credibility by avoiding false precision" [11].

"Within the context of software project management, we are concerned primarily with *productivity and quality metrics*" [12]. However, within the context of aggregate project health and real-time IT strategic alignment, we are concerned primarily with initial estimate and corporate strategy alignment. If the schedule, cost, or resource needs vary (become unaligned) from the original estimates by a certain amount at a given time, then the project should be considered riskier than a project that is in agreement with original estimates. The other side of the coin is the more qualitative alignment of the project with the corporate strategy. If either the corporate strategy has shifted or a project has scope crept, the project can be at risk of not satisfying exactly what the company needs. The addition of such quantitative and qualitative project metrics help the IT PMO better understand the health of the portfolio.

When developing the prioritization process, be sure the selection criteria are simple to use and are tailored to your specific company. Most portfolio selection models imply "a degree of precision far beyond people's ability to provide reliable data" [2]. While a robustly defined selection method may produce results trusted by decision makers, it can result in too much complexity to be usable [13]. For example, larger companies with more entrenched processes and cultures tend to find that the qualitative measures of organizational and cultural fit are often more important. On the other hand, smaller, newer companies with more limited capital resources and nascent organizational structure find that quantitative measures of capital funding or near-term cash flow usually matter more (see Table 9.1) [10].

9.2 Initiative Reviews

Figure 9.1 shows an example of an IT initiative review process. In this case, we start with the ideas that, in turn, materialize as initiative business cases. Before documenting the proposal as a business case, however, the IT PMO provides organizational and technical information specific to the company (e.g., the EBA and the EIA). This allows the idea

Table 9.1
Needs for Qualitative Versus Quantitative Progress Measures
for Large and Small Companies

	Qualitative Measures	*Quantitative Measures*
Old/large company—large portfolio (entrenched processes and cultures)	Organizational and cultural fit—more important	Robust hurdle rate processes (e.g., NPV, IRR, PB) already in place
New/small company—small portfolio (limited capital resources, nascent organizational structure)	More seat of the pants due to limited time and resources	Capital funding or near-term cash flows—more important

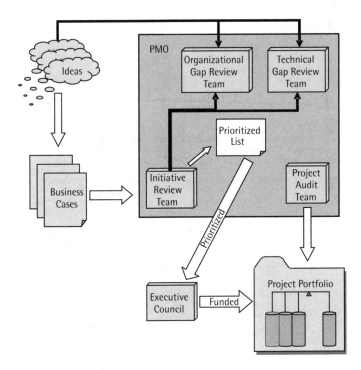

Figure 9.1   Initiative review process flow of an IT PMO using prioritized lists.

generator to be sure that the idea is well aligned. This information can be incorporated into the business case to help boost its eventual rating against other competing business cases. When prioritizing initiatives, the IT PMO also leverages the organizational and technical gap review processes to get a clearer picture of the relative risks of the different initiative proposals. The prioritized list ultimately goes to the executive council to help it determine which projects to fund.

Another example of an IT review process is shown in Figure 9.2. Here, "portfolio selection uses project evaluation and selection techniques in a progression of three phases: strategic considerations (alignment), individual project evaluation (maximization), and portfolio selection (balance)" (see Figure 9.2) [14]. In the previous example, we enhanced this first phase of *prescreening* to include not just strategic alignment review, but also organizational and technical risk/gap analysis. Specifically, we checked to see if the initiative would be organizationally and technically deliverable. In this example, the second major

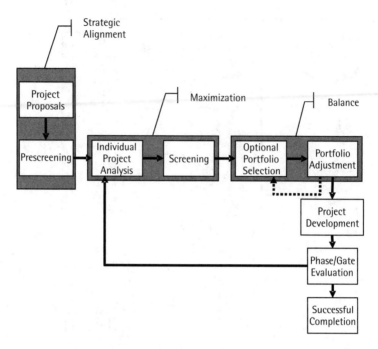

Figure 9.2 When to apply strategic alignment, maximization, and balance during the initiative review process. (*After:* [14].)

step would be to rank the initiatives against each other. The initiatives with the maximum summation of some core set of values such as profitability, strategic alignment, or cost reduction will be ranked highest. Also, interactions between the projects (e.g., interdependencies, competition for resources, and timing) are considered [14]. Finally, the last step focuses on the balance of the portfolio. Here, some projects that show a higher ranking may be rejected in favor of a project that supports a long-term balanced strategic direction.

Earlier, we explained the initiative methodology process that wraps around the core initiative review process. The pipeline feeding the initiative review committee is supported by predefined strategies, architectures, knowledge bases, and business case templates. The pipeline that allows initiatives to begin as projects is supported by efficient review processes and dependable resource management processes. We already found that poor resource acquisition can clog the initiative output pipeline. Yet, how does an inefficient selection process contribute to this malaise? Sometimes, the executive review committee may hold funds until it gets research results from the organizational and technical gap processes of the IT PMO. If this happens, other time-dependent initiatives can get backlogged, waiting for these same funds. One approach could be that a project "could remain on hold for no longer than three months. After that, it is 'up or out'" [2]. Many times, companies lack such gates, and the result is frustrated initiative proposers, unnecessarily waiting for limited funds. On the other hand, other companies that have such gates can impose them too rigorously and fail to give initiatives the complete review they need before rejection or approval. Such balancing between the need for gates and robust initiative reviews, coupled with ongoing resource management, will allow the IT PMO to keep the output side of the IT initiative methodology flowing with dependable projects.

IT initiative prioritization is an important step in managing a solid IT PMO. However, "despite widespread recognition of the front end's importance, there has been limited systematic examination directed at improving its effectiveness" [15]. For an initiative prioritization (filtering) process to be effective, it first has to be measured. While initiative reviews show how to best prioritize the initiatives, project audits focus on how to best measure the initiative's success. The metrics chosen to rank initiatives need to be well correlated with, or identical to, the metrics used to verify project ROI. If this is done, the PMO can trace the effectiveness of an initiative prioritization process all the way down to the aggregate project success level of the IT PMO.

9.3 Project Audits

The project audit review team provides the second source of data for the central IT-based project prioritization list. Figure 9.3 shows how the PMO can conduct organizational, technical, and cross-project gap reviews to update the prioritization lists for the executive committee. Then, funding can continue to go to those projects that are healthy and in alignment with the corporate strategy. While reviewing and prioritizing initiatives is necessary to better distribute funds, it isn't very easy to take funds away from a project that is reviewed poorly. Projects have the

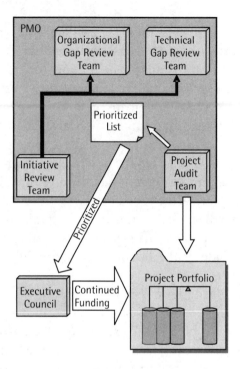

Figure 9.3 Project audit process flows of an IT PMO.

added benefit of momentum—it can be more costly to cancel a problematic project and redistribute the resources than it would if the project were allowed to continue to completion. Nonetheless, the IT PMO audit team needs to quickly find those projects that are spiraling so far out of control that even any future real options have become unattractive. A substantial reduction in wasted development expense can be realized if projects are killed early in their lives [16]. To help stakeholders remove the "horse blinders" they tend to wear on doomed projects, their projects should be reviewed when they reach major milestones, or gates. Running projects should be "re-evaluated at the same time as new projects being considered for selection" [14]. Though the cost of project cancellation should always be included as part of the prioritization calculation, the fact that they are being included in the prioritization list with initiatives helps enhance the view of the IT PPM process in the eyes of the executives [17].

It is important that the project review process be only for review, rather than a platform for micromanaging projects. The IT PMO exists to support projects so that they will be individually successful. As the portfolio of projects, on average, shows improvement, then the project support goals of the IT PMO will have been achieved. If, on the other hand, upper managers or the IT PMO "are held absolutely accountable for the success of every project, it is unlikely they will grant the autonomy that project managers need" [18]. In fact, such an approach could actually degrade the performance of each project and thus the health of the portfolio. "Responsibility for defining a) the tie to strategy and b) interdependencies rests in the hands of the project sponsor and project manager" [19].

This is a particularly sensitive piece of the PMO. The audit team should focus on being an aid rather than a hindrance to a project. The PM should be made aware of how the audit team will be grading the project's health before the audit. Then, while auditing, the audit group should focus on how a project is proceeding rather on the content of the project. For example, if a project has gathered requirements from a set of user interviews, the audit team should focus on giving higher marks for following the interview-to-requirements process rather than lower marks for the quantity or content of the requirements. Grading of content should fall to the PM and to the stakeholders. If the PM has failed to conduct a requirements review with the stakeholders, and the stakeholders have failed to read up on what is considered a quality set of requirements, then the audit team can give lower marks.

When can an IT PMO be most supportive to projects during the audit process? Figure 9.4 shows an example timeline for when such measurements can be taken in the life cycle of a project with three iterations. As can be seen, measurements are taken at the end of each phase within an iteration. In this case, the IT PMO has come up with a set of audit "kits" that can be used on different phases. By modularizing (or in software-speak, objectizing), the audit team has created standard methods for addressing different parts of the auditing process. If changes need to be made, they can be applied to one of these subaudit kits rather than redeveloping one large audit methodology. Figure 9.4 shows four examples of such kits and when they would be used for auditing:

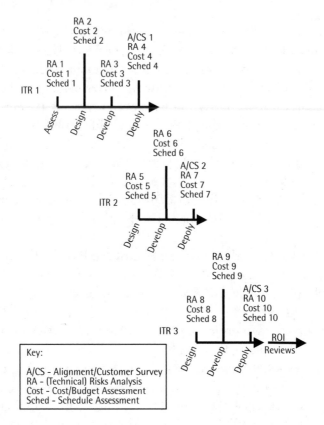

Figure 9.4 When to apply certain predefined audits to a project's timeline.

alignment and customer survey, technical risk analysis, cost/budget assessment, and schedule assessment. As can be seen, these kits were built around the project triad and risk, as introduced in Chapter 2. Such audits are more critical in the early phases of a project because "as the project moves through its life cycle, the ability to influence the outcome of the project declines rapidly" [4]. So, with early surgical audits, the IT PMO can support problematic and flag doomed projects before they drag the company away from its strategic direction.

9.4 Portfolio Maximization

Metric mapping was introduced earlier as a way to verify ongoing project health by linking initial metric projections made in the business case to reality. Let's now look at how such metrics can be chosen by the project sponsor and the PM to show continued value maximization. Because IT projects, like human beings and their personalities, are impossible to clone, a metric set should be chosen to best fit the personality of a given project. Understand what the original motivation was for measuring a part of a project's progress, and "apply measurement to those value areas" [20]. But, how can a central body measure and compare IT project health if every project team is grading itself using different standards? With timelines squeezing and deliverables lists growing, today's IT PM has little time to gather, let alone gather accurate, project metrics. They have enough pressures from stakeholders and team members to worry about before worrying about the process demands of some outside party. However, PMs, like the executive team, need to realize that IT projects should be treated as any other strategic investment where risk monitoring methods should be in place. We assert that if the project metrics are minimized in scope, released carefully, and used effectively, metric tracking from initiative proposal to project ROI will be successful.

Minimize in Scope

Dr. Markowitz defines some rigorous mathematical formulas to monitor and mitigate risk when managing a financial portfolio. Each security's entry in a portfolio must submit to the same risk-monitoring scrutiny that other securities do. So, to accommodate the MPT expectations of the executives and the time pressures of the IT PMs, a middle ground should be defined for an IT project portfolio. While the metric set should be kept small enough not to disrupt ongoing project momentum, it should be robust enough to provide accurately representative reports.

Release Carefully

The Meta Group of Stamford, Connecticut, asserts that IT valuation metrics should be introduced in phases. If the PMO can get PMs to regularly maintain a bare minimum of metrics, the first step to IT valuation will be accomplished. More metrics can be rolled out in later phases once the initial metrics have been embraced by PMs. A good general rule when choosing initial valuation metrics for the portfolio of projects would be to include two quantitative metrics (e.g., budget and schedule) and two qualitative metrics (e.g., business results and risk management). As the project management staff adopts the use of these metrics, the PMO can phase in other metrics that address delivery processes, asset management, and human resources.

Apply Effectively

PMs should understand that the business case describes their project deliverables in terms of the benefits that would be created for the organization. Thus, "with deliverables defined as benefits to be harvested, project tracking should be focused on deviation from delivery of those benefits" [19]. This is why financial measures and customer sign-offs should be just as much a part of the audit as lines of code or function points. As the project progresses, this latter form of internal programming measures produce diminishing returns while financial measures become more relevant [21]. Alternatively, with individual projects, value does not come from improving the results of individual metric measures; rather, it comes from "linking changes in such measures to customer and financial outcomes" [22]. For example, if the earned value analysis of the project in midstream showed marked improvement over a previous measure, this wouldn't add to the value of the project until such a measure could be linked to the combination of ultimate financial outcomes and customer satisfaction. With the portfolio, as a whole, value comes from "the value-enhancing actions that are taken as a consequence of the analysis" [23].

9.4.1 Metrics

When developing the business case templates, the IT PMO review committee will also establish some minimum acceptance hurdles, or gates. These gates can be defined using certain economic models, such as IRR and NPV (the accompanying CD-ROM contains several ROI tools that can be used for this). Then, as the EBA and the budgets shift, the IT PMO can raise or lower these gates to fit changed EBAs or to meet new budget restrictions. When comparing the initiatives for approval, the review teams can use other analytical approaches, such as mathematical programming, decision analyses, and interactive/comparative methods (see Table 9.2). Whichever metrics are used, the project sponsor will ultimately be held accountable for the metrics hurdles they overcame in the initiative review process. In the final project audit, the IT PMO will need to link final metric results back to the financial or customer/user satisfaction goals of the business case.

The following four generic methods list some approaches to tracking these metric areas [5, 13, 24]:

- *Mathematical programming*—Integer programming, linear programming, nonlinear programming, goal programming, and dynamic programming;
- *Economic models*—IRR, NPV, PB period, ROI, cost-benefit analysis, option pricing theory, average rate of return, and profitability index;
- *Decision analysis*—Multiattribute utility theory, decision trees, risk analysis, analytic hierarchy process, unweighted 0–1 factor model, unweighted (1 – n) factor scoring model, and weighted factor scoring model;
- *Interactive comparative models*—Delphi, Q-sort, behavioral decision aids, and decentralized hierarchical modeling.

Not only does this list show how many types of prioritization techniques exist, it also shows how "there is no universal method, dominant theme or generic model" [2]. Rather, the methods and how they are

Table 9.2
Categories of Metrics to Use in IT-Based Business Cases

	Metric Area	Examples
1	Productivity/efficiency	Amount of work completed and amount of time to complete it
2	Quality/effectiveness	Business goals achieved and risks overcome effectively
3	Delivery process	Delivery percentages, backlog costs, rework costs
4	Asset management	Asset portfolio sizes, costs, and distributions
5	Resource management	Turnover and work hour statistics, staff sizes, and costs

grouped tend to be very firm specific. For example, when choosing the minimum acceptance gate metrics for business case submission, it is recommended that the IT PMO look at those used most frequently by their financial department. Aligning these metrics with the internally accepted methods for managerial accounting will help establish IT PMO credibility with the financial department [25].

The metrics used in this list are used to rank order projects against each other to determine which ones offer the greatest return. Mathematical programming and economic models (shown in Chapter 2) provide the calculations that can then be used in the decision analysis and comparative models (real options analysis in Chapter 2 is an example). While such rank ordering of projects and initiatives guarantees a portfolio of high value (or return) projects, there are problems with using only this method of prioritization. For example, if permitted, PMs will tend to manage to short-term financial gains at the expense of long-term benefits (e.g., growth, customer focus, innovation, and employee empowerment) [22]. Moreover, because these types of measures are based on subjective projections, they can be unreliable. Because these unreliable measures tend to be used at the beginning of an initiative, resource-need calculations can be flawed. Ultimately, because such things as defect-free quality and customer satisfaction may not be measured, these narrow-focused financial metrics can cause the portfolio and the associated resource usage to become unbalanced and unaligned [22, 26]. They can end up being so complicated that the PMs won't even use them [27]. While financial measures, on their own, can instill a false sense of project health, if measured consistently across all projects, they give the project sponsors a sense of the relative value of project deliverables.

The business case writer can select metrics beyond the minimal set required by the IT PMO. Taken together, the initiative's metric set should be well rounded to ensure project success. The Meta Group suggests that metrics be chosen from each of the five areas shown in Table 9.2.

Delivery process metrics will help the IT PMO gauge whether the portfolio's health is improving, and asset and resource metrics can be compiled from each project to verify whether the IT PMO is being successful with AARK management. With the first two metric categories, we can begin to see the relation to the project triad and risk analysis presented in Chapter 2 (see Table 9.3).

Robert G. Cooper, Scott J. Edgett, and Elko J. Kleinschmidt, three marketing professors from McCaster University, conducted a groundbreaking survey of 205 responding companies on PPM. The survey asked each company which PPM metrics, out of the following six, they used the most in prioritizing their project portfolio. The metrics tested whether:

1. The projects were aligned with business objectives (*EBA alignment*).

2. The portfolio contained *very-high-value* projects.

3. Spending reflected the business's strategy (*budget/strategy alignment*).

4. Projects were done *on time* (i.e., no gridlock).

Table 9.3
How the Project Triad Affects Metric Choices

	Metrics Chosen	
Productivity/efficiency	Performance to budget (cost)	Measures how actual interim costs are mapping to predicted interim costs.
	Performance to schedule (time)	Maps predicted interim delivery timelines to actual interim delivery timelines.
Quality/effectiveness	Delivery of business results (functionality)	Qualitative measure of how well the interim project results are mapping to shifting business and strategic goals.
	Risk analysis	Each project can list its greatest five risks at the beginning of the project and then track them through the project's lifetime. The number of risks monitored is up to the PM, but a PMO should require some summation of the risks as another metric to help rate the project against other projects.

5. The portfolio had a good *balance* of projects.

6. The portfolio had the *right number* of projects.

They found that the businesses that scored the best from these metrics had processes that:

- Were clearly defined;
- Addressed both initiatives and all phases of projects;
- Were consistently applied;
- Were endorsed by management.

These results highlight the points made earlier that initiative and project methodologies both need to be developed and communicated to the company. These methodologies also need to be applied equally to all projects to maintain the credibility of the IT PMO in the eyes of the business units. Also, a critical first step to the downfall of an IT PMO is when the executive committee fails to select projects for funding from the IT PMO prioritization list (i.e., steps outside the bounds of the initiative methodology). Such a move would be a clear sign that upper management is no longer supporting the IT PMO.

The survey also found that the businesses with higher scores used a hybrid of approaches that were very customized to their business rules. Even more specifically, the two areas in which the top 20% really excelled were [2]:

1. Portfolio balance—achieving the right balance of projects;

2. The right number of projects for the resources available.

Chapter 7 on resource management showed how to avoid project gridlock by constantly leveling the resources. If resources become too scarce, advanced scheduling measures such as critical chain can be used. This next section will present some methods that can help the IT PMO present a prioritized list of projects and initiatives to the executives that will best balance the portfolio.

9.5 Balance

9.5.1 Project Buckets

Earlier, we showed how project investments, as opposed to financial investments, add two elements to the "money out" output: improvements in efficiency and strategic redirection. These two output forms provide the basis for a very common way to categorize the projects in an IT portfolio: separate those projects that improve the efficiency of the company from those that support a redirection in the corporate strategy. Then, divide the "projects into two or three budgets based on the type of investment" [17]. One example would be to split the portfolio into three different budgets: utilities, incremental upgrades, and strategic investments (or *platform, evolutionary,* and *revolutionary* [18]) (see Figure 9.5). First, we create two sides of the project pendulum, called *improve efficiency* and *change business direction.* Then we add the buckets that support these two sides of the pendulum.

Chapter 1 explained that risk is the main determinant in deciding how to balance IT projects across the portfolio. At a high level, risks can change as the market changes. Because the strategies that allow projects to be funded change with the marketplace, the buckets themselves can never be statically defined. So, whenever a strategic shift occurs, the PMO would then need to start rebalancing the portfolio pendulum or

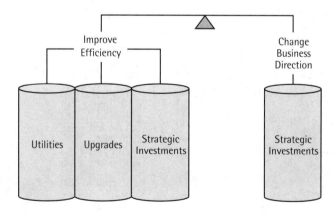

Figure 9.5 Balancing projects between efficiency improvement and strategic change.

start realigning "each project with its contribution to the [new] strategy" [18]. At a low level, risks can differ between the different buckets in the portfolio pendulum. For example, upgrades can be considered relatively low-risk *supporting systems,* and strategic investments can be considered high-risk *disruptive systems* [16].

The riskiness of the portfolio depends not only on the riskiness of its individual projects but also on the extent that they tend to go up and down together—their correlation or covariance. Rather than estimating individual variances, we should build models of technical or organizational covariances [28]. Rather than determining the risk of an IT project portfolio based just on how well risk is distributed among projects, we can determine overall risk based also on how well projects of like categories are progressing. In our case, we use portfolio buckets, balanced on the portfolio pendulum, as our risk covariance model. Figure 9.6 shows three different ways a PMO can bucket projects. It also shows how projects are distributed evenly across the buckets based on risk level. An unhealthy portfolio, on the other hand, would show a

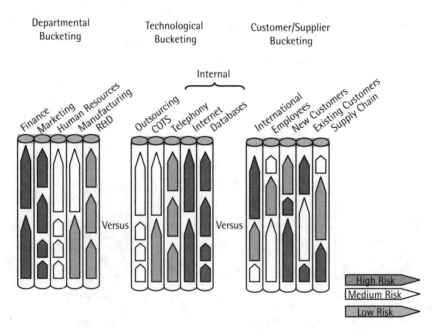

Figure 9.6 Approaches to bucketing projects of varying risk for balance.

preponderance of high-risk projects in one bucket and mostly low-risk projects in another.

Properly designing the buckets can be just as important as properly choosing which projects to finance. "Many companies create buckets associated with departments even though the desired bucket associations should be with customers and corporate strategies"[18]. A poorly chosen bucket suite can incorrectly show a lack of health. This could force the PMO to improperly recommend cancellation of some projects. If buckets are chosen well, on the other hand, some high-risk projects can be saved because the bucket design will show that they are well balanced by low-risk projects in the same bucket. In this case, we can see that a bucket design that focuses on department projects shows that the finance and marketing departments have adopted high-risk projects across the board. We can also see that Internet and database projects that have been financed are also all at high risk. However, a bucket design that focuses on customers, suppliers, and employees shows that the portfolio of project risks is well distributed. Some companies may lean towards certain bucket designs based on past experiences and on their markets. Either way, bucket design should be a part of the corporate strategy (or the EBA).

Figure 9.7 takes the bucket design based on risk mitigation of Figure 9.6 and overlays it with the bucket design based on strategic and efficiency balancing of Figure 9.5. As the company changes strategy (1), not only will the bucket designs need to change (2), but the amount invested in efficiency improvement versus business redirection will need to change. Figure 9.7 shows this by the shifts that can occur in the pendulum. If a company wants to focus more IT project funds on changing the direction of the company, then the pendulum will move to the right (3). This will cause the improvement efficiency side to drop (4). To regain a balance in the IT project portfolio, the PMO would then have to recommend canceling or delaying certain projects in utilities or upgrades. As one can see, such project risk categorization and balancing can be rather subjective. A way to reduce this subjectivity, when balancing the portfolio, is to include some of the metrics described in Section 9.5.2.

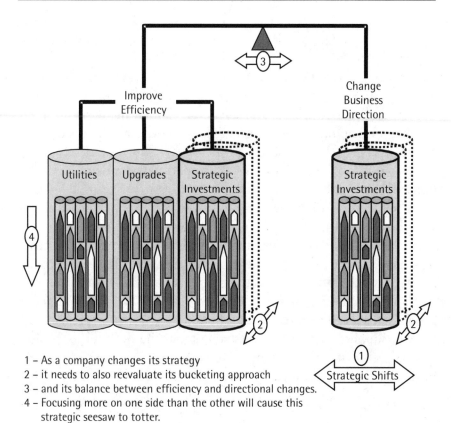

1 – As a company changes its strategy
2 – it needs to also reevaluate its bucketing approach
3 – and its balance between efficiency and directional changes.
4 – Focusing more on one side than the other will cause this
    strategic seesaw to totter.

Figure 9.7 The need for dynamic bucket balancing.

9.5.2 Bubble Diagrams

A very popular way of keeping the cumulative project direction well balanced is through the use of bubble diagrams. Where scorecards will tabulate the values of various metrics for each project, bubble diagrams put these values into multidimensional space. This allows the prioritizing team to see value in a project beyond its total score in a scorecard. While a project may not rate high overall, the bubble diagram will show other strengths that may make the project more appealing than others.

A bubble diagram, otherwise known as a bubble chart or a *portfolio grid* [29], starts off with a two-dimensional graph. Some parameters that can be considered for the axis include resource availability, asset leverage, portfolio leverage, architectural alignment, fit with strategy, cost to complete, and time to complete [26]. When using an X-Y type of grid, it is best to have a qualitative metric on one axis and a quantitative metric on another to help ensure the metrics' variables are independent. Once a grid type and the parameters are chosen, several techniques can be used to represent projects on the grid. Figures 9.8 and 9.9 show an example of Buss's technique for rank ordering projects, which uses four bubble charts concurrently [29].

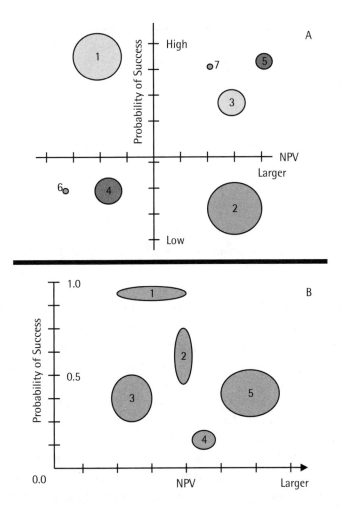

Figure 9.8 Other graphical approaches to balancing a project portfolio (A and B).

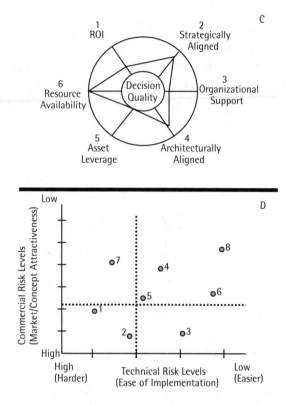

Figure 9.9 Other graphical approaches to balancing a project portfolio (C and D).

Chart A shows the Y axis as the qualitative *probability of success* metric and the X axis as the quantitative *NPV* metric. The areas of the circles represent resource usage. More advanced bubble diagrams will calculate the summation of the areas of the circles and ensure that this sum stays constant (representing the constant number of resources available to the portfolio). The colors can represent the state of the initiative (e.g., imminent launch or on hold) or the progress of the project (e.g., 50% complete or in rollout phase of last iteration). Rather than depict resource usage, chart B shows how the circles can become ovals to show range of error while calculating the metric values. Chart C shows a spider diagram depicting the relationship among six requirements for a single project. Though spider diagrams only represent one project, they show six dimensions (or metrics) at once. To compare projects using this form of diagram will require the prioritizer to hold up multiple diagrams at once. Finally, the IT PMO can create a chart that includes hurdle gates. Chart D shows where the cutoff points are set for commercial risk levels (horizontal line to the Y-axis) and for technical risk levels (vertical line to the X-axis).

9.6 Summary

Keep in mind that bubble diagrams are not an end to the portfolio-balancing problem; they are meant to serve only as a decision-enabling tool. Another tool that assists with balancing is the bucket concept described earlier. A manager can stare at a set of diagrams forever, "but unless a portfolio was obviously and extremely out of balance, how does one know whether or not one has the right balance?" [26]. Ultimately, balancing the portfolio requires just as many subjective decisions as those used to estimate financial ROI and strategic alignment. The best mix and quantity of metrics depends on the individual company. We pointed out that some companies develop prioritization lists more aligned with qualitative measures, while others do better with quantitative measures. Cooper, Edgett, and Kleinschmidt's survey showed that using more criteria is associated with better performing companies; "the top performers, on average, rely on 6.2 criteria for project selection, whereas the poor performers use only 4.4 criteria, on average" [8]. As long as each of the three prioritization approaches are represented, the IT portfolio can, at the same time, stay both flexible to strategic shifts and focused on corporate growth.

References

[1] Crawford, J. Kent, *The Strategic Project Office*, Monticello, NY: Marcel Dekker, 2004.

[2] Edgett, Scott, Elko Kleinschmidt, and Robert Cooper, "Portfolio Management in New Product Development: Lessons from the Leaders, Phase II," in *Project Portfolio Management*, Lowell D. Dye and James S. Pennypacker, (eds.), West Chester, PA: Center for Business Practices, 1999, pp. 97–116.

[3] Markowitz, Harry M., *Portfolio Selection*, London, England: Basil Blackwell, 1992.

[4] Cleland, David, "The Strategic Context of Projects," in *Project Portfolio Management*, Lowell D. Dye and James S. Pennypacker, (eds.), West Chester, PA: Center for Business Practices, 2002, pp. 3–22.

[5] Bridges, Dianne, "Project Portfolio Management: Ideas and Practices," in *Project Portfolio Management*, Lowell D. Dye and James S. Pennypacker, (eds.), West Chester, PA: Center for Business Practices, 2000, pp. 45–54.

[6] Spring, Steve, Beebe Nelson, and Bob Gill, "Building on the Stage/Gate: An Enterprise-Wide Architecture for New Product Development," in *Project Portfolio Management*, Lowell D. Dye and James S. Pennypacker, (eds.), West Chester, PA: Center for Business Practices, 1999, pp. 87–96.

[7] Ferranti, Marc, "Gartner—Align Thyself," *CIO Magazine*, November 15, 2001, http://www.cio.com/archive/111501/align.html (last accessed on January 15, 2004).

[8] Edgett, Scott, Elko Kleinschmidt, and Robert Cooper, "Best Practices for Managing R&D Portfolios," in *Project Portfolio Management*, Lowell D. Dye and James S. Pennypacker, (eds.), West Chester, PA: Center for Business Practices, 1999, pp. 309–328.

[9] Frame, J. Davidson, "Selecting Projects That Will Lead to Success," in *Project Portfolio Management*, Lowell D. Dye and James S. Pennypacker, (eds.), West Chester, PA: Center for Business Practices, 1999, pp. 169–182.

[10] Tjan, Anthony K., "Finally a Way to Put Your Internet Portfolio in Order," *Harvard Business Review*, February 1, 2001, Reprint R0102E.

[11] Keelin, Tom, and Paul Sharpe, "How SmithKline Beecham Makes Better Resource-Allocation Decisions," in *Project Portfolio Management*, Lowell D. Dye and James S. Pennypacker, (eds.), West Chester, PA: Center for Business Practices, 1999, pp. 329–338.

[12] Pressman, Robert S., *Software Engineering: A Practitioner's Approach*, 3rd ed., New York: McGraw Hill, 1993.

[13] Ghasemzadeh, Fereidoun, and Norman Archer, "Project Portfolio Selection Techniques: A Review and a Suggested Integrated Approach," in *Project Portfolio Management*, Lowell D. Dye and James S. Pennypacker, (eds.), West Chester, PA: Center for Business Practices, 1999, pp. 207–238.

[14] Ghasemzadeh, Fereidoun, and Norman Archer, "An Integrated Framework for Project Portfolio Selection," in *Project Portfolio Management*, Lowell D. Dye and James S. Pennypacker, (eds.), West Chester, PA: Center for Business Practices, 1999, pp. 117–134.

[15] Khurana, Anil, and Stephen R. Rosenthal, "Integrating the Fuzzy Front End of New Product Development," in *Project Portfolio Management*, Lowell D. Dye and James S. Pennypacker, (eds.), West Chester, PA: Center for Business Practices, 2001, pp. 339–362.

[16] Kaplan, Jeffrey D., "White Paper: Strategically Managing Your IT Portfolio," *PRTM's Insight*, April 1, 2001, http://www.prtm.com (last accessed on January 15, 2004).

[17] Berry, John, "Tools Bring ROI into Focus—Software That Calculates Return On Investment Helps Companies Determine," *Internet Week*, December 10, 2001, http://www.portfoliomgt.org/ForumItem.asp?itemID=965 (last accessed on January 15, 2004).

[18] Englund, Randall, and Robert Graham, *Creating an Environment for Successful Projects*, San Francisco, CA: Jossey-Bass, 2002.

[19] Combe, Margaret W., "Project Prioritization in a Large Functional Organization," in *Project Portfolio Management*, Lowell D. Dye and James S. Pennypacker, (eds.), West Chester, PA: Center for Business Practices, 2000, pp. 363–370.

[20] Pastore, Richard, "Noodling Numbers," *CIO Magazine*, May 1, 2000, http://www.cio.com/archive/050100/advice.html (last accessed on January 15, 2004).

[21] Mayor, Tracy, "Value Made Visible," *CIO Magazine*, May 1, 2000, http://www.cio.com/archive/050100/method.html (last accessed on January 15, 2004).

[22] Norton, David P., and Robert S. Kaplan, *The Strategy-Focused Organization*, Boston, MA: Harvard Business School Press, 2001.

[23] Kutoloski, David M., and C. Thomas Spradlin, "Action-Oriented Portfolio Management," in *Project Portfolio Management*, Lowell D. Dye and James S. Pennypacker, (eds.), West Chester, PA: Center for Business Practices, 2000, pp. 261–270.

[24] Mantel, Samual, and Jack Meredith, "Project Selection," in *Project Portfolio Management*, Lowell D. Dye and James S. Pennypacker, (eds.), West Chester, PA: Center for Business Practices, 2001, pp. 135–168.

[25] Reifer, Donald J., *Making the Software Business Case: Improvement by the Numbers*, Reading, MA: Addison-Wesley, 2004.

[26] Kleinschmidt, Elko, Scott Edgett, and Robert Cooper, "Portfolio Management in New Product Development: Lessons from the Leaders, Phase I," in *Project Portfolio Management*, Lowell D. Dye and James S.

Pennypacker, (eds.), West Chester, PA: Center for Business Practices, 1999, pp. 97–116.

[27] Traynor, Ann Jensen, and Anne DePiante Henrikson, "A Practical R&D Project_Selection Scoring Tool," in *Project Portfolio Management*, Lowell D. Dye and James S. Pennypacker, (eds.), West Chester, PA: Center for Business Practices, 1999, pp. 239–260.

[28] Harder, Paul, "A Conversation with Dr. Harry Markowitz," *Gantthead.com*, 2002, http://www.eitforum.com/ForumItem.asp?itemID=1158.

[29] Menk, Michael, and J. Matheson, "Using Decision Quality Principles to Balance Your R&D Portfolio," in *Project Portfolio Management*, Lowell D. Dye and James S. Pennypacker, (eds.), West Chester, PA: Center for Business Practices, 1999, pp. 61–70.

[30] Low, Lafe, "How Citigroup Measures Up," *CIO Magazine*, April 15, 2004, http://www.cio.com/archive/041504/citigroup.html (last accessed on June 25, 2004).

Appendix 9A: Case Study—CitiGroup—IT PPM Software

Many software companies have built software products that support IT PMOs (see the accompanying CD-ROM for a sample listing). However, rather than purchase a software package that provides IT PPM functionality, CitiGroup's Global Corporate and Investment Banking (GCIB) group built its own from scratch. The group's goal was to build a tool to automate many of the features normally found in an IT PMO. The internal product was called Mystic (short for my systems and technology information center) and provided the following functionality:

- *Project health status.* This is a *project prioritization system* that monitors the project portfolio in real time. PMs regularly enter the status of their projects so that executives can view summarization reports.

- *Citigroup technology catalog.* This is an *asset management* system that tracks CitiGroup's servers, network routers, and packaged applications.

- *CitiGroup systems inventory.* This is another *asset management* system that tracks custom, internally developed applications.

- *Customer satisfaction surveys.* This is a *knowledge management* system that allows for post-mortem input from the project sponsor on how the project staff performed.

- *Reusable asset manager.* This is a second *knowledge management* system that stores reusable software and project collateral.

- *Global talent manager.* This is a *resource management* system to track the skill levels of the IT talent available to support IT-based projects.

It took GCIB's CIO, Thomas Sanzone, over two years to roll this system out to the IT department to support the 15,000 ongoing projects. Since the initial rollout, project on-time delivery has improved 15%, while the number of projects has grown 50%. Not only is this system used to support current projects, it is also used to improve the portfolio at the initiative approval stage. While a CIO council has final approval on project funding, initiatives are first required to consult the

CitiGroup technology catalog in Mystic for approved and supported software. Such control helps reduce overall portfolio costs by ensuring architecture alignment and asset reuse within the project pipeline.

This approach to IT PPM rollout uses the IT department as a pilot department first before engaging the rest of the company. With organizational acceptance as the greatest hurdle to IT PPM success, any IT PPM initiative will have gained a solid advantage if it has worked out the technical kinks beforehand with such a pilot. An error-prone software solution that supports a grand organizational shift such as IT PPM can lead to severe backlash and ultimate failure. Besides smoothing out the quality of the system, Sanzone also understands that the Mystic system will need to allow for metrics to be more flexible to the various business units before rolling it out to non-IT sponsored technical projects. This is similar to the need for dynamic KPIs in the Balanced Scorecard (see Appendix 3A). In short, whether you buy or build an IT PPM software solution, be sure to couple its rollout with continual internal marketing and software quality assurance [30].

10

Organizational Support

IT people have a reputation of wanting to crawl into a closet and be left alone until they are ready to release whatever they are working on. Only PMs who have sprung from these ranks understand how this sort of psychology is actually a necessity to maintain focus. The business leaders who are financing these IT-based projects, however, want a continual feed of results, not mid-stream *vaporware*. An IT PMO rollout can solve a similar conflict by allowing the IT PMO staff to focus on successful completion of modules that show early wins. According to Graham's second law, "If they know nothing of what you are doing, they assume you are doing nothing" [1]. Through phased releases and intense organizational involvement, a small PMO development group can prove ROI of itself and valuation of the portfolio to CFO staff quickly and successfully. Then once the value of IT PPM is embraced by the organization, the IT PMO "can transcend the IT organization (where it usually originates) to achieve an even broader impact on the enterprise's portfolio of transformational business initiatives" [2].

Many new strategic initiatives, such as PMOs, kick off with great fanfare only to wither due to organizational resistance and diminishing executive participation. Another way to counter such resistance is to persistently prove the value of the PMO. That is, you will need to continually stress and visibly demonstrate that the project office adds value to the organization [3]. One early way to show this is by focusing on the projects that are underway. Because CFOs are always eager to view the valuation of a company's project portfolio, showing this would be a great early win for the PMO initiative. At the very least, the PMO organization needs to be able to explain exactly what it is trying to derive from such a valuation. Is it to prioritize projects for budget cuts? Is it to understand skill gaps on projects? According to Greg Smith, executive consultant for Compass America, "There has to be a business driver for valuation" [4]. Where the previous chapters showed the business value of each of the IT PPM building blocks, this chapter will illustrate a way that these building blocks can be effectively rolled out to the organization.

10.1 Marketing IT PPM

When selling the concept of a PMO to an organization, the two primary audiences will be the executives and the middle managers. With these two groups looking at initiative proposals from two different perspectives, a PMO marketing pitch should be segmented to get the best results from each group. (Be sure to review the contents of the accompanying CD-ROM for graphics, PowerPoint presentations, and bibliography links to help sell your IT PPM initiative internally.)

Where executives will be more interested in viewing aggregate project health and IT valuation to make strategic decisions, middle managers will be more interested in attaining high ROI from their IT projects. Therefore, because certain building blocks satisfy the needs of one of these two groups more than the other, building block rollout should be timed so that both groups are constantly satisfied. In short, to gain support from either group, not only do the objectives need to be tied to the goals of the PMO, the objectives also need to be measurable as the PMO develops.

When rolling out the IT PMO, early wins are critical to get buy in from early adopters. While "we want to establish a longer-term vision to guide our immediate tactical choices" [5], we still need to get early tactical wins to create the base of early adopters. One marketing model that applies to IT PMO acceptance can be represented by Geoffrey A. Moore's classic bell curve of new product adoption. When rolling out a new organizational process such as a PMO, project and business unit managers need to be continuously sold on the benefits of IT PPM. If an IT PMO lead thinks that he will get buy in through executive declaration, he is dreaming. While complete executive support is a requirement, so is passionate adoption by the troops. The IT PMO needs to prove true ROI for those projects that are the first to leverage the benefits of the IT PMO (innovators and early adopters in Figure 10.1). These early pilot users (PMs and business unit sponsors) are the same resources that made up the virtual IT PMO support teams. Assuming that most of them will realize benefits from the IT PMO, it is now the job of the core IT PMO staff to get the IT PMO across the chasm. That is, the IT PMO team will need to ensure that the early adopters efficiently market their success to help establish the early majority adopters of PMs and sponsors. Only then can momentum and executive decree be leveraged to bring the "late majority" and "laggards" to adopt the support of the IT PMO.

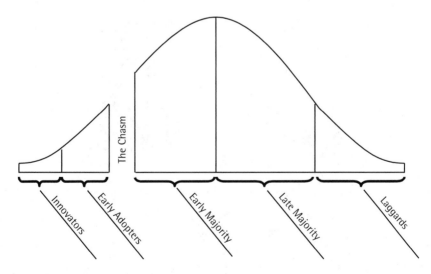

Figure 10.1   Phases of product adoption. (*After:* [6].)

Imagine a situation where one-third of the PMO support teams haven't been completely sold on the benefits of the PMO after they have had a chance to reap its benefits. This is the one-third of PMs and sponsors that the PMO staff will need to focus on primarily for adequate marketing. For if the PMO team allows this one-third to leave with less than optimal reviews of the PMO, their word-of-mouth marketing will propagate to their peers and subordinates. While most of the PMO's marketing energy will be focused on diminishing the expansion of the "reds" (or dark grays in Figure 10.2), they need to also focus on those support team members who support the PMO's purpose but fail to adequately build an expanded base of early adopters. In this case, the PMO team needs to supply these "yellow" (or light gray) leaders the appropriate marketing tools (the perennial presentations and T-shirts) and marketing support.

10.2 IT PMO Rollout

In our example, we will present a three-phased approach to rolling out an IT PMO. Most companies will already have some of these building

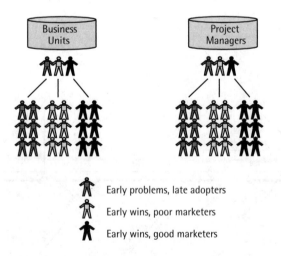

Figure 10.2 Distribution of IT PMO supporters in business units and project management staff.

blocks in place. By seeing its position in the context of an IT PMO, however, a company can realize it is missing some critical pieces. Phase 1 will focus on first establishing organizational support through strategy definition, methodology creation, asset inventory, and PPM software tool rollout. Phase 2 will evolve from the deliverables of phase 1 with methodology training, project methodology pilots, EBA and EIA definition, portfolio reviews and audits, and KM. Finally, phase 3 will roll out architecture management, resource management, and portfolio valuation and ROI. Before the IT PMO begins each phase, it should review the following five SMART questions [7]:

- *Specific.* Is the IT PMO sized and tailored to the business?
- *Measurable.* Are ROI goals defined for the IT PMO early, to then be reported on periodically?
- *Agreed upon.* Do the organization and the executives show cultural readiness and commitment?
- *Realistic.* Is the timeline achievable and are the projected costs accurate?
- *Time constrained.* Are there a finite number of milestones documented to reach completion?

10.2.1 Phase 1

Complete valuation of projects is usually not possible given a small audit team and a large portfolio of projects. With the CFO driving the CIO to get valuation results as soon as possible, something needs to be delivered in the early implementation phases of a PMO. One way to do this would be to have all PMs grade their projects on a published set of metrics. Then, the PMO team would take a random sampling of all projects and verify some of the grades. Two quantitative metrics that could be used are project cost or the more subjective long-term cost and ROI (i.e., after project completion). A qualitative metric would be to verify how their project supports one or more of the corporate strategic goals. Such a project valuation effort should start in the early part of PMO phase 1, so that the compiled results can be passed up by the end of this phase. Eventually these metrics will become part of the business case template used when submitting a business initiative (an initiative methodology). In both cases (in early valuation or as an initiative methodology), quick PMO marketing wins would result:

- They would forge and enforce an alignment between the IT function and business strategy.

- They would require all parties to articulate what their goals and expectations are for a given IT project.

- They would help business executives map out a clear hierarchy of priorities.

10.2.1.1   Portfolio Management Teams and Committees

In Chapter 1, we introduced the building blocks of IT PPM and then arranged them in certain ways to show how to best create organizational support. Figure 1.14 showed these blocks resting on spires of organizational support from representatives of three committees: business units, PMs, and architects. These three groups, along with the executive committee, make up the extended, virtual IT PMO. Rather than creating another bureaucratic gorilla, this approach keeps the IT PMO small and reactive. Chapter 4 showed that as the IT PMO evolves, the IT PMO staff needs to support different activities and committees. Where the top two teams will support portfolio prioritization and valuation to the executive committee, the lower four teams will support the health of the portfolio through AARK management (see Figure 10.3).

A good technique to acquire and maintain buy in of a PMO is to keep everyone affected by the IT projects involved with the PMO. Populating committees with resources from the various IT-reliant departments will do this. For example, the business unit committee should be made up of representatives of the various business units, and the architecture committee should be made up of senior architects from the IT department. "The legitimacy of the [teams are] only seen after it becomes instrumental in project success. After initial success the [teams] can be expanded with increased authority to solve interdepartmental conflict" [1]. That is, start the teams small, create successes, then use early team members as evangelists to preach the value of the PMO to new members of larger teams.

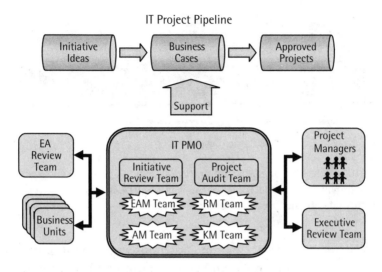

Figure 10.3 Virtual IT PMO—overall team view.

Before the teams in the IT PMO can conduct their ongoing tasks of supporting projects and the executives, they need to work on building the IT PMO itself. They need to split up into "rollout" teams that help:

1. Executives maintain the strategy.

2. Business units develop the initiative methodology.

3. PMs develop the project methodology.

4. Architects conduct the asset inventory.

They will also need to purchase and roll out a project prioritization software tool across the enterprise. Figure 10.3 shows the virtual PMO as four organizational support committees and the IT PMO staff. These groups need to be created and sold on the concept of the support teams delivering under the guidance of the IT PMO.

10.2.1.2 Deliverables

In Phase 1 (see Figure 10.4) we can see the first building blocks that the IT PMO will guide the support teams in delivering:

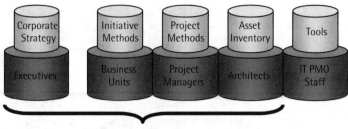

Organizational Support

Figure 10.4 Phase 1 deliverables of an IT PMO rollout. (The accompanying CD-ROM provides an animated version of Figures 10.4 through 10.6 in the "IT PPM Intro" PowerPoint presentation.)

- *Corporate strategy.* Chapter 2 demonstrated the importance of defining, maintaining, and communicating the corporate strategy. This needs to not only be the primary, but also the ongoing, task of the executive committee. If the executives are not able to keep the strategy in tune with the market, then the IT PMO will not have a bell weather to guide them during initiative prioritization processes. Such a lapse by the executive committee would result in undermining the success of the IT PMO.

- *Initiative methodology.* At the same time as the strategy is being developed by the executive committee, the IT PMO needs to work with the business units on a standard method in which all IT-based business initiatives should be presented to the IT PMO review committee. Such a methodology would include things like business case templates, submission guidelines, IT PMO contact names, minimum acceptance measures, and review timelines (see Chapter 3).

- *Project methodology.* This process solicits input from PMs in selecting some industry-standard IT project methodologies and then attaching company-specific audit points to them. Once this is done, then the IT PMO can develop training curricula and assign pilot projects in phase 2 (see Chapter 3).

- *Asset inventory.* This step involves understanding what asset base the company is relying on before developing an EA. Phase 2 will then draw on such an inventory and on the EBA to develop a current-state EIA. From the EIA, the architects will then know whether they should evolve the architecture or scrap it for some new direction.

- *Tools.* If a company has several projects running concurrently, it would be nearly impossible for a three-person audit team to sufficiently check the health of every project. Therefore, it is important that some sort of workflow tool be implemented and used by all PMs. Such tools provide PMs a way to keep a PMO team aware of the status of projects. If all the PMs are using the tool consistently, then a small audit team will be able select which projects to audit based on some predetermined flags. For example, a workflow tool should be able to print out a list of all projects sorted by cost, health (as determined by the PM entries), size, and actual-to-estimated timelines. The audit team can then conduct audits using the Internal Revenue Service model: audit the highest risk and highest cost projects, then audit a random sampling of the remaining projects. This next section goes into more detail on some of the options that are available for software PPM tools.

10.2.1.3 Software Tools

Scott Berinato, writer of "Do the Math," in *CIO Magazine*, believes that the evolution of a project portfolio focuses around project valuation through a phased implementation of technology [8]. In phase 1, he recommends collecting basic information on all projects and then putting them in a central database. Phase 2 is reached when those projects are prioritized against each other. An IT organization has satisfied phase 3 when the projects are categorized (or bucketed) for budgetary reasons. Finally, phase 4 is reached when PMs can enter their project metrics into the database easily (i.e., through a tool), and when executives can view real-time project health.

While improving the efficiency of project valuation, a PPM tool will also improve communication among the PMs. One of the more common implementations of PPM tools is the *red light, green light* rating. When a project is running at low risk, it gets a green light. Conversely, when a project is in a state of high risk, it gets a red light. This is simply a way to summarize the tracking metrics for quick review. It allows for an easy way to list and rate all of the projects where everyone sees everyone else's performance and where "integrity becomes self-policing" [9].

Fortunately, IT performance monitoring need not be complex or time consuming. A "dashboard" of project metrics will suffice. Metrics such as schedule slippage and time to completion are typical high-level performance indicators that serve as good "warning lights" that a deeper problem may exist [10]. Further drill down can come if yellows and reds show up. Such automated tools should be leveraged to provide this efficiency not only in the collection of tracking metrics, but also in the ability of executives to drill down and receive simple reports on the portfolio.

When rolling a PPM software solution out, the organization needs to be trained properly to garner the most acceptance. For example, "educate PMs and team members that red does not mean 'bad,' it means 'help.'" Such summary scoring as this also helps gauge aggregate project stability over time [11]. A list of those authorized to enter predetermined project metrics needs to be documented. Then, once these individuals are trained, their audit entries can be policed by the IT PMO.

There are many tools that support the entry and reporting of metrics:

- *EIS tools* mine data sprinkled within the corporate databases, apply statistical algorithms, and then produce summarization reports. EISs were developed to give the executive team a summarized, real-time picture of their company's activities.

- *ROI tools* compute project ROI as well as discounted cash flow methods such as NPV and PB period. Examples of these tools include those sold by Glomark Corp. and CIOview Corp. [12]. (The accompanying CD-ROM contains tools provided by Nucleus Research, Inc.)

- *Collaboration tools* allow for multiple individuals or groups of individiuals to communicate and strive for common goals. A simple version of this would be an e-mail system. An advanced version can include Web-based white boarding, videoconferencing, chat rooms, and multiuser project management tools. Lotus Domino, Nexprise, and Alventive are examples of collaboration tools.

- *Enterprise project management tools* are a form of collaboration tools that allow for PMs to enter asset, resource, and project information into a central enterprise project management database. The enterprise project management system then produces reports that rate the different projects. Other output is available, such as time and expense accounting, integrated skills scheduling, and KM. Examples include PlanView, Primavera, eLabor, Prosight, and Artemis. (The accompanying CD-ROM contains a more extensive list of EPM tool vendors.)

- *Business intelligence solutions* are an extension of EIS tools in that they provide consolidated views of information found in various corporate systems. Where EIS systems drastically summarize data for time-strapped executives, business intelligence systems allow for more extensive drill-down capabilities. Business intelligence tools are available from vendors such as Cognos, Inc., Business Objects SA, and Brio Technology, Inc.

While ROI tools are used primarily for project-level reporting and EPM tools are used for portfolio monitoring, the more generic business intelligence, EIS, and collaboration tool solutions can be used for both project and nonproject-related information.

10.2.2 Phase 2

Phase 2 (see Figure 10.5) of the IT PMO rollout will provide the first opportunity for the IT PMO to show portfolio valuation. After rolling out the prioritization tool, a view of the current state of the portfolio will be available. Then, as the IT PMO commences implementation of the AARK management processes, they will be able to show real-time portfolio valuation improvements. Phase 2 will also provide the IT PMO with its first opportunity to create its core support teams: the initiative review team, the project audit team, the EAM team, and the KM team. While the EAM team will start working with the architects and

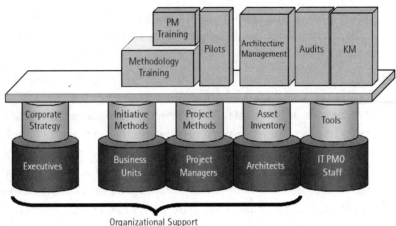

Figure 10.5   Phase 2 deliverables of an IT PMO rollout.

the business units to develop the EIA and EBA, respectively, the KM team will begin developing the central project knowledge base and a process to roll out project-specific knowledge bases. The next two sections will describe the value of project pilots and training during this phase.

10.2.2.1 Methodology Piloting

When tailoring the methodologies, it is critical to solicit the input of a council of PMs. If they are allowed to contribute to the development of the corporate software development methodologies, they will be more likely to use them. Once the first, usable versions of the project methodologies are ready, they should be rolled out to pilot projects. As the organization learns, adopts, and gets comfortable with the basics, other elements of the methodology can be added: document templates, instructions, and process guides. This approach should start with true believers who demonstrate through small wins the benefits of the standardized methodologies. Improved project health ratings will then help develop credibility and offer something to show the "show-me gang." When they are converted and critical mass of two thirds of the organization is achieved, it may be necessary to apply a little top-down command to convince the die hards. Remember, antagonists who become converts often become your biggest allies and advocates [3]!

10.2.2.2 Training

Once the initiative methodology has been approved by the executive sponsor and the business units, and the project methodology has been approved by the project management super-user group, the rest of the organization needs to be trained. Two training curricula need to be created for each methodology: one for upper management and one for the troops. The shorter, higher level training plan will be given to business unit and IT upper management. The longer, more detailed training will be given to the individuals who will be implementing the methodology. While the upper management needs to be trained in the value such methodologies will bring to the organization, implementers need to be trained on how to be successful with the methodology.

Once the PMs have been trained to use the methodology, they then need to be trained on some of the more subtle aspects of project management. Everything from human resources issues to project time and cost estimation, and from interproject communication to facilities management, needs to be packaged into a training curriculum. Then a follow-up road show to the methodology training course needs to be conducted [3].

10.2.3 Phase 3

This final phase is where the IT PMO will be able to show the most return on IT PPM investment to the executive committee. By this time, the project portfolio should be showing clear signs of improvement via the portfolio health monitoring software (see Figure 10.6). This health will have been boosted by better KM, architecture management, initiative filtering, and methodology usage. With these last four components in place and working, IT PMO staff members will be able to focus on developing asset-managing autotrackers (with the asset management team) and advanced resources management approaches such as drum schedules (with the KM team). Keep in mind, as these new building blocks are added, training curricula may need to be altered. Combining improved portfolio valuation with these last building block additions, the IT PMO will be able prove ROI to the executive sponsors. If you don't prove ROI at this point, the IT PMO will become just a flash in the pan rather than be embraced as a new direction for the company [3].

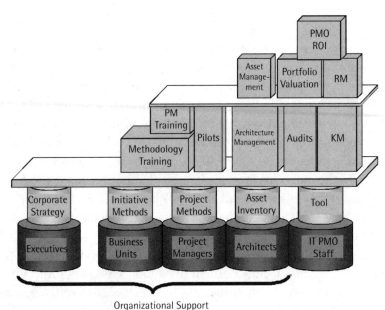

Figure 10.6 Phase 3 deliverables of an IT PMO rollout.

10.3 Bringing It Together and Making It Happen

10.3.1 Bridging IT and Business Functions

A basic barrier that IT departments face in most companies is in how to best communicate their reason for being to the finance department. This book introduced IT-based PPM concepts not only as a way to prioritize and improve the health of IT-based project portfolios, but also as a way to bridge the communication gap that exists between IT and finance staff. Chapter 1 first explained how similar IT PPM is to classical financial portfolio management by drawing links to Dr. Markowitz's MPT. Chapter 2 showed the importance of first establishing a corporate strategy and then continuously mapping IT-based initiatives and projects to the ever-changing substrategy map. Chapter 3 balanced the financial and the IT perspectives even more by showing how to develop and then link business initiative and project management methodologies. By reviewing the techniques used by financial and IT experts, both parties can become better able to communicate the strengths of IT PPM to each other.

10.3.2 Balancing the Two IT PPM Directions

Many companies will already have many, if not all, of the building blocks of IT PPM in place. Problems arise when they don't know how to leverage the pieces or how to make the pieces work together. One way to improperly implement IT PPM concepts is with an IT PPM vision that is too narrowly focused in one direction. For example, many believe that IT PPM exists to either support the executives in valuating their IT portfolios or to support the health of the portfolios as extensions to program and project offices. This book has argued that one direction cannot be successful without also pursuing the other direction. Figure 10.7 shows that the IT PMO conducts initiative reviews and project audits to provide updated prioritization lists to the executive committee. Such lists allow the committee to view real-time project portfolio valuations

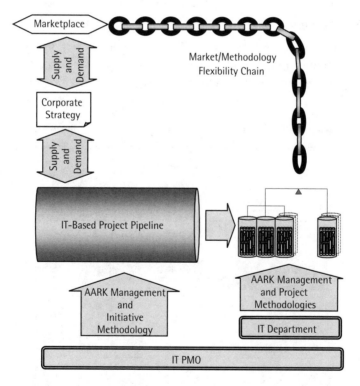

Figure 10.7 Central tasks of the IT PMO and the executive committee in supporting the IT-based project pipeline.

and to provide new and continued funding. As an analogy, forced ranking is a concept that can be used to clean house of the lowest 10% of a company's workforce at many companies. Portfolio prioritization provides executives with the same opportunity to cross check poorly conceived projects that sneak into the portfolio.

While the process shown in Figure 10.7 is central to IT PPM, Figure 10.8 shows the other IT PPM processes needed to keep the project portfolio flexible to the needs of the marketplace. Chapter 2 showed how the supply and demand pipeline for IT-based solutions starts at the marketplace and works its way through the layers of the strategy down to the IT initiative review committee of the IT-based project pipeline. Then, if the IT PMO supports a healthy, well-balanced portfolio, through AARK management and iterative methodology auditing, the company will have established a strong, yet flexible, market/methodology chain.

10.3.2.1 Accountability

Figure 10.8 also shows that IT PMO support starts well before project kickoff. Then, while the IT department is supporting the individual projects after they start, the IT PMO continues to provide cross-project

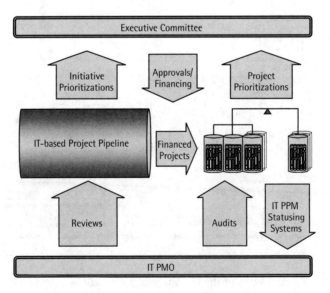

Figure 10.8 The market-methodology flexibility chain.

support. But what exactly is the IT PMO accountable for? Because IT projects are ultimately owned by the business unit sponsors who finance the projects, these sponsors are also the ones that need to be held accountable for the project's success. This is balanced by an IT PMO that is held accountable for the entire project portfolio. Where the project sponsor has control over project success by having a direct hand in planning and managing the project, the IT PMO has control over the portfolio by having a direct hand in choosing which projects get added to and stay in the portfolio. Such checks and balances allow PMs to maintain creative freedom when satisfying microstrategy demands but prevent their hidden agendas from driving the whole portfolio.

10.3.2.2 Early AARK Management

A key to successful IT project portfolio support is to be involved in the project life cycle early. AARK management is more effective if it supports the proposed initiatives and not just the approved projects.

- *Assets.* Early participation allows IT PMOs to help IT departments manage assets not just from a reactive mode, but also from a proactive mode, by having a clearer picture of projects in the pipeline across the enterprise. Help desk managers can determine staff training costs and systems administrators can evaluate lab space availability for the business case writers before they submit their proposals.

- *Architecture.* If IT architects are involved in the early phases of initiative submission, the architectures of these initiatives can be influenced to better fit with the current corporate architecture. On the other hand, if the initiative requires technology that is not a part of the EIA, then at least the help desk will be given early preparation to train and support the deliverable.

- *Resources.* Project kickoff timing depends on when the deliverable is needed by the company, when the financing will be available, when the solution will be technically feasible, and when resources will be freed up (to name a few). The IT PMO has the opportunity to ease the headaches associated with this last hurdle to starting a project.

♦ *Knowledge.* IT systems, their original "current state," their "to be" requirements, and their design documents act as building blocks to the EBA as well as the EIA. Many companies may develop detailed process diagrams to meet ISO 9000, TQM, or Six Sigma requirements. While such documented processes can also add to the business architecture, they tend to collect dust over time. Enterprise-level knowledge bases that are continually updated by IT-based projects, on the other hand, help keep architectures current and IT-based initiative proposals aligned.

10.3.3 Organizational Change

To help cross the chasm of IT PPM rollout, Chapter 1 explained the need to market horizontally to the various business units as well as vertically to the different layers of management. Chapter 2 explained the need for early and sustained strategic design by the executive team. Chapter 3 highlighted the need for methodology ownership by the project and business unit managers. Chapter 4 showed how to minimize additional bureaucracy and how to mitigate the risk of initiative bottle-necking. Chapters 5 through 8 detailed how to leverage the power of the organization to not only guarantee IT PMO acceptance, but also IT PMO delivery success. All of these approaches to getting IT PMO support are important tools to gaining ultimate and sustained support by all of the early and late majority. Finally, this chapter provides a stepwise approach to rolling out an IT PMO solution to all areas of the organization. Ultimately, the glue that holds a successful IT PMO together is the complete integration of the rest of the business in a virtual IT PMO.

10.3.3.1 Virtual IT PMO Synergy

Synergy is defined as the extra output that results when individuals work as a team rather than separately. The virtual IT PMO creates synergy by building a healthy IT project portfolio above and beyond what is possible if project sponsors worked independently. As an example, the IT department will support IT assets after a project is complete, but many times not before; it will manage IT department resources, but not functional or outsourced resources; it will develop and maintain IT architectures, but not business architectures; and it will have no reason to maintain project collateral. All of these are examples of holes that a virtual IT PMO and its associated committees can fill. The architecture committee will maintain awareness and prepare support for new assets as they are proposed, the business unit committee will guide the IT PMO in distributing drum resources to prevent portfolio bottlenecks, and the IT PMO will ensure business architectures and other project collateral are saved in the knowledge base for future project usage.

Without cooperation and teamwork, IT-based initiative proposals and approved projects will not only need to navigate the problems associated with their own projects, they'll also need to navigate the potholes created by a fragmented portfolio. With a lack of initiative methodology, they'll have to rely more on political maneuvering than fair review processes. With a lack of standardized, iterative project methodologies, they'll have to depend on the hope that their original requirements will still support strategic demands upon delivery. And with a lack of fair project-monitoring tools, no one will know which projects are advancing the company's goals or dragging the company behind the competition. The committees of the virtual IT PMO act as a platform where such methodologies and tools get approved with consensus and are used with enthusiasm by the organization. Thus, transfer of ownership of the PMO to the business units, the IT architects, the executive committee, and the PMs not only helps eliminate the organizational buy-in hurdle, it also increases the opportunity for synergy.

Over the last decade, corporate business units have seen IT organizations balloon and then deflate as projects come and go. After a large percentage of these projects fail, business units find they are left with bloated IT departments that can't even respond to a nonmanager help desk request. With IT having a historical reputation of overhyped project successes and budget drain power, the last thing these business units want to support is another push for IT-based bureaucracy. While many IT departments are well-oiled efficiency machines, the perception that has grown among non-IT-heads has become their "reality." What IT departments are starting to discover is that the only way to get business units to accept IT growth is to get them more involved as success stakeholders. While Chapter 3 showed how a small IT PMO can distribute deliverable ownership to a set of such committees, the rest of the book expanded on the definition of the virtual IT PMO.

Market-methodology flexibility, the virtual PMO, and organizational change are three important foundations to any IT PPM initiative. Inflexible IT projects, additional bureaucratic walls, and organizational resistance all can trigger the downfall of a well-designed IT PMO. Therefore, with the new urgency for risk control (recent government regulations), IT project alignment (more unpredictable marketplace), and IT portfolio scrutiny (loss of visibility via offshoring), IT PPM is a solution worth reviewing. Moreover, as technology-enhanced businesses cross borders, the flexibility that IT PPM provides is critical for quick reaction to the global marketplace shifts.

References

[1]   Englund, Randall, and Robert Graham, *Creating an Environment for Successful Projects*, San Francisco, CA: Jossey-Bass, 2003.

[2]   Meta Group, "Centralizing Management of Project Portfolios," January 29, 2002, http://www.umt.com/site/Documents/IT_World_-_Leading_Organisation_Centralize_Management_of_Project_Portfolios_-_29Jan02.pdf (last accessed on January 15, 2004).

[3]   Young, D. Allen, "Project Office Start-Up," *PM Network*, February 1, 2001, http://www.pmi.org/info/PIR_PMNetworkOnline.asp (last accessed on January 15, 2004).

[4]   Mayor, Tracy, "Value Made Visible," *CIO Magazine*, May 1, 2000, http://www.cio.com/archive/050100/method.html (last accessed on January 15, 2004).

[5]   Goldratt, Eliyahu, *Critical Chain*, Great Barrington, MA: The North River Press, 1999.

[6]   Moore, Geoffrey, *Crossing the Chasm*, New York: Harper Perennial, 1999.

[7]   Crawford, J. Kent, *The Strategic Project Office*, Monticello, NY: Marcel Dekker, 2002.

[8]   Berinato, Scott, "Do the Math," *CIO Magazine*, October 1, 2001.

[9]   Norton, David P., and Robert S. Kaplan, *The Strategy-Focused Organization*, Boston, MA: Harvard Business School Press, 2001.

[10]　Kaplan, Jeffrey D., "White Paper: Strategically Managing Your IT Portfolio," *PRTM's Insight*, April 1, 2001, http://www.prtm.com (last accessed on January 15, 2004).

[11]　Mayor, Tracy, "Red Light; Green Light," *CIO Magazine*, October 1, 2001, http://www.cio.com/archive/100101/red.html (last accessed on January 15, 2004).

[12]　Berry, John, "Tools Bring ROI into Focus—Software That Calculates Return on Investment Helps Companies Determine," *Internet Week*, December 10, 2001, http://www.portfoliomgt.org/ForumItem.asp?itemID=965 (last accessed on January 15, 2004).

Selected Bibliography

Barker, Joh, and Stephen Smith, "Benefit-Cost Ratio: Selection Tool or Trap?" in *Project Portfolio Management*, Lowell D. Dye and James S. Pennypacker, (eds.), West Chester, PA: Center for Business Practices, 1999, pp. 281–286.

Bazley, John, *Financial Accounting: Concepts and Uses*, Denver, CO: University of Denver, 2002.

Berardino, Joe, "Enron: A Wake-Up Call," *Wall Street Journal*, December 4, 2001.

Boer, F. Peter, "Real Options: The IT Investment Risk-Buster," *Optimize Magazine*, July 1, 2002, http://www.optimizemag.com/issue/0009/financial_p3.htm.

Borck, James R., "As E-Collaboration Tools Mature, They Can Help You Work Out a Competitive Advantage," *InfoWorld*, November 27, 2000, http://archive.infoworld.com/articles/op/xml/00/11/27/001127opborck.xml.

Bredemeyer, Dana, and Ruth Malan, "Creating an Architectural Vision: Collecting Input," 2000, http://www.eacommunity.com/articles/art17.asp.

Brenner, Merrill S., "Practical R&D Project Prioritization," in *Project Portfolio Management*, Lowell D. Dye and James S. Pennypacker, (eds.), West Chester, PA: Center for Business Practices, 1999, pp. 239–260.

Brown, William H., *AntiPatterns: Refactoring Software, Architectures, and Projects in Crisis*, New York: John Wiley & Sons, 1999.

Buss, Martin D. J., "How to Rank Computer Projects," in *Project Portfolio Management*, Lowell D. Dye and James S. Pennypacker, (eds.), West Chester, PA: Center for Business Practices, 1999, pp. 183–192.

Copeland, Tom, "The Real-Options Approach to Capital Allocation," *Strategic Finance*, October 1, 2001.

Fabrycky, Wolter J., and G. Chris Moolman, "A Capital Budgeting Model Based on the Project Portfolio Approach: Avoiding Cash Flows Per Project," in *Project Portfolio Management*, Lowell D. Dye and James S. Pennypacker, (eds.), West Chester, PA: Center for Business Practices, 1999, pp. 287–308.

Galucci, Sam, "SFA Systems: Managing the Behavior and Cultural Changes," *The Journal of Customer Relationships,* Issue 9, 1998.

Goldratt, Eliyahu, *Necessary But Not Sufficient*, Great Barrington, MA: The North River Press, 2000.

Gotta, Mike, "Web & Collaboration Strategies," *Meta Group*, November 14, 2001, http://www.metagroup.com/products/insights/wcs_1_sco.htm.

Hammond, Chad, "Using Business Intelligence Applications," *InfoWorld,* February 5, 2001.

Jiang, James J., and Gary Klein, "Information System Project-Selection Criteria Variations within Strategic Classes," in *Project Portfolio Management*, Lowell D. Dye and James S. Pennypacker (eds.), West Chester, PA: Center for Business Practices, 1999, pp. 193–206.

Luehrman, Timothy, "Strategy as a Portfolio of Real Options," in *Project Portfolio Management*, Lowell D. Dye and James S. Pennypacker, (eds.), West Chester, PA: Center for Business Practices, 1999, pp. 71–86.

Manasco, Britton, "Dow Chemical Capitalizes on Intelectual Assets," *Knowledge Inc.*, March 1, 1997, http://www.webcom.com/quantera/Dow.html.

Manasco, Britton, "Leading Firms Develop Knowledge Strategies," *Quantera*, October 1, 1996, http://webcom.com/quantera/Apqc.html.

McCarthy, Dennis G., *The Loyalty Link*, New York: John Wiley & Sons, 1997.

Moore, Geoffrey A., *Crossing the Chasm*, New York: Harper-Perennial, 1999.

Noyes, Katherine, "Take It Slow," *CIO Magazine*, October 1, 2000, http://www.cio.com/archive/100100/tl_itvalue.html.

Pringle, David, "Learning Gurus Adapt to Escape Corporate Axes," *Wall Street Journal*, January 1, 2003.

Ritchie-Dunham, James, and Hal Rabbino, *Managing from Clarity*, New York: John Wiley & Sons, 2001.

Roberts, Bill, "Ratings Game," *CIO Magazine*, October 15, 2000, http://www.cio.com/archive/101500_rating.html.

Roetzheim, William, "Improving Our Track Record," *SD Times*, http://www.costxpert.com/resource_center/sdtimes.html, last accessed on September 28, 2004.

Royce, Mark, "Elements of an Architecture Review," http://www.eacommunity.com/articles/art2.asp, last accessed on September 28, 2004.

Ruport, Mark, "The Hidden Treasure of Business Process Automation: Six Steps to Improving ROI," *Optika*, December 23, 2001, http://www.ebizq.net/topics/bpm/features/2591.html.

Sims, David, "Connected Enterprise Architecture Components," http://www.eacommunity.com/articles/art16.asp, last accessed on September 28, 2004.

Sims, David, "Enterprise Architecture: The Executive Advantage," http://www.eacommunity.com/articles/art10.asp, last accessed on September 28, 2004.

Wheelwright, Steven C., and Kim B. Clark, "Creating Project Plans to Focus Product Development," in *Project Portfolio Management*, Lowell D.

Dye and James S. Pennypacker, (eds.), West Chester, PA: Center for Business Practices, 1999, pp. 371–388.

Winters, Frank, "Insuring Success: PMO's Bring IT Together," *Gantthead.com*, 2001, http://www.gantthead.com/Gantthead/departments/features/1,1523,12,00.html.

List of Acronyms

AARK	Architecture, asset, resource, and knowledge
B2B	Business to business
BPI	Business process improvement
BPR	Business process reengineering
CEO	Chief executive officer
CFO	Chief financial officer
CIMOSA	Computer-integrated manufacturing open source architecture
CIO	Chief information officer
COO	Chief operations officer
COCOMO	Constructive cost model
COTS	Commercial off-the-shelf (software)
CRM	Customer resources management
DBA	Database administrator

EA	Enterprise architecture
EAM	Enterprise architecture management
EBA	Enterprise business architecture
EIA	Enterprise IT architecture
EIS	Executive information system
EPMO	Enterprise project management office
ERP	Enterprise resource planning
FDA	Federal Drug Administration
FOL	Facts of life
GCIB	Citigroup's Global Corporate and Investment Banking
GIS	GPS information system
GUI	Graphical user interface
IRR	Internal rate of return
IT	Information technology
KM	Knowledge management
KPI	Key performance indicator
LAN	Local area network
MPT	Modern portfolio theory (for financial portfolios)
NASA	National Aeronautics and Space Administration
NPV	Net present value
PB	Payback
PERA	Purdue enterprise reference architecture
PI	Profit index
PM	Project manager
PMBOK	Project Management Body of Knowledge
PMI	Project Management Institute

PMO	Portfolio management office
PPM	Project portfolio management
PV	Present value
ROI	Return on investment
RUP	Rational Unified Process
S&P	Selection and prioritization criteria for financial and project portfolios
SA	Systems administrator
SBU	Strategic business unit
TCO	Total cost of ownership
TPR	Technical process reengineering
TQM	Total quality management
UML	Universal Modeling Language
WAN	Wide area network
XP	Extreme Programming

About the Author

Stephen S. Bonham is the president of TrueCourse Solutions, Inc., an IT strategy consulting company that specializes in customized IT PPM solutions. Before starting this company, Mr. Bonham held a wide range of positions during his 15 years in the IT industry. He started his career as a systems administrator and a software engineer for small and large companies. After completing his M.E. in computer science, he then worked for several IT consulting companies that specialized in computer/telephony solutions, CRM and ERP implementations, custom software development, and enterprise-level systems integrations. During this time, he held positions as project manager, program manager, engineering manager, enterprise IT architect, and IT management consultant.

Mr. Bonham has published several articles on organizational change and IT PPM in various trade journals. He is a certified project management professional (PMP) and has an M.B.A. from the University of Denver.

Index

O

Operational asset management, 155–56
Operational concepts, 75
Organization, this book, xi–xii
Organizational change, 104–12, 240–42
  benefits, 104–7
  governance, 107–12
  impediments, 104
  tasks for TPR, 135
Organizational risks, 6
Organizational support, 223–42
  balancing two PPM directions, 237–40
  bridging IT/business functions, 236
  marketing, 224–26
  organizational change, 240–42
  rollout, 226–36
Organizations
  cultural readiness, 106
  large, PMO structure, 96–102
  matrixed structure, 163
  small, PMO structure, 102–4
Outsourcing, 172–75
  avoiding, 173–74
  as competitive thrust, 173
  risk mitigation, 173
  upsurge, 175
  use of, 172–73
  See also Resource management;
      Resources

P

Payback (PB) period, 69, 70–71
Penker-Erikson extensions, 129–31
Personal KM, 185, 190
PMO structure, 96–104
  large, project-centric companies,
      96–102
  small, less project-centric companies,
      102–4
  See also IT PMO
PMO-supported KM, 184–90
  KM team, 188
  organizational support, 188–90
  personal KM, 185
  project KM, 185–87
  rollout, 188–90

See also Knowledge management
Portfolio grid, 214
Portfolio prioritization, 195–217
  audits, 201–4
  balance, 211–17
  criteria development, 197
  initiative reviews, 198–201
  maximization, 204–10
  methods, 195
  process, 196–98
  process development, 198
  qualitative measures, 197
  quantitative measures, 197
  review teams, 196–97
  summary, 217
Portfolios
  balanced, 19–20, 93
  building/maintaining, for strategic
      alignment, 18
  flexibility, 59–85
  maximization, 195, 204–10
  metric mapping, 75–76
Portfolio selection, 16–21
  balance, 19–20
  maximization, 16–17
  resource allocation, 20–21
  strategic alignment, 17–19
Preliminary initiative plans, 65
Prescreening, 199
Private risks. *See* Unique risks
Processes
  business, 1, 42
  delivery, 208–9
  development/support, 26–27
  rigid workflow, 151
Product adoption phases, 225
Productivity, 47–49
Profit index (PI), 69, 70–71
  as cumulative value, 72
  defined, 70
Project buckets, 211–14
  approaches, 212
  design, 213
  dynamic balancing, 214
Project investments, 6–9
  risk cost, 8

Recent Titles in the Artech House Effective Project Management Series

Robert K. Wysocki, Series Editor

Critical Chain Project Management, Second Edition,
  Lawrence P. Leach

IT Project Portfolio Management, Stephen S. Bonham

The Project Management Communications Toolkit, Carl Pritchard

Project Management Process Improvement, Robert K. Wysocki

For further information on these and other Artech House titles, including previously considered out-of-print books now available through our In-Print-Forever® (IPF®) program, contact:

Artech House
685 Canton Street
Norwood, MA 02062
Phone: 781-769-9750
Fax: 781-769-6334
e-mail: artech@artechhouse.com

Artech House
46 Gillingham Street
London SW1V 1AH UK
Phone: +44 (0)20 7596-8750
Fax: +44 (0)20 7630-0166
e-mail: artech-uk@artechhouse.com

Find us on the World Wide Web at:
www.artechhouse.com